Health Policy in Transition

Health Policy in Transition

A Decade of Health Politics, Policy and Law

Edited by Lawrence D. Brown

Duke University Press Durham 1987

The text of this book was originally
published without the present preface
or index as volume 11, number 4 of the
*Journal of Health Politics, Policy
and Law.*

Copyright © 1987 Duke University Press
Printed in the United States of America
on acid-free paper ∞

Library of Congress Cataloging-in-Publication Data
Health policy in transition.
Includes index.
1. Medical policy—United States—History. 2. Medical
care—United States—History. I. Brown, Lawrence D.
(Lawrence David), 1947–   . [DNLM: 1. Delivery of
Health Care—trends—United States. 2. Health Policy—
trends—United States. WA 540 AA1H24]
RA395.A3H4256   1987   362.1'0973   87-13714
ISBN 0-8223-0776-6
ISBN 0-8223-0790-1 (pbk.)

Contents

Editor's Preface

This volume began life at a conference held at Duke University in April 1986 to observe the tenth anniversary of the *Journal of Health Politics, Policy and Law*. Having witnessed a decade of unusually rapid change in the health care system, we decided to tackle what we took to be basic and central themes, enduring and recurring issues, each of which invites both a sorting out of past developments and conjectures about the future.

In the introduction, I offer a brief overview of the major sources and patterns of transition. Then Robert Evans examines the last decade's preeminent preoccupation, how to contain the rising costs of health care, drawing lessons for both policy analysts and policy makers from recent experience in Canada and the United States. Theodore Marmor uses cross-national inquiry to set the U.S. system in the larger political context of the "crisis" of the welfare state in advanced democracies. Harvey Sapolsky ponders the promises and problems of the prospective payment system adopted in 1983—surely the most important legislative change in Medicare since its enactment in 1965, and a major break with our idiosyncratic system of payment based on retrospective calculation of actual costs instead of prospectively negotiated rates. Frank Thompson addresses the politics of health policy in the U.S. intergovernmental system, disentangling deeper from more transient trends in the various "New Federalisms" envisioned in Washington. Deborah Stone casts a skeptical eye on everyone's favorite progressive policy measure, prevention, posing some troubling questions that lie beneath the surface of what were once widely endorsed "answers." Finally, Clark Havighurst explains the rediscovery of market principles and solutions in law and policy in recent years, and explores their implications for consumers and providers.

We are well aware that these issues do not exhaust the list of major concerns in health politics, policy, and law. We might have included (for example) the evolution of the Medicare program and the tumultuous developments in bioethics, had we not recently addressed the former in a special issue of the *Journal of Health Politics, Policy and Law* (Fall 1985) and the latter in a special section on the medical treatment of handicapped newborns (Summer 1986). Likewise, long-term care is surely a central issue. But it was our view that the health arena has largely dodged, not confronted, its challenges in the past decade; and our intent was to investigate concrete developments, not stalemated debates.

Though our choice of topics is not comprehensive, and our analyses do not pretend to offer the last word, we hope that this volume will be a rich source of evidence and argument for readers trying to make sense of the recent past and likely future of the U.S. health care system.

Many contributors helped make the volume possible. A special word of warm thanks is due to The Commonwealth Fund, which assisted our conference and the preparation of the special issue of the *Journal* in which these articles first appeared; to Joan Aberbach, who adroitly managed the logistics of assembling the articles; and to Kathy Brodeur, whose sound judgment and exemplary editing skills enhanced the quality of this volume in countless ways.

Introduction to a Decade of Transition

Lawrence D. Brown, University of Michigan

Abstract. A brief review of the last decade or so of developments in health politics, policy and law suggests that health is no longer a field of mere "dynamics without change." Responding not only to economic strains but also to new conceptual challenges to the assumptions of the traditional medical model, in the 1970s and 1980s policy makers have launched various competitive and regulatory programs aimed mainly at containing costs. These interventions, however, have mainly sought savings through reductions in waste and inappropriate utilization; they have done little about deeper cost-increasing forces such as demographic trends, technology, and personnel patterns. Nor have these innovations on the cost side of the policy ledger been matched by action on the benefit side. Such changes await reconceptualization of the practical meaning of social justice and of the role of government in the health field.

In scanning the past decade of developments in health politics, policy, and law, there is a sense of entering (in 1976) at the early twilight of an ancien régime, of witnessing the rise and diffusion of important changes, and then (in 1986) observing the gradual but firm consolidation of a new order. Because the forces for change have been at work continually over the decade, it may be useful to begin with a quick year-by-year review of some of the high points. Indeed it may be well to begin a decade and a half ago, in 1972, the year that Robert Alford depicted a health care system beset by "dynamics without change."[1]

1972   Amendments to the Social Security Act establish professional standards review organizations (PSROs), capital expenditure review under Section 1122, and new authority for federal support for rate-setting demonstrations in the states, all major steps on the road toward regulation.

1973   The Health Maintenance Organization Act passes, a step along the road to competition.

1974   The Health Planning and Resources Development Act establishes local health system agencies and requires that states adopt certificate-of-need programs; Marc LaLonde's *New Perspectives on the Health of Canadians* appears, calling new attention to the importance of prevention in health policy.

1975   The Ford administration proposes block grants for various health programs. This notion, absent from Nixon's New Federalism agenda six years earlier, will reappear six years later in Reagan's New Federalism.

1976   Amendments to the HMO law suggest that Congress means business about competition and will work to try to get it "right"; a new manpower law offers incentives to medical schools to increase the ranks of general practitioners and encourages medical school graduates to work in underserved areas.

1977   Six months after Gerald Ford signs the HMO amendments, the new administration of Jimmy Carter unveils a hospital cost-containment bill that would impose annual limits on hospital revenues and capital spending. The hospital industry counters this regulatory scheme with a "voluntary effort" to prove that it can cut spending on its own.

1978   The Carter plan triggers an intense debate about the relative merits of competition and markets versus regulation and public controls as means of containing costs.

1979   The Carter plan dies in the House of Representatives. The "voluntary effort" dies with it. Meanwhile the Federal Trade Commission rules against efforts by the American Medical Association to restrict advertising by physicians.

1980   Ronald Reagan wins the presidential election. His advisors and designees pledge to avoid—indeed, repeal—regulatory approaches to health cost containment, vowing to rely instead on market-based approaches. Meanwhile, scholarly studies showing the effectiveness of some state rate-setting programs in containing costs begin to attract attention in Washington.

1981   Provisions of the Omnibus Budget Reconciliation Act create block grants for certain health programs, impose cuts on Medicare and Medicaid, and introduce into Medicaid substantive changes that encourage states to adopt gatekeeping and managed care systems.

1982   The long-awaited procompetitive cost-containment plan promised by the Reagan administration fails to arrive. Congress declines to kill PSROs, instead transforming them into peer review organizations (PROs). The Tax Equity and Fiscal Responsibility Act cuts Medicare payments to providers, changes the system for paying hospitals in the program, calls on the Department of Health and Human Services to deliver a full-blown prospective payment plan for Medicare payments to hospitals (which the department supplies in December), liberalizes Medicare payment methods for HMOs, and introduces new hospice benefits in Medicare.

1983   Congress debates, but fails to enact, new health insurance provisions for the unemployed, and adopts a prospective payment system for Medicare payments to hospitals. Throughout the nation interest grows in "prudent purchasing," "preferred providers," and local cost-containment coalitions.

1984   Congress adds the Child Health Assurance Program to Medicaid and, in the Deficit Reduction Act, imposes a temporary freeze on physician fees in Medicare. Amendments to the Child Abuse Prevention and Treatment Act pass, involving the states and infant care review committees in medical decisions about the treatment of handicapped newborns. At the state level, laws sanctioning "living wills" proliferate, and throughout the nation bioethical debates heat up.

1985   The Reagan administration renews (this time as part of a tax-reform package) its call for a cap on the exclusion of employer contributions to worker health benefit plans from the taxable income of the employee; the proposal continues to find little favor in Congress. Many states begin debating, and a few begin acting on, the problems of the medically indigent and uncompensated care in the new era of prudent purchasing.

1986   In the Consolidated Omnibus Budget Reconciliation Act, Congress imposes new obligations on employers to permit dismissed employees to continue their health insurance at group rates.

In short, the last fifteen years have seen the adoption of (depending on how one counts) about a dozen major pieces of federal legislation, some of which (especially OBRA and TEFRA) made myriad modifications in existing programs. Moreover, this is only one man's count of high points, mainly at the federal level; the addition of other, more minor federal enactments, changes in agency regulations, federal proposals that generated much debate but failed to pass, and state and local developments enhances the impression of steady, significant change.

This overview suggests that over the last decade or so health has moved from a policy area constrained, indeed often paralyzed, by professional dominance (Freidson's term), monopoly (Alford's), and sovereignty (Starr's),[2] and beset by "dynamics without change," to one exhibiting both colorful dynamics and genuine change. These changes do not constitute a revolution overthrowing existing institutions in its wake, but neither are they a collective expression of false consciousness that leave "real" economic interests and professional power undisturbed. Starr's term, "transformation," is apt. Although this is not the place for comparing policy arenas, it seems fair to say that such fields as education, housing, transportation, and welfare policy have seen no remotely similar transformation over the same period. Indeed one wonders whether any policy field in the United States has ever sustained a transition as compressed and far-reaching as that of the last decade in the health field.

Sources of transition: ideas and values

Any effort to contrast in a few words the central conceptual and normative foundations of the "old" versus the "new" systems runs an obvious risk of oversimplification. Be that as it may, one may begin by boiling down the foundations of the "old" system to six propositions.

First, health status outcomes depend critically on the structures and processes of the health care system. An improved health care system means better health for much of the population. The central function of the system is curing illness.

Second, one of the main problems with the system is that there is too little of it. More is better; a "supply side" strategy is indicated. Specifically, the system needs more biomedical research and technology, more hospitals, and more physicians. Policy makers should subsidize these resources, as they certainly did, encouraging biomedical research with funds for the National Institutes of Health, hospital construction with monies in the Hill-Burton program, and an increased number of physicians with programs authorized in a series of legislative enactments. Between 1945 and 1965, these subsidy programs were the heart of federal health care policy.

Third, the second (and only other) serious problem with the system is limited financial access to mainstream care among disadvantaged citizens, notably the poor and the elderly. The just and logical solution is a set of entitlement programs—Medicare, Medicaid, and (ultimately) national health insurance—that would eventually make accessible to all society a single-tiered system of care.

Fourth, payments for professional and institutional services should be based on measures of the true, fair value of providers' work, which means payment of the actual incurred costs of hospitals and the usual and customary charges of physicians, so long as these are reasonable. Medical professionals should be left free to work as, and charge what, they think appropriate, at least within broad limits.

Fifth, in health care, markets do not and cannot work. Price competition is infeasible and undesirable for a host of reasons—the supplier's power to define demand, the consumer's limited information, and more.

Sixth, in health care, regulation is the wrong answer to market failures. Inevitably it leads to inefficiencies, inequities, perverse incentives, sacrifices in quality, and the capture of public power by private interests.

By the early 1970s, all six propositions had come under challenge. Public opinion, policy analysts, and policy makers had begun to reconceptualize the workings, achievements, and costs of the system. As a result the traditional assumptions suffered a loss of credibility, which opened wide the door to practical innovations responding to the new public sensibility.

First, troubling questions were pressed about the relation between health provision and health status outcomes. The contribution of personal prevention to improved health received increased emphasis. If it was indeed the case that diet, smoking, exercise, driving habits, stress, and the like were prime determinants of health status, then provider and institution-specific variables mattered less than previously thought. Health, it appeared, was in the main a matter of "pre-" or "non-" provider variables. Moreover, the distinction between curing and caring was more sharply drawn. Much illness gets better by itself; other ailments are insusceptible to cure. If, as one physician put it, "that leaves only 10 percent of cases in which scientific medicine—at considerable cost—has any value at all,"[3] much of the nation's medical bill was not buying cures. Caring is a vital function, to be sure, but the questions naturally arose: should it cost so much, and are doctors and hospitals the right agents? Analysts also gained new awareness of the psychosomatic, as distinct from the organic, sources of patient complaints. On some estimates perhaps 60–70 percent of the ailments patients bring to physicians originate in psychological, not physical, sources, a datum that of course also highlights the distinction between cure and care.

As these points—all of which sharply challenged the traditional model—sank gradually into the national consciousness, society watched national health care spending approach and then exceed 10 percent of gross national product, contemplated health costs rising two or three times faster than the annual rate of general prices in the early 1980s, heard projections of a multibillion dollar deficit in Medicare's hospital insurance trust fund by the early 1990s, learned that the federal health budget was doubling every five years, and discovered that the nation's annual health care bill might well hit $1 trillion by the mid-1990s.[4] In short, learning about results (outcomes) was on a collision course with learning about spending (inputs).

Second, in the 1970s public and elite opinion came rather abruptly to recognize that the health care system is in major respects too large, not too small. Biomedical research remained highly popular, but it was increasingly understood that the unconstrained diffusion of medical technology could lead to excessive tests, treatments, risks, and costs, and, in some cases, exposure to danger in institutions with a volume of procedures (heart surgery, for example) too low to ensure quality. By the mid-1970s experts agreed that the nation had a sizable bed surplus; indeed perhaps 10–20 percent of capacity might be unneeded. The worrisome doctor shortage had by the mid-1970s turned into a surplus of disturbing proportions. The concerted force of professional norms demanding that physicians do everything possible for their patients, malpractice incentives working in the same direction, Roemer's law (which contends that excess beds generate excess use), and the "target income" hypothesis (which postulates that physicians can manipulate demand to generate the remuneration to which they think themselves entitled) argued that excess supply was a direct and immediate source of unnecessary use and unjustified cost.

Third, some observers began to doubt aloud whether public entitlement programs that bought access for the disadvantaged to mainstream care were affordable and desirable after all. National health insurance, often portrayed as "imminent'' in the 1970s, was a dead letter by 1980. Critics wondered if society should struggle to afford its swelling public health care budget, and reopened debate about the definition of need that justifies an entitlement. The universalistic philosophy that supported Social Security and Medicare was challenged: Would not targeting on ''true'' need make more sense? Would not means testing be fairer and more efficient? Discussion turned to vouchers, capitation schemes, higher cost sharing, and managed care systems (which might abridge the consumer's freedom of choice of provider) in Medicare and Medicaid. Some deplored these retreats from the theory and practice of a one-tiered health care system for everyone. Others argued that the retreat was mere realism in a system devoted (as Uwe Reinhardt put it) simultaneously to egalitarianism in the distribution of health care and to libertarianism in its production. Reinhardt, for instance, concluded that the notion of equal access most consistent with American values ''implies that the probability of surviving a medical condition after medical treatment, and the degree of recovery, be independent of the patient's socio-economic and insurance status but that the amenities accompanying the delivery of care and the degree of freedom of choice among providers may vary systematically by socio-economic class.''[5]

Fourth, evidence accumulated showing that the rates and costs of treatment within and between small areas vary enormously and without apparent demographic or medical justification. The traditional view that each medical decision about utilization was a micromanifestation of objective, scientific, professional judgment was undermined by the findings of John Wennberg and others, which seemed to suggest that such decisions often depend heavily on personal practice patterns, local medical cultures, and perhaps income-increasing objectives. But if much utilization was, in this sense, ''arbitrary and capricious,'' then payment methods presupposing that the actual cost of care was (in effect) some type of objective entity to be accurately measured, carefully studied, and faithfully remunerated lost much of their normative appeal. Increasingly, costs have been viewed as a social definition, a policy construct, sums to be defined by payers and providers in the course of negotiations. And average, not actual or usual, costs have increasingly seemed an objective and fair basis for payment.

Fifth, although markets in health care remain empirically and ethically problematic, analysts and practitioners have reconsidered the possibility that price competition involving providers and payers might help contain costs after all. The key developments of the 1970s were a growing consciousness in all quarters of a sizable surplus of hospital beds and physicians and new availability of data on who uses how much care and for what purposes. The combination of providers, anxious to secure their market share, and payers, newly enlightened by extensive evidence on utilization and cost patterns, was the foundation for the prudent purchasers and preferred providers of the 1980s. It is still unclear whether price competition can lower costs in the system as a whole, but competition (some on price, some not) is a fact of life in the new system now emerging.

Sixth, the same intellectual forces that prompted a reconsideration of markets and competition also led to a new pragmatic tolerance for regulation in the health care system. Over the 1970s regulation was increasingly viewed as a necessary evil or even a positive good. In a system rife with overutilization, physician peer review could not be discarded. In a system in which resources bear an imperfect relation to need, planning was an important if elusive goal. If the diffusion of technology and the unconstrained construction, modernization, and expansion of hospitals raised costs, some form of capital expenditure review would remain on the policy agenda. If retrospective costs were in retreat, rate setting by means of prospective payment methods would come to the front. Given the growing perception that the loosely regulated status quo harbored a vast array of inefficiencies, perversities, inequities, and departures from sound quality, it became ever harder to argue that regulation must aggravate the situation, and much informed opinion urged that regulation be allowed to take its place and play its role alongside other policy strategies.

A system in transition: programs and policies

These six "revisionist" propositions are the conceptual and normative core of the "new" health care system unfolding in the mid-1980s. But changing ideas and attitudes could transform the health care system only to the degree that they found practical expression. These did so with remarkable rapidity.

The birth of the new system may be captured by an imaginative step backward to 1970. The Nixon administration had been in office for a year and felt rising pressure to counter the expanding costs of Medicare and Medicaid. None of the "logical" solutions was attractive. The administration could have sought cuts in benefits in these federal programs, but it was chary of appearing anti-old and anti-poor. It could have promoted a national health insurance plan that balanced broader benefits with stronger cost controls, but it feared that Senator Edward Kennedy, the AFL-CIO, and the Democratic-dominated House and Senate would carry that ball in directions it neither controlled nor desired. It could have resorted to regulation, but this was antipathetic to its Republican principles. Then, as if on cue, Paul Ellwood, a physician and policy analyst, reminded high officials in the Department of Health, Education, and Welfare of the virtues of the Kaiser-Permanente health care system and of prepaid group practice plans in general, and explained how PGPs could be transmuted into a more flexible model with an appealing modern name—health maintenance organizations. The administration was easily sold: HMOs reduced no one's benefits, took no steps toward national health insurance, and were nonregulatory. Rather they employed such good Republican means as market competition, expanded consumer choice, and correct incentives.[6]

Thus began more than a decade of federal efforts to encourage what might be termed "decentralized market building." The federal government would commit small catalytic sums in the form of grants and loans; entrepreneurs would respond by building HMOs all over the land. The combination of modest federal stimulus and creative local response would strike a blow for cost containment. "Change the incentives" became the battle cry of the 1970s.

Federal efforts at decentralized market building have not been a notable success. In 1970 there were about 100 HMOs, enrolling about 2 percent of the population. In 1980 about 235 HMOs served about 5–6 percent of the population. In 1986 the nation had more than 500 HMOs, with about 8 percent of the population enrolled. Penetration, in short, has been significant but slow—far too slow to serve as the engine of a new system.

Recognizing the limits of this strategy, some critics called in the late 1970s for a shift to *centralized* market building. The decentralized route was too occasional, too random, too ad hoc. Real change demanded that the federal government alter the rules of the game by which health insurance is sold and bought in the United States; the right changes might produce the right incentives after all. Analysts urged three steps in particular. First, employers should be required to offer their workers a choice of multiple health plans. Second, they should be required to make equal contributions to the premiums of the several plans, leaving employees who insisted on the extras associated with "inefficient" plans to bear the additional costs out of pocket. Third, the government should cap the dollar value of employer contributions to employee health insurance that is excluded from the taxable income of the employee. (Some argued too for a fourth innovation, a cash or tax rebate to workers who chose "efficient" plans.)

These proposals were advanced and debated in the late Carter and early Reagan years. On the whole, they have not come to much. Strong political opposition by labor, the elderly, and most provider groups is part of the explanation, but conceptual difficulties are at least as important. The basic problem is that if the government made *only* the changes listed above it would probably segment the health insurance market. Young, healthy low utilizers would gravitate to plans with cheap premiums, shallow coverage, and significant out-of-pocket costs; older, sicker high utilizers would be attracted to plans that might cost more but offered comprehensive coverage and low cost sharing. Over time the dynamics of adverse selection could sink the latter plans, which include, of course, the efficient HMOs and HMO variants some analysts hoped to encourage.

The dilemma split the camp of the market builders. One faction contended that government should establish the conditions for the free play of markets and then be content to live with the results. Another school countered that not all competition is socially desirable in the health field, that the proper object of reform is to promote competition among organized, efficient plans like HMOs. This latter strategy, Alain Enthoven argued cogently, demanded correlative federal requirements setting standards for the benefits the plans offered, their enrollment practices, how they set premiums, and more.[7] So large a dose of "procompetitive regulation" found little favor with the purer free marketers or with the Reagan administration, however. The centralized market-building effort had collapsed by 1982, leaving as its meager legacy a continuing, inconclusive debate about the merits of a cap on the tax exclusion.

This brief review supports a simple conclusion: after more than fifteen years of effort the federal government has not managed, by means of *policy,* to change incentives on any significant scale. The tangible results of the procompetitive, market-building strategy, in both its decentralized and centralized guises, have been entirely minor. Yet this conclusion conflicts with the palpable growth of competition throughout the system, and the widespread view that market dynamics stand at the center of the transition now underway. The simple, and probably accurate, solution to the puzzle is that although federal policy has done little directly to change incentives, the debate about why and how to try to do so has helped change the way society *thinks* about incentives. These changing attitudes have combined with other, non-policy-specific variables to promote competitive forces that are gaining new prominence in the mid-1980s.

The first element in an explanation for the rise of competition in the 1980s is what might be called the social symbolism of scary numbers. The main horrors were mentioned earlier: over 10 percent of GNP devoted to health care, an impending Medicare hospital insurance trust fund deficit, projections that the national health bill would hit $1 trillion annually by the mid-1990s, a federal health budget doubling every five years, and health costs rising at a rate well above that of general prices. These figures, well publicized and falling hard upon one another, raised very sharply the question whether these levels of spending and rates of increase were supportable or desirable.

As spokesmen for the American Medical Association sometimes remind their critics, however, who is to say how much is enough? Why not 15 or 20 percent of GNP and $2 trillion a year? Is health not worth it? These caveats were largely neutralized by a second element in the explanation—the range of arguments, increasingly pervasive and persuasive, suggesting that Americans do not in fact realize proper value for money in the system. New perspectives on prevention, on the distinction between curing and caring, and on the importance of psychosomatic as distinct from organic sources of ailments all dramatized the limits of curative medicine and therefore of the traditional model.

Society might have reached a consensus that health spending was too high without coming to detailed agreement on where to make cuts. In fact, however, in the late 1970s and early 1980s a third element entered the equation—an explosion of data documenting major areas of overuse and suggesting plausible candidates for economies. These data came both from academic studies of small area variations and from regulatory bodies—for example, peer profiles of physicians assembled and analyzed by the PSROs, community data incorporated in HSA plans, and peer comparisons of hospitals along dozens of measures constructed by rate-setting bodies. As a consequence, utilization patterns lost much of their mystery—at least enough of it to embolden laymen to ask tough questions and demand cogent answers.

These challenging findings might have made little impact if they had been confined to academic journals and the counsels of planning and regulatory bodies.
As it has happened, however, these data were disseminated and debated in larger
forums that reached both elite and mass opinion. Lengthy television features and
newspaper articles and series have examined the health cost problem and creative
approaches to solving it. Local business and community coalitions, assisted by
such national groups as the Washington Business Group on Health and the "Big
Six" organizations convened by John Dunlop, have acquainted organizational
notables with the latest thinking on savings. The computer revolution and the
proliferation of health data firms have enabled businesses, large and small, to
print out in their own benefit offices profiles depicting who is a preferred provider
and who is not, and to use this information in efforts to purchase health coverage
more prudently.

Purchasers might have these data and the most prudent of intentions yet be
unable to act on them for want of concrete alternatives with which to do business.
But since the mid-1970s alternative delivery systems (ADS), including HMOs,
PPOs, and variations on these themes, have grown substantially. In 1976 such
"experiments" were taboo among physicians and radical to many purchasers; a
decade later they are mainstream in everyone's eyes. For the new legitimacy
enjoyed by ADS federal market-building efforts can properly claim much credit.

Such alternatives might fail as realistic options if providers endorsed them in
theory but worked to defeat them in practice. Yet since the late 1970s growing
awareness of the sizable surplus of hospital beds and physicians has sapped both
the ability and the will of providers—who are increasingly anxious to secure their
market shares by contracting with fixed and stable sources of demand—to thwart
these changes. Unable to beat ADS, many providers have agreed to join them.

The result of this sequence of developments is a new competitive dynamic that
cannot be explained adequately by invoking changes in economic incentives. The
principal basis of this competitive energy is changing ideas, especially the notion
that in health care economic discipline presupposes organizational discipline,
which in its turn demands improved management. So strongly rooted is this conviction that today one can speak of a "managerial imperative" whose main competitive expressions are HMOs, PPOs, managed care systems, and gatekeeping
techniques. This is a major departure: managers are no longer viewed as glorified
clericals or the obedient servants of medical professionals. This deep and broad
trend—of which the much-discussed "corporatization" is but one expression—
will probably continue to gain strength.

The managerial imperative has regulatory as well as competitive manifestations; today's fascination with the novelty of the latter should not obscure the
importance of the former. At the dawn of the new era in the 1970s policy makers
were warned that they must choose between competition and regulation as vehicles of cost containment. Sensibly replying (in essence) that such a stark choice
was both premature and unrealistic, they experimented with decentralized ver-

sions of both strategies. While attempting to launch HMOs they also set in motion regulatory programs that embodied two distinct theories. The PSROs, HSAs, and CON programs shared three basic properties. First, they were examples of "behavioral" regulation, scrutinizing detailed decisions about utilization, expansion, modernization, and acquisition by providers and trying to block those (and only those) that were not necessary and appropriate. Second, working within the framework of the traditional cost-based reimbursement system, they hypothesized that if the system could be pruned around its edges to eliminate waste it could, so to speak, be saved from itself. Third, these programs had a federal blueprint. There were to be about 200 PSROs and a roughly equal number of HSAs with federally mandated structures and procedures; and under the planning legislation of 1974 each state was to adopt a CON program that met federal standards.

Rate setting differed on all three counts. First, it represented budgetary, not behavioral, regulation. The idea was not to scrutinize and then approve or deny specific decisions made by providers (a battle very hard for layman regulators to win), but rather to set dollar limits on rates or revenues, leaving it to administrators and medical staffs to adapt managerially. Second, rate setting explicitly broke with the traditional payment approach. Its premise was that *prospective* reimbursement was necessary for improved efficiency, though the units and methods of prospective payment could take many forms. Third, rate-setting programs in the states developed with federal funds, technical assistance, and waivers, but without tight federal constraints. Self-selection among the states was allowed and encouraged, programs differed with state preferences and politics, and the federal system was permitted to play its fabled role as a laboratory of innovation and an arena of experimentation. By the early 1980s experience and evaluation called the first (behavioral) approach severely into question but suggested that, at least in certain sites and under favorable circumstances, the budgetary strategy might achieve significant savings.

In short, by 1980 policy makers had planted the conceptual and programmatic seeds of new competitive *and* regulatory interventions. Meanwhile events were planting the political seeds of a new synthesis of competitive and regulatory approaches that would add momentum to the gradually accelerating transitions of the 1970s. Briefly, the main developments (noted above) were these. In 1977, President Jimmy Carter introduced his hospital cost-containment plan. Resolved to defend the status quo, the hospital industry countered with its "voluntary effort." In 1978 the Carter plan was debated, attacked, and amended. In 1979 it was decisively defeated in the House of Representatives, and the hospitals' "voluntary effort" collapsed. In 1980 Ronald Reagan won the White House and promised to replace regulatory with competitive solutions in the quest for health cost containment. The regulatory slate, it seemed, would soon be wiped clean. Hospital costs soared. In 1981, hospital expenditure increases edged toward 20 percent, while Reagan failed to deliver a procompetitive cost-containment plan. Meanwhile, evidence was accumulating on the savings in both HMOs and rate setting, and it began increasingly to be noticed that these supposedly antithetical competitive and regulatory approaches shared a common element—prospective payment. Both Congress and the executive branch, feeling in some measure betrayed by the hospitals, began talking up prospective payment and warning that change was in the wind. In 1982 Congress passed the Tax Equity and Fiscal Responsibility Act, which made sharp cuts in Medicare payments to hospitals and instructed HHS to deliver a prospective payment plan by year's end. In December HHS presented its plan, which had been for some time under development in the Health Care Financing Administration. In 1983 the PPS became law with little debate, embraced by a coalition that included members who viewed it as regulated competition and others who considered it procompetitive regulation. The parallel lines of competitive and regulatory policy had, so to speak, converged, leaving a system in which measures of competition *and* regulation that had been unthinkable ten years earlier were not only present but accepted and applauded.

The limits of transition

How does one evaluate these transitions? On some counts the system (both public and private) surely earns high marks. It has been flexible and responsive; it has experimented and innovated; it has not been paralyzed by antique ideas or omnipotent interests. It has even acted rationally in the sense that (if the analysis offered here is accurate) there is a pattern of trial, error, and adaptation in the comings and goings of strategies and programs.

From the standpoint of the health care system as a whole, however, these transformations, important as they have been, remain confined to a rather narrow sphere. Most of them address what might be called the "profligate provider" model of rising health care costs. The comforting assumption is that once overutilization, abuse, waste, and unnecessary and inappropriate care have been sufficiently curtailed, all will be well.

Even if this happy outcome were achieved, however, the "price of progress" model, which concentrates on costly developments that have little to do with waste and inefficiency, will continue to challenge policy makers to reduce the growth of costs without unacceptably restricting the scope of true medical benefits. Three ingredients of this latter model are of special importance.

The first is demographic trends, especially patterns of aging. As an ever-larger portion of the population lives to ever-greater old age it will demand more medical, custodial, and social services. Yet the United States has hardly begun to formulate a coherent and humane long-term-care policy.

A second set of "progressive" costs derive from medical technology, which is inherently innovative and often cost-increasing. Some believe that an effective assault on current wasteful practices in the system could easily free sums large enough to support artificial hearts and other organs for all who need them. Others contend that even with reasonable efficiencies, technical progress will eventually become so costly that care sometimes will have to be denied to patients who would derive significant benefit from it. This, of course, raises the spectre of rationing, a moral and practical challenge policy makers have not yet confronted.

Third, change—and resistance to change—in patterns of personnel, the largest source of costs in this the nation's second-largest industry, raise perplexing policy issues. In general, the larger the numbers of workers absorbed into the health services sector, the higher the costs of sustaining that sector, and the stronger the political pressure to curb the growth of those costs. On the other hand, the larger the size of the health sector personnel component, the stronger the potential constituency against cost controls, or, at any rate, against controls that threaten employment. Today fiscally pressed hospitals are increasingly cutting costs by discharging more expendable personnel, which may aggravate unemployment in disadvantaged communities; at the same time new jobs are arising in a wide range of alternative delivery systems, which may generate new political constituencies in support of arrangements about which little is now known.

A final limitation of the transitions of the last decade is the most important of all: the system's laudable flexibility and innovativeness have been directed almost wholly to cost containment, scarcely at all to issues of equity and the distribution of services in relation to need. On these latter counts, alas, the system has been depressingly stable, disturbingly continuous. The portion of the population lacking health insurance has risen during the 1980s and now may stand near 15 percent. Despite recent modest reforms, those who lose their jobs may lose their health insurance, too. Many risk bankruptcy as a consequence of catastrophic illness. Others might reap benefits from preventive measures that policy does not provide, fund, or encourage. Half of the poor fail to qualify for Medicaid, a program whose original intent—to aid the younger, welfare poor—has largely collapsed, as about half its dollars go to nursing homes. In these areas of policy there are transitions devoutly to be wished.

Those who hope that the policy process will soon address these equity questions in earnest sometimes assume that the correct course is a major expansion of the role of the federal government in establishing new entitlements along universalistic lines. This path may lead nowhere, however, for attitudes toward the meaning of justice in social policy and toward the role of government are now also in transition. The conviction that health care is a right to which everyone should be entitled at government expense (or subject to government guarantees) has never been very strong in the United States, and what little strength it has retained is rapidly ebbing. The notion that a right to care embraces all the innovative, costly, and sometimes doubtfully effective products of medical progress is increasingly implausible; interest in "minimum adequate standards" (perhaps amounting to an unmistakable second tier of care) and rationing of costly procedures is likely to grow. At the same time entitlements to health care (however circumscribed) at public expense for all citizens regardless of their resources seem increasingly extravagant given the high and rising cost of care, the difficulties in providing adequate care for the poor and the "truly needy," and the claims of policy areas other than health, some of which may have a stronger influence on health outcomes than does health policy itself. Therefore policy makers are likely to explore various forms of targeting, probably including means testing and other retreats from universalism.

Meanwhile, the post-Depression image of the federal government as society's salvation from erratic and catastrophic market forces and overwhelmed subnational governments has been badly strained as that government has, especially since the mid-1960s, assumed many new commitments and fumbled some of them. Although much of this fumbling results not from intrinsic ineptitude but rather from the complexity of the tasks government set itself, federal "failures" have fueled enthusiasm for private-sector, market-based approaches, competition, and incentives. And the pitfalls of "trying to run the country from Washington" have brought renewed attention to the merits of devolving policy to the state and local levels of government, which are supposedly more flexible and closer to the people.

Policy that sets aside the quest for uniformity and centralization in favor of targeting, efficiency, reprivatization, and devolution is bound to be even more fragmented than that to which the system is congenitally accustomed, harder to ground in general normative categories, and less conducive to amalgamating groups into political coalitions. Defining "true need" as a precondition for governmental assistance can easily bog down in the fine print of empirical distinctions, as one sees from the debate about health coverage for the medically indigent—some of whom are unemployed, but others of whom have part-time jobs, are occasionally employed, have full-time jobs with few or no fringe benefits, or have spouses in one of these situations, each of which carries distinct policy implications. The closer and longer policy makers ponder the "technical" heterogeneity of the group to be assisted, the harder it is to maintain focus on the moral dimensions of their need and to assemble a coalition for change.

Likewise, a governmental commitment to fund only services that pass clear benefit-cost or cost-effectiveness criteria would create much methodological and other confusion, as the debates about the merits of various preventive services shows. Determination to adjust government's rules so as to enlarge the roles and free the energies of private-sector organizations can mortgage action to debate over theoretical scenarios whose merits may remain in doubt for years (the systemwide savings of HMOs, for example) or may paralyze policy by holding out prospects that are impeccable in the abstract but improbable in the political arena (such as reform of the tax treatment of health benefits, vouchers, and "consumer choice" health plans). And a larger role for the states, which are supposedly closer to the people, may put vulnerable citizens at the mercy of policies about which the rest of "the people" have little information or understanding (for example, Medicaid policies on eligibility, payment levels, services, provider payments, and the distribution of spending among groups).

Those who retain their allegiance to New Deal notions that firmly equate equity with uniformity and universalism and policy with programs of the federal government may want to think again. Those who would see new and better benefits find their place on the public agenda alongside cost-containment issues may need to map a transition from the comfortable traditional liberalism to a new progressivism, its basic features as yet obscured by experiment and conjecture.

Notes

1. Robert R. Alford, "The Political Economy of Health Care: Dynamics Without Change," *Politics and Society* 2 (Winter 1972): 127–64.

2. Eliot Freidson, *Professional Dominance* (New York: Atherton, 1970); Robert R. Alford, *Health Care Politics* (Chicago: University of Chicago Press, 1975); Paul Starr, *The Social Transformation of American Medicine* (New York: Basic Books, 1982).

3. Letter to *Medical Economics,* quoted in Victor R. Fuchs, *Who Shall Live? Health, Economics, and Social Change* (New York: Basic Books, 1974), p. 64.

4. Robert M. Gibson et al., "National Health Expenditures, 1983," *Health Care Financing Review* 6 (Winter 1984): 1; Mark Freeland and Carol Ellen Schendler, "National Health Expenditures Growth in the 1980s: An Aging Population, New Technologies, and Increasing Competition," *Health Care Financing Review* 4 (March 1983): 3; "Summary of the 1983 Annual Reports of the Medicare Board of Trustees," *Health Care Financing Review* 5 (Winter 1983): 2–3.

5. Uwe E. Reinhardt, "The Problem of 'Uncompensated Care' or Are Americans Really as Mean as They Look," in *Proceedings—Uncompensated Care in a Competitive Environment: Whose Problem Is It?* 13–14 September 1984, HRP-0906304 (Washington, DC: U.S. Department of Health and Human Services), p. 20.

6. See Lawrence D. Brown, *Politics and Health Care Organization: HMOs as Federal Policy* (Washington, DC: Brookings Institution, 1983), chapter 5.

7. Alain C. Enthoven, *Health Plan* (Reading, MA: Addison-Wesley, 1980).

Finding the Levers, Finding the Courage: Lessons from Cost Containment in North America

Robert G. Evans, University of British Columbia

Abstract. "Learning" is broader and more complex than simply the orderly acquisition of new knowledge. At least as important is the evolution of the background of assumptions and beliefs held by the community, or its principal decision makers, and implicit in its institutions and policies. These may bear only a loose relation to evidence or knowledge narrowly defined. The pressures of cost escalation over the past twenty years, and the attempts at containment in the U.S. and Canada, have added substantially to our knowledge of how the health care system works. Containment is possible, and the successful mechanisms, thus far, are quite specific. But the results of these attempts and (in the U.S.) the continued escalation have also significantly shifted the broader set of assumptions in the community about appropriate priorities and policies in health care. Attitudes towards physician supply, variations in practice patterns, capitated practice, and for-profit organization, for example, have changed radically, although the supporting evidence has not. But cost pressures have created an audience which wants to hear, whose background assumptions provide a different "fit" for the evidence.

Expenditures on health care in the United States have been rising at a faster pace than the general rate of growth, and therefore taking up an ever-increasing share of national income, roughly since the end of World War II. Health care cost escalation has thus been the experience of an entire generation. For the first half of this period, roughly until the mid-1960s, this expansion was regarded (by most of those who were conscious of it at all) as a "good thing," a humane and proper way to spend, or even invest, the extra production of a growing economy.

Concerns about the "cost spiral," however, began to emerge during the 1960s. These concerns have become increasingly acute as the upward trend has continued, with periods of apparent stabilization followed by resurgences of growth. By 1985 the United States was devoting 10.63 percent of its gross national product to expenditures on health care, up from 5.94 percent in 1965 and 4.06 percent in 1948; expenditures are projected to be over 12 percent by 1990.[1] This escalation has kept health care cost containment near the top of the domestic policy agenda, and a number of general strategies and specific policies have been suggested in response. Some have even been tried.

None, however, have worked. Proponents of the currently fashionable strategy of relying on competition, for-profit motivation, and the forces of the marketplace continue to see light at the end of the tunnel. Competition, in some broad sense, will eventually limit the escalation of costs, although exactly when is obscure. (Most economic analysis is based on static equilibrium models, which are silent as to the time path of adjustment.) And it may be so, but by 1986, after several years of such policies, it has not happened yet.

This record of failure suggests that the principal lesson to be learned from cost control is that it cannot be done. Then, human nature being what it is, the next step is a "sour grapes" argument that control is probably an inappropriate objective anyway, although this conclusion is more popular among academic analysts (and, of course, health care providers) than among those who pay the health care bills.

But this conclusion, though in one sense comforting as an explanation or excuse for the American record, is incorrect. A closer examination of the evolution of health care expenditures and of efforts to control them, particularly in the light of comparable international experience, yields a number of inferences both about the way in which the health care system functions and responds (or fails to respond) to particular incentives, and about the sorts of policies which are likely to work in the future.

Moreover, and perhaps most important, the experience of the past twenty years has brought about a significant shift in the way in which the rest of society, or at least many of its key decision makers, view the health care system. "Learning" is much broader and more complex than the orderly acquisition of new knowledge, "scientific" or otherwise. It includes the evolution of the broad general background of assumptions and beliefs which people bring to particular issues and problems. Very rarely, if ever, is the knowledge base sufficiently complete and secure to provide a definitive answer to a real-life policy question. Rather, as Samuel Butler noted, "life is the art of drawing sufficient conclusions from insufficient premises."

In the process, we draw on a large, semiconscious collection of "things we believe when we do not know," a sort of set of default assumptions. And it is this set of assumptions, at least insofar as they relate to the provision and pricing of health care, which have been shifting over time. If we think of "learning" as changing the way we think about the world, this shift may be the most significant and consequential form of learning from cost containment.

Patterns in U.S. health care expenditures: The possibility of policy

The argument that cost control is impossible or in any case undesirable has its roots in two separate and to a considerable extent conflicting intellectual traditions, whose conflicts are nevertheless frequently misunderstood or deliberately glossed over in debate. These are the economic theory of consumer choice, and the clinical determination of medical need. We will deal with the former here: the latter will be deferred because it addresses only desirability and because it raises more complex issues.

The "consumer choice" view treats health care as just one more bundle in the general universe of commodities, from which fully informed and rational consumers each choose, subject to the constraint of limited resources, the set that gives them the greatest satisfaction. Health care cost escalation is then reinterpreted as indicating that care is a "luxury" good on which people choose to spend more as their incomes rise. One should therefore not be surprised or concerned that the share of national income spent on health care is rising; it is a natural consequence of growing wealth that people change the mix of commodities that they buy. This view is then buttressed by reference to international data, which show that there is indeed a significant positive correlation between a country's national income per capita and the share of that income devoted to health care.[2]

This view has always been rather unconvincing because it rests on the assumption that the utilization of health care *can* in fact be usefully analyzed in the framework of informed consumer choice, an assumption which has no very obvious a priori appeal and has been rich in challengers. Moreover, it is notorious that ill health is associated with poverty, not wealth, so if health care were treated as a luxury good, its distribution at any point in time would be perverse from a clinical standpoint.

It is also notable that cost escalation has been to a large extent driven by increases in the relative prices of health care services, a form of sector-specific inflation which has been continuous for forty years. Absent this, and the increase in actual utilization of health care which has been taking place would be a roughly constant share of U.S. national income. If, therefore, informed consumers are "choosing" to spend more on health care as their incomes rise, it is odd that they should be "choosing" higher prices. These quibbles can be circumvented by a suitable combination of conceptual redefinition, unsubstantiated references to supply elasticities, and confident assertion, but the analysis loses clarity and conviction.

For our purposes, however, the international comparisons are more interesting. The most recent comparative analysis of health care spending, by Poullier for the OECD (Organization for Economic Cooperation and Development) countries, confirms a general positive relationship between per capita income and percent spent on health care, with an income elasticity of $+1.3$—that is, each 10 percent increase in income is associated, on average, with a 13 percent increase in health spending. But this is an average; at least as interesting is the pattern of variation around the average. The OECD study reports that countries at the top of the "league tables" with similar levels of per capita income—the U.S., Canada, Sweden, Norway, and Switzerland—spend remarkably different amounts on

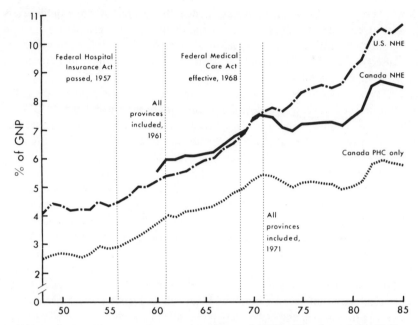

Figure 1. Health Expenditures as a Share of GNP, Canada and the U.S., 1948–85

health care. "Socialist" Sweden and the "capitalist" U.S. spent the largest shares, 9.6 percent and 10.8 percent of GDP respectively in 1983, but Canada and Switzerland spent 8.2 percent and 7.8 percent, and Norway was down at 6.9 percent.[3]

It is difficult for an external observer to assess the significance of the very large discrepancy between Norway and Sweden. But the Canada–U.S. divergence is well established. The message of the international comparisons is not that health cost escalation is a natural, unavoidable, and indeed desirable consequence of increasing income, but that there is a great deal of variety in national experience. High incomes and low, or at least lower, health spending are quite compatible. The U.S. has taken the high road, but others were available.

In particular the Canada–U.S. comparison, which has been frequently noted but even more frequently discounted or ignored in the U.S., shows that societies with very similar populations, environments, and cultures, and even very similar health care delivery (though not payment) systems can show very different records of cost control. Figures 1 and 2 display the historical trends in health care expenditure relative to GNP for Canada and the U.S. over the postwar period.[4] Abstracting from the recession-induced jump of 1982—a recession from which Canada has never entirely recovered—the Canadian ratio has been roughly stable since 1970. For hospital and physician care, the 1982 recession only brought the Canadian percentage back up to its 1970 level.

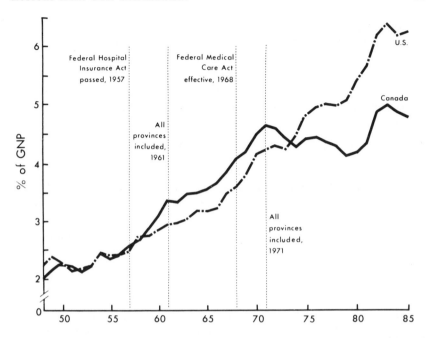

Figure 2. Hospitals and M.D. Expenditure as a Share of GNP, Canada and the U.S., 1948–85

Figures 1 and 2 declare, about as loudly and clearly as it is possible to do, that costs *can* be contained over a long period of time. They emphasize the critical role of the public insurance program in achieving this stability, because it is quite obvious that the cost patterns in the two countries only begin to diverge, and the Canadian to stabilize, after the completion of the universal, comprehensive public insurance programs at the end of the 1960s. Moreover the divergence between the two countries' experience only shows up in those sectors—hospital and physician services—which are covered by the Canadian public plans.

But the lessons from past efforts at cost control are by no means all Canadian success and American failure. The most recent U.S. experience, and in particular the 1984 data, which triggered (somewhat prematurely) announcements of success in the struggle against rising health care costs, yield some important findings. Total health spending as a share of the U.S. GNP actually fell between 1983 and 1984 from 10.49 percent to 10.36 percent, although a strong general economy in 1984 contributed to this, and the ratio appears to have rebounded to a new peak of 10.63 percent in 1985. But the real action is in the hospital sector.

Spending on hospital care rose 6.1 percent between 1983 and 1984, but all of this was due to price increases.[5] Adjusted for increases in the prices of hospitals' services, total expenditure did not rise at all. But the population served increased by about 0.9 percent and its average age increased. Aging per se is currently contributing about 1 percent per annum to hospital utilization, ceteris paribus.[6]

So hospital expenditure per capita in constant dollars, adjusted for population age, actually *fell* by about 2 percent in one year.

This is in striking contrast to the previous record of continuous growth in real, per capita hospital spending. From 1965 to 1975, hospital spending per capita rose on average 4.3 percent per year, over and above the increases in hospital prices. From 1975 to 1983 it slowed to 3.0 percent per year, still about 2 percent above the estimated impact of population aging on utilization.[7] Then in one year the rate of growth of real spending swung down from 2 percent above to 2 percent below the growth of age-adjusted population.

The preliminary 1985 National Health Expenditure data do not report the change in the hospital price index, but the overall increase in hospital spending is 5.6 percent, down from 6.1 percent in 1984. The Consumer Price Index component "hospital and other medical services" for December 1985 over December 1984 is up 5.0 percent (compared with the All-Items Index at 3.8 percent),[8] suggesting that real expenditures per capita have fallen by another half a percent, and age-adjusted use by about 1.5 percent.

This shift in spending patterns is both unprecedented and massive. If the pre-1984 trends had continued, hospital spending would have been about $6.3 billion higher in 1984, and perhaps $10–12 billion higher in 1985. The U.S. would have reached 11 percent of GNP spent on health care. This did not happen, for reasons which are only partly understood.

The easy explanation is that the change in the U.S. Medicare reimbursement system, from cost reimbursement to prospective payment by admission, created incentives for shorter lengths of patient stay. The average length of stay in U.S. hospitals fell to 6.7 days in 1984. But total patient days in hospital dropped 8.6 percent, as a combination of a 3.7 percent drop in admissions and a 5.1 percent drop in lengths of stay, whereas prospective payment should if anything create incentives to *increase* admissions. Furthermore, since the population was both increasing and aging, and since these factors should have tended primarily to increase admissions (although elderly people also have longer stays), the fall in admissions on a per capita age-adjusted basis was well over 5 percent, or at least equal to the fall in lengths of stay.

Thus, the neat temporal conjunction of the change in the Medicare payment system (October 1983) with the massive and sudden shift in expenditure patterns in U.S. hospitals provides only part of the explanation. Something else was also going on; either other forces also bore down sharply in 1984, or they had been generating a cumulative pressure which finally triggered a response in that year, perhaps assisted by the influence of the prospective payment system (PPS).

The fact that utilization also fell among the under-65 population, very few of whom are covered by the U.S. Medicare system, emphasizes the inadequacy of the simple-minded reimbursement incentives story. But the generalization that "third parties have assumed a more active role in determining which services will be consumed and how many"[9] leaves open the obvious question: Why in

1984? Why did everything happen at once, when general, systemwide tendencies usually unfold over a number of years?

For our purposes, however, the critical observation is that *something happened*. A big shift in behavior occurred suddenly, which significantly reduced the rate of growth of a key expenditure component, and for the moment this shift is persisting. What we can learn from this U.S. experience, as from the international comparisons, is that cost patterns are not immutable, dictated by fundamental laws of nature or social behavior. If one finds the policy lever, the system responds. One may or may not fully understand the nature of the lever—as noted above, there is apparently a lot more going on besides PPS and DRGs—and we may not be sure if the response is good or bad, but the supertanker *can* be steered. Policy is possible.

Equally important, however, are the patterns which did *not* change after 1983. The changes in behavior were not only large, but localized, implying either tightly targeted incentives or very specific possibilities for response. The change in behavior is entirely located in hospital utilization, both in admission rates and in lengths of stay. The prices of hospital services rose, on average, by about 6 percent, or about 1.6 percent faster than the Consumer Price Index at 4.3 percent. This continues a long-established historical pattern of prices in the hospital sector rising more rapidly than in the general economy, whether the economywide inflation rate is high or low. Whatever the measures which induced the massive shift in hospital utilization patterns, they had no impact on relative price increases in that sector.

Expenditures on physician services were likewise wholly unaffected. Despite the continuing steady growth in physician supply, which outstrips the growth of population by about 2 percent per year, and the widespread commentary about increasing competition in the market for physician services, the U.S. Consumer Price Index component of "physician fees" rose by 7.0 percent in 1984, or 2.6 percent faster than the general increase in prices. In 1985 (December over December), fees rose 6.9 percent, or 3.0 percent faster than the CPI at 3.8 percent, and in the first half of 1986 they grew at a remarkable 9.2 percent annualized rate, while the increase in the CPI held at 0.4 percent.[10]

Physician fees have outpaced the general rate of inflation in the U.S. almost every year in the last forty,[11] but the long-run gain has been between 1 percent and 1.5 percent per year. Since 1980, however, the annual margin has widened significantly; from 1980 to 1982 physicians gained an average of 2.75 percent per year over the All-Items CPI. The 1984 and 1985 data continue this more rapid fee inflation, and the preliminary data for the first half of 1986, if they hold up, show a spectacular further surge. Whatever changes may have occurred in the provision and reimbursement of physician services in the last five years, they have as of 1986 had no detectable controlling effect on physician fees—quite the contrary.[12]

Of course, expenditures on physician fees depend not only on fee levels but also on rates of utilization. Conceivably a more competitive environment could yield either more careful "shopping" or biases in the measurement of fees actually received (discounting) such that reported utilization fell. But this too has not happened.

Constant dollar expenditure on physician services rose 3.0 percent in 1984, while a combination of population growth and aging (which has much less effect on physician use, about 0.33 percent per year per capita) would have accounted for about 1.25 percent to 1.33 percent. The 1985 increase, comparing a 9.8 percent increase in expenditures with a 6.9 percent increase (December over December) in fees, was about 2.7 percent. Per capita age-adjusted use is thus still rising steadily, in proportion (and by no means coincidentally) with the increase in physician supply. There is something of a long-term slowdown in the growth of utilization of physician services, from annual rates of over 4 percent in the late 1960s and early 1970s, but there is no dramatic shift in pattern after 1983, or anywhere else in the record.[13] If anything, it appears that a slight slowdown in the rate of increase in utilization per capita has been offset by an increase in the rate of escalation of (inflation-adjusted) fees, nothing more.

Nor is there much else of interest in the 1984 and 1985 data, with one dramatic exception. In general the shifts in shares of different components seem to be a consequence of the change in hospital utilization: if one item falls, the shares of the others have to rise as a result. In particular, after 1983 there is no sign of a rise in expenditures on nursing home care, which one might have expected to be offsetting some of the reductions in hospital use if patients were being transferred earlier and sicker. There is a long-term rise in the share of GNP going to nursing homes, but there is no significant change between 1983 and 1985. (The 1984 share is actually down slightly.)

The one other significant change after 1983 is in the costs of program administration and health insurance (overhead costs, or premiums less payouts). These shot up from $14.5 billion in 1983 to $19.1 billion in 1984, and again to $26.2 billion in 1985—or from 0.426 percent of GNP to 0.507 percent and 0.655 percent. Figure 3 shows the trend in this component over the last 25 years, with Canadian data for comparison, and emphasizes both the much greater overhead costs of operating a payment system with a diversity of funding sources and methods, and the long-term uptrend and recent acceleration in those costs. In 1960, when the U.S. and Canadian insurance systems had only begun to diverge (the Canadian universal hospital insurance plans were established in the late 1950s), the two countries spent similar amounts for this purpose. Now, the U.S. spends a share six times as great.

Looked at another way, if the U.S. had spent at the Canadian rate in 1985, the savings would be over half a percentage point of GNP, or nearly $22 billion— not much less than the entire cost of dentist services. About one quarter of the difference betwen Canada and the U.S. reported in Figure 1 is now the difference in the costs of running the payment system itself, as opposed to providing care. Indeed, if the share of GNP devoted to such costs had even remained constant at its 1983 level of 0.426 percent, total health outlays in 1985 would have been

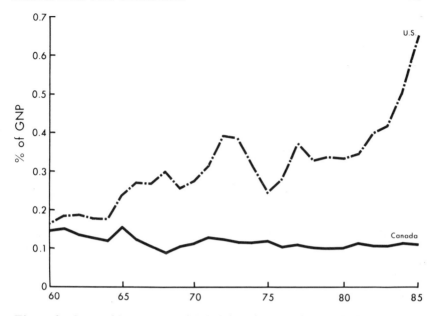

Figure 3. Costs of Insurance and Administration as a Share of GNP, Canada
and the U.S., 1960–85

lower by just over $9 billion. This is not far off the rough estimate above of the "savings" from reduced hospital utilization.

Various explanations may be offered for the post-1983 increase, including short-term adjustments in the reserve position of insurers, or windfall gains in new markets which have not yet been shaken out by competition. It is tempting to hypothesize, however, that this increase represents at least in part the costs of increased administrative effort required to control hospital utilization—the costs of saving money. If in fact this pattern persists, it may be that the U.S. experience after 1983 represents merely a transfer of outlays and incomes from hospital patient care staff to managers and investors, with no net saving to payers. If so, the implications for cost-control strategies would be profound, as it is by no means clear in what sense this would be an improvement for patients or anyone else (except, of course, for managers and investors).

Comparisons with the Canadian experience: The dimensions of reference

The U.S. experience after 1983, with sudden and major shifts in two components of health expenditures and "business as usual" elsewhere, is in this precise targeting similar to the longer-term Canadian record. Figures 1 and 2 were referred to earlier to indicate that cost control was in fact possible in a society, economy, and health care system very similar to that of the U.S. But they also show that the shift from cost escalation to stability, at least in terms of share of GNP, took place quite rapidly. The Canadian trends break sharply at the beginning of the 1970s. Cost control was not a gradual process, in which expansionary pressures slowly weakened and/or restraints were progressively tightened. It *is* true that both institutions and perceptions of policy priorities have evolved over time. But the shift from escalation to control was associated with a decisive and quite specific break in the institutional environment: the introduction of public, universal, comprehensive, first-dollar medical insurance. In the same way the American experience, at least with respect to hospital expenditure, shifts discontinuously between 1983 and 1984.

Moreover, the post-1971 Canadian pattern is not one of general cost control. The large discrepancy between Canada and the U.S., which by the 1980s reached 2 percent of GNP, is almost entirely located in hospital and medical costs—the sectors which are reimbursed through the public and universal plans. There are some cross-border differences in other sectors—the U.S. spends much more on program administration and net insurance costs, as noted, and Canada spends more on nonhospital institutional care. But in total these other categories have moved more or less in parallel on both sides of the border. Within the hospital and medical sectors, moreover, it turns out that the discrepancy is almost entirely due to diverging trends in two factors, physician fees and "intensity of servicing" in hospitals.[14]

In Canada, physician fees rose much less rapidly than the general inflation rate in the early and mid-1970s, thus falling in real terms, while in the last decade they have more or less kept pace. In the U.S., as noted above, fees have consistently outrun inflation, and by an increasing amount in the 1980s. Meanwhile, the supply of physicians and the utilization of medical services per capita have increased steadily and at about the same rate in both countries. In neither country is there any sign of "saturation" or falling average workloads per physician (as measured by total expenditures adjusted for fee increases and divided by the supply of physicians) in response to increased supply. Nor has the difference in out-of-pocket costs (virtually zero in Canada, but about one-third of all physician bills and perhaps 60 percent of ambulatory bills in the U.S.) resulted in any difference in utilization trends.

In the hospital sector, again, the Canada–U.S. trends are roughly parallel with one exception. In both countries, hospital prices have for decades outrun general inflation rates. Utilization of services as measured by patient days and admissions first rose through the 1950s and 1960s, then peaked and began to drift down. But the key difference is in "intensity of servicing"—the cost per patient-day or per capita adjusted for price changes—which represents the volume of services provided/received during the period. This has risen much faster in the U.S. than in Canada, and is the dominant factor in explaining (in an accounting sense) the difference in hospital cost patterns.

The fact that the Canada–U.S. cost differential can be so specifically located in particular components of the total of health care costs is indicative of its dependence on particular institutional/policy differences. The divergent trends in physician fees demonstrate the differing effectiveness of countervailing power and of "market" forces, however competitive or otherwise these are perceived to be.

In Canada, uniform fee schedules are negotiated annually between the medical association of each province and the provincial reimbursement agency, and all medical practitioners in private fee-for-service practice are reimbursed by the province, not the patient, on this schedule. "Extra-billing" the patient above this schedule has been a contentious issue for years, but has never been large, and is now effectively nonexistent. The result of fee control has not been an offsetting surge of additional bills (although that pressure does exist, and there is much more to fee schedule negotiation than simply limiting increases), nor has it been an exodus of physicians or a drying up of recruitment. Rather, the result has simply been lower fees—and lower rates of cost escalation.

The hospital picture is more complex. Hospitals are reimbursed for their operating costs on an annually negotiated global budget, with separate grants for their approved capital expenditures. While U.S. hospitals, reimbursed (for a significant part of their case load) by the procedure at a rate covering both operating and capital costs, have (had) every incentive to encourage high levels of procedural intensity, Canadian hospitals do not, at the margin, earn more by doing more. The result, as noted above, is that in the U.S. hospital system the amount of servicing, the number of person-hours and procedures per patient-day, has risen significantly faster than in Canada.

But there is another dimension to this contrast. Average lengths of stay in acute-care hospitals are substantially longer in Canada, and have not been falling as in the U.S. They currently average about 11 days, compared to the 6.7 reported for the U.S. in 1984. An increasing proportion of patient-days are accounted for by people staying for 60 days or more, and physicians speak of "bed blockers" who tie up capacity and prevent them from admitting acute patients for whom they could provide (and bill for) services.[15]

The U.S. has found a way to bribe or browbeat hospitals into discharging patients earlier, or not letting them in at all, with corresponding sharp drops in occupancy rates, bed closures, and perhaps hospital bankruptcies. In Canada, beds are "withdrawn from service" by being occupied by de facto long-term patients who are less intensively serviced on a per day basis. The Canadian approach maintains the jobs of nurses and provides long-term care; the U.S. discharges the nurses and hires managers and technicians, and emphasizes machines and procedures. In both systems, the availability of acute-care beds is reduced, but the style of care, and the mix of people earning incomes from providing it, is different.

The implications of these contrasting experiences in cost control are profound. The shift in U.S. hospital utilization patterns after 1983 is clearly traceable in part (and perhaps in whole) to changes in administrative procedures. These changed the incentives faced by hospitals, to be sure, and thereby changed their behavior. But incentives are not the exclusive property of "competitive" or "market" mechanisms. All administrative processes embody incentives as well. The introduction of the prospective payment system was a change in the administrative environment, a regulatory change in a broad sense, and it worked.

In the case of physician services, on the other hand, there has been no major change in the administrative environment. There has been much rhetoric about a more competitive market environment, and certainly the supply of physicians has risen rapidly and is continuing to rise, but there is no sign, as yet, that such increasing competition either in the conventional fee-for-service system or through the multiplicity of alternative purchasing arrangements such as PPOs, HMOs, and IPAs has had any impact at all on the long-term historical trends of increased utilization and sector-specific inflation. And the latter, at the moment, is accelerating.

Such inflation *can* be controlled—the Canadian experience is conclusive— but it has been done through fee bargaining and bilateral monopoly, backed up by a regulatory framework which does not permit physicians to have direct access to the patient's wallet. It may be that "the marketplace" in some form can also impose control; perhaps the present U.S. ferment needs more time or further fine tuning.[16] But such a view can at present only be a statement of faith in a result no one has ever seen in the U.S. or anywhere else.

The hospital sector experience is more ambiguous. As noted above, the timing of the post-1983 shift is consistent with a PPS effect, but the changes among classes of patients which it does not affect, and particularly the drop in admissions, emphasize that a broader shift is underway. This may reflect the effects of a number of other forms of administrative intervention, by both public and private insurers, galvanized by the shift to the PPS. But one might also argue that it is in part at least a response to the development of competitive forms of delivery. Perhaps the rapid spread of HMOs has finally resulted in an impact on overall utilization rates.

There seem to be two weaknesses to this line of argument. First, as noted above, it is difficult to see why such a long-term and gradual movement as the spread of HMOs should be reflected in a sudden and large trend break. One could offer the explanation of critical mass, except that the market penetration of HMOs varies widely across the U.S., so that different areas should "go critical" at different times, thus "smearing" the aggregate response. Second, recent case studies, reported in this journal, have shown that in those regions with the greatest market penetration by HMOs—Minneapolis, Hawaii, and Rochester, NY— there has been no detectable impact on hospital cost trends in the region as a whole.[17] Again one may argue that more mass is needed (though not so long ago, advocates were arguing that a small but aggressive entrant could force competitive behavior on an entire market). But if the regions where HMOs are strongest have yet to show a response, it is hard to argue that the national shift between 1983 and 1984 is driven by HMOs. Again one is brought back to the "regulatory," or at least the administrative, explanation.

But if the American cost experience confirms the potential effectiveness of administrative mechanisms for cost containment, and thus far fails to support the market approach, then it also has powerful implications for the continuing debates over the role of the consumer in the cost escalation process—implications which are reinforced by the Canadian comparison.

Many U.S. observers, particularly economists, have long maintained that health care cost escalation is at root the result of the behavior of *patients*—who "demand" increasing amounts of services and thereby drive up prices as well as utilization, or at least do not "shop" carefully enough to hold down prices— backed up by excessively comprehensive insurance coverage which relieves them of the financial consequences of their behavior. This coverage is in turn alleged to be the result of misguided government policy, which both supplies overly generous coverage to part of the population, and subsidizes it (through the deductibility of employer-paid premiums) for much of the rest.

The strength of this conviction has always seemed mysterious to external observers, who note that the U.S. has long had a combination of the world's highest and most intractable health costs, and the highest proportion (among developed nations) of expenditures funded by direct charges. But the interesting feature of the post-1983 break in hospital use is that nothing at all happened to the out-of-pocket costs of consumers. In 1983, hospital patients paid 8.6 percent of their hospital costs as direct charges; in 1984 they paid 8.7 percent. Yet patient-day utilization fell by 8.6 percent, or about 10 percent on an age-adjusted per capita basis, in one year. In 1985, the preliminary data report that direct charges did rise a bit, to 9.4 percent of the total, but it is hard to see why a utilization response should *precede* a price increase.

In fact, the share of government in U.S. health care spending has been remarkably stable over time. From 1950 to 1965, all governments in the U.S. accounted for just over one-fifth of health spending. Medicare and Medicaid pushed this up to about one-third in the mid-1960s, and further benefit expansions in the early 1970s increased the share to just under 40 percent, but it has held steady at that level for over a decade. U.S. governments have certainly participated in funding the cost escalation, but they have not led it. Neither the acceleration in physician fees in the 1980s nor the contraction in hospital use after 1983 bear any obvious relation to any shift in either the level of public funding or the extent of patient direct payment.

The Canadian experience, moreover, recasts the debate over the role of the consumer in a very different light. The combination of cost control with universal comprehensive coverage is not merely coincidental, but causal. Universal coverage is a necessary condition for government to engage in bilateral negotiations, to exercise the leverage whereby cost escalation can be controlled. So long as there are multiple funding sources, whether private insurance or direct charges to patients, providers can always find ways to expand their billings.

Indeed this view is strongly supported by physician organizations in Canada, who argue for the reintroduction both of the right to bill patients directly and of private insurance, precisely *because* they believe that this will increase costs. They argue that the current system is "underfunded," that an increase in expenditures (and in their incomes) is essential, and that universality and comprehensiveness are the features which lead to underfunding—the coin whose obverse is cost control.[18]

The U.S. arguments for direct charges and against universality are thus turned on their heads, both by supporters of the Canadian system and by opponents of it. Or rather, the experience with cost control in both countries suggests that the U.S. arguments are already standing on their heads; the Canadian debate puts them on a solid footing again.

The costs of cost control: Prescriptions painful to whom?

The two-sided coin that cost containment is also "underfunding" brings us back to some unfinished business. We noted at the outset that while analyses rooted in the economic theory of informed, rational consumer behavior raised questions as to the possibility and desirability of cost control, those rooted in the clinical assessment of medical need addressed more specifically its desirability. In the Canadian context, spokesmen for providers recognize only too well the fact, not merely the possibility, of cost control through regulatory mechanisms. Their claim of "underfunding" reflects a judgment, or at least a claim, that this is bad policy, and that continued cost escalation through a combination of public and (to a greater extent) private funding would be preferable.

There are, however, two parts to the "underfunding" case which must be carefully distinguished. As a matter of simple accounting definition, the total expenditures on health care (or anything else) in any society must be identically equal to the incomes earned by all those who participate in its provision. Cost control means income control, or it does not mean anything at all. In particular, expenditures on physician services make up the gross incomes or receipts of physicians; thus when the Canadian provinces limit the escalation of physician fees, the action has direct repercussions on the incomes of physicians. On the other hand, the continuing escalation of fees in the U.S. represents a continuing transfer of wealth from the rest of society to physicians. To a large extent, therefore, the claim of "underfunding" is simply a statement by Canadian physicians that they would like higher incomes.

Such a statement is no doubt true, but it is neither unique nor particularly compelling. So would I. To generalize the argument, it is necessary to show that the wider society, and patients in particular, have an interest in increased expenditure. Efforts to show that if physicians are not paid more they will all emigrate or leave the profession, or that enrollment in medical schools will fall, have been singularly unsuccessful due to the intractability of the data. All that remains is an exiguous claim that underpaid physicians will feel unappreciated, that their morale will suffer, and that quality of care will deteriorate. But no suggestion has ever come forward as to how this claim might be tested.

The fairly obvious lesson is that there will always be an automatic constituency *against* cost control which will become more active as and if successful control measures are developed, and will target its attacks on the measures most likely to be effective. But support of cost inflation per se, no matter how sincere, is a poor basis for building a coalition, so the expressed policy positions and prescriptions of providers are generally more subtle and require a certain amount of "unpackaging" to establish their net effects.

In the case of hospital services, however, the issue is less clear. It is important not to fall into the trap of assuming that whatever measures the providers of care, or their official and unofficial spokesmen, attack (or support) are always the most (or least) likely to control cost escalation. The rule is generally but not universally reliable. At the core of the issue is the question of whether constraints on cost escalation lead to a reduction in utilization (in the number, complexity, or sophistication of interventions) such that patients are denied care which would have been effective in improving their health status. Or more accurately, since the context is a dynamic one in which costs are in fact rising, the question is whether growth in hospital costs (in Canada) is too slow to keep pace with the growth in the scope of effective interventions, such that patients are being denied opportunities for benefit. In the clinical context, "underfunding" is equivalent to "unmet needs."

It is at this point that the Canadian debate joins the set of arguments in the U.S. which can be summarized as "painful prescriptions" and which display considerable ambiguity on the issue of cost control.[19] These arguments, or scenarios, start from the assumption that "needs" for care are without limit, which may well be true, depending on how one defines needs. For practical purposes, of course, all health care systems embody mechanisms for determining which needs are worth meeting, as there are no infinitely large health care systems.

But whatever mechanisms are employed, the ever-expanding reach of medical technology is constantly redefining needs by increasing the numbers and types of potentially effective interventions—and their costs. Thus a static health care system will confront an ever-increasing amount of unmet need as the range of potentially effective interventions left undone expands. Moreover the aging of the population will for the foreseeable future continue to increase the proportion of the population in vulnerable age groups, those with deteriorating health and accumulating needs for which medical interventions of all types are both increasingly effective and increasingly costly.

The essential ambiguity of the argument emerges from its conflicting long-run and short-run applications. If we accept the assumptions, the "painful prescription" asserts that we are caught in a cruel dilemma: either we must spend an ever-increasing share of our national income on health care, or we must accept a growing burden of unmet need in the sense of increasing numbers of effective interventions which we cannot afford to, or choose not to, provide. Nor can any increases in the efficiency with which health care is provided, or reductions in the prices or incomes of providers, or care in weeding out the ineffective from the effective interventions do more than postpone the inevitable. Eventually we must "ration" access to lifesaving and life-improving care because our resources simply cannot expand as fast as our needs.

Of course, like most economic arguments, this one is true, or at least consistent, if we accept its assumptions and wait long enough for the "long run" to arrive. But the assumptions are in fact highly questionable; as noted above, the impact of population aging per se on health care costs is in fact much lower than commonly imagined—about 1 percent per capita per year in aggregate, or well within the capacity of normal rates of growth of the general economy—and this has been demonstrated by every analyst who has examined the question. What is really happening is that the intensity of servicing (the number and cost of interventions) is rising relatively rapidly among the elderly themselves; the age-use profiles are shifting upwards and twisting.[20]

So the "inevitability of rationing" boils down to an assumption about the future of medical technology, in particular that it will continue to generate predominantly "half-way" technologies of great cost and limited effect rather than decisive breakthroughs which lower the costs of providing care. It is at least arguable that the direction of technological progress depends on the economic payoff to different types of innovation, and that as the U.S. moves away from cost reimbursement, the demand for innovation will shift toward more cost-saving technologies. There is no shortage of potential candidates; if progress in organ transplantation threatens to break the bank, that in genetic engineering holds out economic as well as clinical hope.

But these are long-run issues. The short-run implications of the "painful prescription" view of the world are distincly inimical to cost control. By focusing on the assumed inevitable long-run, it encourages the foreshortening of the policy horizon and distracts from or distorts the possibilities in the present. There is today, as the U.S.–Canada comparisons make clear, a great deal of scope for cost control, without an inevitable cost in terms of "unmet need." For that matter the Norwegian numbers suggest, and Canadian experience makes clear, that Canada is by no means the last word in efficiency either. The extent of unevaluated, or known ineffective, care, delivered in ways known to be unnecessarily costly by people for whom less costly substitutes have long been identified, is impossible to determine with precision, but could easily run between a quarter and a third of current U.S. outlays. That is enough of a challenge for one generation; who knows what the next generation's technology may bring?

It is not surprising, however, that the providers of care (whose incomes are drawn from current outlays) would prefer not to discuss these issues, but would rather focus our attention on the costs in "unmet need" of cost control. The focus on a hypothetical long run serves this purpose admirably by assuring us that current efforts to improve efficiency and effectiveness can only defer the inevitable, and thus are by implication unimportant, as well as by emphasizing the painful trade-off between expenditure escalation and unmet need, a trade-off which is either here or at least just around the corner.

But the possibility of cost control through improved efficiency and effectiveness of care, such that the growth of the health care sector can be reined in to that of the rest of the economy, is no guarantee of its attainment. It must be conceded that, in the hospital sector at least, the record of cost containment thus far will support a certain degree of unease.

The average length of stay in U.S. hospitals cannot fall without limit. However much "fat" is believed to be in the system in the form of unnecessary utilization, there must be some point at which increasingly early discharges begin to put the health of patients at risk. Some will claim that this has already happened; others point to a lack of any conclusive evidence. But stable costs achieved through falling average lengths of stay is not itself a stable situation. It looks rather more like the temporary respite from escalation predicted in the "painful prescription" scenario.

The downward trend in admission rates is somewhat more encouraging. There is probably a good deal more scope for both reductions and consequent savings through avoiding unnecessary admissions in the first place than there is through sending patients home earlier. The large and long-emphasized differences between hospital utilization rates in HMOs and those in comparable fee-for-service practice indicate the possibility of reductions of 20 to 40 percent in utilization rates without harm to patients, although some cracks may be appearing in that conventional wisdom.

But in the end the savings from better management of utilization are still bounded, even if large. At some point the escalation of hospital prices must be brought under control. In principle, the prospective payment system embodies incentives for hospitals to contain price increases as well as to shorten the lengths of patient stays. Competitive pressures bearing on HMOs should have similar effects, but so far this has not been observed. The successes of both HMOs and the administrative pressures applied through and alongside PPS after 1983 have come through reductions in utilization in the context of continuing escalation in prices/unit costs.

Moreover, both have run into trouble in translating sectoral savings into overall savings. As noted above, the post-1983 savings in hospital costs have been almost matched by extraordinary increases in the costs of program administration and overhead costs of insurance, suggesting that they may have been dissipated by the processes needed for their achievement. Meanwhile, the U.S. regions most deeply penetrated by HMOs do not show any resulting change in their overall cost behavior—for the region as a whole it is business as usual. And in the physician services sector, neither competitive forces nor administrative mechanisms have yet had any detectable impact. In the light of this experience, claims as to the inevitability of escalation and the temporary nature of any relief through either better management or more competition become understandable.

They do not, of course, become valid. The Canadian record of long-run cost stability is still there to be confronted. The important thing to note is that this stability has been achieved not by indirect means, by trying to create a more competitive environment for physicians or by paying hospitals in such a way as to encourage them to cut costs. Rather it has been the result of direct controls, such as face-to-face fee bargaining between physicians' representatives and the payers for care, and global budgeting for hospitals. Total spending is not completely locked in, as the volume of servicing by physicians is an uncontrolled variable, and hospitals can occasionally work their way around the "globe." But the scope for manipulating billing patterns is surprisingly limited when the structure of the fee schedule is itself negotiated. The control does not work with pinpoint precision, but it works.

Or does it? Do we know for sure that the consequence of controls is *not* unmet needs—potentially effective interventions foregone because the health care system is being starved for funds, or more accurately, because it has not expanded to keep pace with the growing capabilities of technology and needs of patients? No. The restraint on hospital expansion in Canada has been no more backed by careful evaluation and hard evidence than has the unrestrained expansion in the U.S. The difference is rather between an approach of "when in doubt, don't" and one of "when in doubt, do."

New and expensive technologies thus proliferate much less rapidly in Canada than has historically been the case in the U.S. (Things may be different under PPS.) In the case of innovations which turn out to be significant advances, some patients may suffer from this delay. On the other hand, it is notorious that new interventions in the U.S. have tended to proliferate too rapidly, far in advance of their evaluation, so that patients are exposed to unproven technologies which may turn out be of little value or even harmful in some or all of their applications (extracranial/intracranial bypass surgery is a recent case in point).[21]

The continued pressure applied to hospital costs by Canadian governments rests not on a firm foundation of clinical epidemiology or of evaluative studies demonstrating which interventions are effective and which are not, but rather on a much more impressionistic sense that when resources are limited, clinicians will make the appropriate decisions about which interventions to carry out and which to forego. Constant provider complaints and cries for more are to be expected, but if a real problem develops, the tone of the cry will change and something can be done about it.

Further, it is implicitly assumed that there is enough slack in the system as a whole so that new technologies can be funded at an appropriate level out of efficiencies in other areas, helped along by net expansion at about the same rate as the general economy. Overall restraint is consistent with reallocation of priorities and some net growth, and therefore does not result in increasing levels of unmet need as technology progresses. In any case, while the system remains overwhelmingly popular politically and relatively stable financially, no evidence has emerged that the health of patients, as opposed to the ambitions of providers, is suffering from the restraint.

Of course this may all be true, and the Canadian funding system may be as good a compromise among clinical, political, and economic forces as one can expect. But it would be nice to be sure that if constraints on expenditure growth *did* start to threaten the effectiveness of the system, we would in fact know about it. Just because providers cry "Wolf!" as a matter of course is no guarantee that there are no wolves out there or that none will ever arrive. On the other side of the coin, just because the escalation of costs has been controlled in aggregate, we have no warrant to assume that there are not still a number of activities going on which are highly questionable as to effectiveness or efficiency. Perhaps we could do a lot better.

The system of global constraint through political processes creates no inherent demand, by providers or payers, for sound evaluation of the effectiveness of current practices. Neither side in the dialogue has thus far shown any great interest in taking the risks implicit in a serious scientific evaluation of either current practices or new proposals. Providers might find themselves trying to justify current practices which turn out to be wholly or largely ineffective; payers might discover that they were refusing to fund the expansion of a proven beneficial innovation. From time to time it may be advantageous for either advocates or opponents of particular clinical activities to base their positions on evaluative research; but in general rhetorical arguments over global "less or more"—underfunding or cost explosion—are safer and less intellectually demanding.

On the other hand, it is not obvious that the competitive marketplace has generated any demand for evaluative research either, or that it will in the future. If the marketing process is to elicit information, there must be sophisticated buyers who can recognize and demand reliable information. The market share of providers must somehow be linked to the energy with which they seek out and offer therapeutically effective interventions and remove ineffective or harmful ones from their product lines.

But this sophisticated buyer is not the individual patient—that has never been and never will be true outside the mind and models of the odd economic theorist. Can the individual hope to be better informed as a buyer of insurance contracts, deciding which future therapeutic option packages are worth paying for? Will the paternalistic corporation as employer, or the union, have an incentive to demand effectiveness information on the basis of which to make choices for employees/members, and succeed in receiving such data? Perhaps, but this has yet to be shown. The art of marketing has rarely had much acquaintance with the generation and dissemination of scientific information.

A competitive marketplace displays a great deal more product innovation and change than a bureaucratically constrained system, for fairly obvious reasons. But there is no basis for any a priori assumption that in a highly "information-impacted" environment the result will be a more effective, much less a more cost-effective, health care system. So far, the U.S.–Canadian comparison suggests the reverse.

The shifting burden of proof: Changes in the intellectual background

It is helpful to back away from the most recent collection of statistical entrails, however, in order to identify a more important trend. We suggested at the beginning of this paper that perhaps the most significant lessons which had been learned from two decades of attempts at the control of health care costs across all developed countries took the form of a shift in the attitudes and background assumptions, the policy-relevant priors, of those whose decisions shape health policy. There are several specific examples.

A recent study by workers at the Rand Corporation has shown large variations across regions in the frequency with which beneficiaries of the U.S. Medicare system utilize different medical and surgical services, variations which were not traceable to measured characteristics of the populations served.[22] This is not news; such variations have been demonstrated by a number of different researchers for many different populations over at least twenty years. Studies by Bunker, Vayda, Wennberg, and Roos and Roos come immediately to mind, and there are others. But the Rand study is one more body of corroborative evidence, and it is also a large one.

The authors insert the customary caveats for interpretation. One cannot assume that high rates of servicing mean overservicing, because from the data alone it is equally possible that people in low-use regions are underserviced. For that matter the populations may differ in ways which the aggregate data do not reflect, but which clinicians on the spot recognize and respond to. The addition in the most recent paper is the authors' plea to their clinical colleagues to take these discrepancies seriously, not just because they may reflect opportunities to improve the quality of clinical practice, but because nonclinicians increasingly regard such variations as prima facie evidence of overservicing.

Twenty years ago, providers of care could ignore or dismiss such findings on the grounds that they did not constitute proof of inappropriate clinical behavior. Implicitly, clinical behavior was its own justification: if the doctor did it, it must have been right. Now, many dollars and years later, the burden of proof has shifted. A recent U.S. survey of private sector approaches to cost containment states baldly: "there is no medical excuse for the variation in care which now exists."[23] If physicians cannot find ways either to justify or to correct these variations, others will intervene.

They are beginning to do so, although with what success or side effects it is too early to say. The same source describes a number of initiatives by private payers to influence patterns of medical practice. For our purposes, however, the interesting fact is that the linkage from observed variation to inappropriate servicing is little more secure than it was twenty years ago. Our "scientific" knowledge on this point has increased somewhat, with additional demonstrations of widespread and large variations in clinical practice. For particular procedures, which are well documented and have well-defined indications, the weight of evidence certainly suggests some inappropriate servicing. But this is not proof of a general linkage. Yet the underlying default assumptions have now been reversed, in response primarily to the unrelenting pressure of cost escalation.

Physician manpower policy reflects the same reversal. The number of physicians per capita has been rising in both Canada and the U.S. since about 1950, roughly doubling over that time, and on present projections of population and physician supply will go on rising into the next century at least. Twenty years ago, this trend was viewed as a healthy response to a physician "shortage"; today it feeds a growing "surplus." Yet now as then, it is a standard debating trick of defenders of the status quo to issue the challenge, "Define the optimum level." The implication that if one cannot define the optimum, one cannot identify a surplus (or shortage) and therefore that present policies should be maintained is of course a glaring non sequitur. But it illustrates an important point.

With very few exceptions, attempts to define optimum levels of physician supply reduce, after a certain amount of number juggling of greater or lesser sophistication, to an assumption that current levels of utilization are appropriate, or at least not too high. Certain regions or specialties may be undersupplied, as evidenced by observed differentials in capacity or utilization. But as in the interregional variations case, clinical behavior is implicitly its own justification. With such a basis, as numerous critics have pointed out, surpluses are ruled out a priori. [24]

Over time, one finds that the optimum level posited by successive manpower studies rises more or less in proportion with the supply of physicians, because utilization rises along with physician supply. The planning exercise does not disturb the status quo; rather it provides a comfortable justification that all is well, and that whatever is, is right. [25]

In the U.S., this position is buttressed by "economic" arguments from those who still find the economic theory of the perfectly competitive marketplace a plausible way of thinking about medical care. In this world the correlation between supply and use is not causal (in the sense of additional physicians either generating or enabling additional use) but accidental, the result of parallel trends. Some can still repeat with straight faces the textbook homily that the price of physician services is the appropriate indicator of surplus or shortage. Using this argument there is still a shortage, since physician fees in the U.S. are still rising in real terms, and the actual numbers are irrelevant. Indeed, on the basis of the preliminary data above for the first half of 1986, the shortage must be becoming more acute.

In the real world, however, Doctor Pangloss receives less respect. It is now commonplace among Canadian ministers of health, for example, that each additional physician entering practice costs the taxpayers an additional $400,000 or $500,000 or some such amount, depending on the place and year. The strong correlation, across time and place, between physician supply and utilization is taken for granted as causal by those who pay for services. The easy steps to limit supply—cutting back on immigration—were taken as long ago as 1975, and now governments are finally raising courage enough to cut back on training places.

For immediate effect, however, one province (British Columbia) has placed limits on the numbers of new physicians permitted to bill the public insurance plan in regions designated as ''over-doctored''—a measure whose constitutionality is still in the process of being determined. If it is upheld, it will give the provincial government direct and immediate control over what it perceives to be a major component of its costs. If other provinces follow suit, new entrants may find practice opportunities severely curtailed throughout Canada.

In the U.S., by contrast, the physician surplus is being interpreted by many as an opportunity, not a threat. Alternatives to fee-for-service practice now have much less difficulty in recruiting physicians, and the diversity of forms of delivery is growing rapidly. As a result, the residual traditional fee-for-service market is becoming much more crowded more rapidly than the overall national picture indicates. Tarlov projects that by the year 2000 the average population per physician in the U.S. may be 429, but that outside the prepaid group practice sector it will be down to 310. The overall average in 1978 was 585.[26]

Such projections suggest that the pressures of competition on U.S. physicians have hardly begun to be felt. If so, this tends to support the position of the advocates of competition that the rock-solid stability of the long-run trends in physician fees, utilization, and costs is nearing its end. When twice as many physicians are trying to make a living from the same number of patients, something will break. Exactly *what* will break, however, and who will gain or lose as a result, is much less clear than simple-minded competitive theory would predict.[27]

Whether one views the surplus as threat or opportunity, the now-dominant perception is that there is now or will soon be a surplus. Yet the nagging question of ''What then is the optimum?'' has no better answer than it ever did. The ''market'' never saturates; even at 300 people per physician Israel's doctors remain busy. The North American ratio has just dipped below 500; there is still some distance to go. And a recent report of the Ontario Council of Health has shown that it is still possible to generate estimates of a physician ''shortage'' by the old tried and false methods.[28] Manpower needs are no better rooted in epidemiological data than they ever were, to say nothing of the extensive data on optimal manpower mixes which have been accumulated but ignored.[29]

The critical factor is that nearly forty years of growth in physician supply have gone by, accompanied in the U.S. by steady rises in costs and the consistent failure of all efforts at control. In Canada control has been established over fee escalation at least, but the political costs are high and may be rising. The trends in physician supply, and their cost implications, were clearly visible more than ten years ago. But once again, the general shift in perceptions followed after, and from, the experience of cost control: as Pogo said, "Man never reads the writing on the wall until his back is against it."

Yet a third area in which the data have not changed but the policy response has shifted is the HMO movement. The observation that capitated group practices are less expensive than comparable fee-for-service practice, and in particular that they make substantially less use of hospital care for their patients, is of very long standing; detailed empirical comparisons date from the 1950s. The standard responses have been to cast doubt on the comparability of the patient bases served or on the therapeutic outcomes—another instance of the "burden of proof" problem. The evidence has accumulated steadily over at least thirty years, yet a major review of the HMO experience in 1981 reported that it was still unclear exactly why HMOs were less expensive.[30]

By the 1980s, however, the background assumptions have changed. Everybody knows that HMOs are more efficient; the burden of proof rests squarely on anyone who would argue otherwise. Interesting questions about capitation still remain. There is room for a large amount of detailed work on the measurement of therapeutic outcomes, to deal with the question central to the whole process of health care delivery: How do utilization patterns link to outcomes? What is worth doing? But at the aggregate level, two obvious issues stand out. The first has been referred to above: if HMOs are less costly than fee-for-service practice, why is there as yet no evidence that their growth has lowered the growth of overall health costs in the regions where they are best established? The second issue arises from their changing sponsorship.

Virtually all the accumulated evidence on the comparative performance of HMOs has been derived from their historically dominant form, the not-for-profit prepaid group practice. This form established itself in American medicine in the 1940s and 1950s against intense opposition, but until very recently has been a small and geographically localized institution with a slowly growing market share. The explosive growth at the end of the 1970s and early 1980s has coincided with the entry of for-profit HMOs into the market, demonstrating the truth of the argument that for-profit competitive institutions are more dynamic.

But little or nothing is known about the performance, in terms of costs and effectiveness, of for-profit HMOs competing aggressively for market share in a highly competitive environment. All the previous research studied not-for-profit institutions, which were motivated by an alternative view of how medicine should be practiced (clinical and social objectives), struggling to survive in a hostile environment which was constantly looking for evidence of inadequate quality of care and would be provoked by overly aggressive expansion to retaliate through professional, not market, channels.

May one justifiably cheer on the new organizations, on the basis of the evidence from the old? A priori, one might expect performance of for-profit HMOs to be different. Professional hostility and competitive markets both impose powerful incentives, but to different forms of behavior. For-profit HMOs may be quite different from their not-for-profit forerunners. The fact is, however, that at this point we do not really know. Twenty years ago this ignorance would have counted strongly against for-profit HMOs; now it seems not to enter into the discussion. The pressures on U.S. business and government to contain costs have again reversed the burden of proof—a form of organization which promises savings does not have to justify itself on other grounds. It is the critics, now, whose case is all to make.

Of course, the shift in attitudes towards HMOs and similar alternative organizations is taking place within a broader shift in the assumptions about the appropriate form of organization for health care delivery—i.e., the balance of for-profit and not-for-profit (or not-only-for-profit) firms. For most of this century, there has been a consensus in at least the industrialized countries of the world that the delivery of health care was special, for a variety of reasons, and that the organizations providing it directly to patients should be motivated by considerations other than profit maximization. The supporting industries—drug and equipment manufacturing, for example—might be left to the for-profit sector, but hospitals in particular should be not-for-profit. The position of the physician was left in comfortable ambiguity, since the self-employed physician clearly receives the profits from the practice as an economic enterprise. Implicitly, the assumption was that physicians might receive profits and even be motivated by them, but that effects that were potentially harmful to patients would be mitigated by physicians' simultaneous pursuit of other and more "professional" objectives, backed up by peer group sanctions.

This view was never universal; in the U.S. a residual for-profit hospital sector has always persisted. But in the mid-1960s it seemed to be disappearing. In Canada, the much smaller and less firmly rooted for-profit sector *did* disappear. Twenty years later, however, the U.S. for-profit sector is not only alive and well, but growing rapidly. It is generally regarded as the wave of the future by supporters and opponents alike. The question now may be whether the *not-for-profit* sector will disappear.

The rhetoric of the marketplace has replaced that of the clinic; for-profit organizations are lean and efficient, flexible and responsive to consumer wants, and technically and administratively innovative. Concern that they might cut corners on quality, exploit the ignorance of patients, and "skim off the cream" of patients able to pay their own bills for relatively straightforward and profitable procedures are dismissed as self-serving pleas by inefficient organizations whose participants have been extracting above-market incomes (in cash or kind) under the cover of altruistic, "nonprofit" motives.

But again, what of the evidence? *Are* for-profit hospitals more efficient, in the sense of providing as or more effective care at lower cost? The question is, as always, complex, and the evidence is both mixed and remarkably scanty. In the hospital sector, however, such evidence as there is indicates the contrary. It appears that for-profit hospitals are *more* costly and spend *more* on management, administration, and marketing and less on patient care. Indeed, in an imperfect market they behave just as a priori economic theory would suggest, promoting the utilization of and raising the mark-ups on those services about which patients are least able to make independent decisions.[31]

The empirical evidence is, of course, contentious. That can be taken for granted both because the research process in a complex world is inevitably rough-edged, and because the associated large political and economic interests and ideological preconceptions enter into research methodology as well as into interpretation and reporting.[32] But the interesting shift is that analyses showing for-profit organizations to be *less* efficient—which in the hospital sector at least seem to have the better of the empirical argument[33]—are now subjected to the most searching criticism, and required to bear the burden of proof.

Twenty years ago, everybody knew that for-profit motivation was a menace to the health of patients and the finances of payers. Evidence to the contrary, if it received a hearing at all, could expect to be dismissed as failing standards of proof which could in turn be set high enough to ensure the desired outcome. Now that the shoe is on the other foot, serious concerns about the cost-effectiveness of for-profit institutions can be ignored, or dismissed by appeal to trivial nit-picking to undermine the empirical evidence.

Of course, part of the explanation is a more general change in the zeitgeist, in public attitudes toward the state and the marketplace. But it appears that to a large extent the transformation in the U.S. in particular is the outcome of twenty years of failed cost control. Just as victims of cancer, when the conventional treatments offer no hope, turn to laetrile and other nostrums, so the U.S. has turned to "free enterprise," competition, and the profit motive—rhetorical symbols which give great comfort (as well as substantial profit opportunities)—to solve an apparently intractable problem. The belief in efficacy stems not from the evidence, which is not there, nor from the a priori argument, which as always points both ways, but from the acutely felt need for a solution.

No other nation has gone this route, nor is likely to, partly because the symbolism of "free enteprise" does not evoke the same visceral response elsewhere (other countries have different "religions") but also because the experience with cost control has been different. The process of control is difficult, imperfect, and in a number of ways unsatisfactory, but it has not heretofore been an obvious failure. In Canada the cancer is in remission; we are not so interested in laetrile.

This language implicitly assumes that the current approach to health care cost containment in the U.S. will be ineffective. As emphasized above, that may be premature. The evidence so far is negative; numerous examples of apparent localized "successes" add up to aggregate "business as usual," which is failure. If this continues, then it seems virtually certain that the wheel will turn again, and the marketplace will fall out of favor.

There are of course those for whom the free market plays the same role as God did for the eighteenth-century deists; from that perspective process, not outcome, is the desideratum. The free market is not preferred because it achieves other objectives, whether of cost, quality, or access; it is *itself* the objective, and whatever emerges from the market is right. If free competition among for-profit providers leads to further cost escalation, then so be it; that must be the socially preferred outcome.

This normative position, as a number of observers have noted, is not merely intellectually isomorphic with religion, it *is* a religion. The liturgy is frequently expressed in the peculiar jargon of economic analysis, just as the Roman Catholic church for most of its history carried out its ceremonies in Latin. And the set of values and beliefs which it embodies seem to have a particular appeal to economists, who ironically teach the distinction between normative and positive propositions as routinely and as confidently in the classroom as they confuse it outside. But the political advocacy of particular tenets of faith does not thereby become economics.

This rather peculiar sect will probably not be decisive. If it is true that the broader appeal in the U.S. of for-profit institutions and the "competitive marketplace" are a response to the failure of more traditional forms of organization and regulation to control costs, and if these newer appraoches fail in their turn, as they appear so far to be doing, then the fall-back position that escalation is no longer "bad" but now "good" because it is happening in a competitive environment is unlikely to carry much weight among those who pay the costs.

Something else will be tried, most probably (like PPS) some expanded form of public regulation. The recent report of the Harvard Medicare Project clearly points in this direction, recommending binding negotiated fee schedules for physicians, with mandatory assignment (in Canadian terms, no extra-billing), and global expenditure caps with prorating. For hospitals, some form of state-based all-payers budget determination looks very much like global budgets, while the report recommends less reliance on direct charges and more on premiums, but with the latter income-related, so looking rather like a tax . . . [34]

The whole package, in the sincerest form of flattery, appears to be an attempt to move as close as possible to Canada without actually going there. It raises a host of debatable issues; but the key fact to which it responds is that displayed in Figures 1 and 2. If the objective is access plus cost control, the Canadian package works. If the present U.S. trends turn around, and the competitive approach also "works," the Harvard report will presumably gather dust, surviving only in the occasional footnote. But if not, it may well usher in the next wave.

However the institutional mix unfolds in the U.S., or indeed anywhere else, the shift in assumptions about particular institutions seems to reflect a change in fundamental attitudes toward or assumptions about clinical practice. The basic principle of the clinical freedom of the physician is being eroded both by increased competition among providers in the U.S. and by the public regulatory system in Canada and elsewhere.

As noted above, the changed interpretation of interregional variations in utilization patterns and of the linkage between physician supply and overall utilization rates reflects an erosion of the assumption that clinical behavior is its own justification, that whatever doctors do must be right until (rigorously) demonstrated otherwise. The increased acceptance of for-profit organizations and alternatives to fee-for-service practice is similarly a rejection of the principle that the individual clinician, uninfluenced by external constraints—whether from the market or from public or private managers—is the best judge of the patient's interests.

In the U.S., this erosion has been accompanied by the fall of a supporting principle, that of "free choice of physician" whereby the payer for services was barred from restricting the patient's choice. This of course was always a disability imposed on patients in that it did not permit them to contract away their "right" of free choice in return for other advantages such as lower premiums (or for that matter to exercise it with respect to nonlicensed practitioners). But this principle buttressed clinical freedom by making it difficult for third-party payers to select among (and thereby to negotiate with) practitioners on the basis of either fees or practice patterns.

In Canada, as in other countries with universal payment systems, free choice has thus far been maintained, and clinical freedom has been restricted only indirectly through the fee schedule and the hospital budgetary process. But the trends, as in the U.S., seem clear. The lesson of cost containment appears to be that, in the long run, it is incompatible with the clinical freedom of the practitioner, although the form of the resolution of this contradiction is not yet clear and may be quite different in different countries.

Research resonance: The evolving audience for policy analysis

The emphasis on the importance of changes in background or default assumptions, on what policy makers believe when the evidence is incomplete, does not imply that nothing useful is learned from health care research, whether at the "hard end" of the randomized controlled trial or in the softer form of policy analysis which attempts to organize and weigh incompletely specified probabilities with incomplete and imperfect data. Obviously much *is* learned, not least by those who carry out the research. But this learning takes the form of incremental changes in a broader belief framework. Research results are never decisive, because they are almost never conclusive, and even when they are, they can fairly easily be misinterpreted or suppressed.

The experience with cost control illustrates the critical importance of the policy audience, the putative customers for research results. What they are able to hear is heavily influenced by what they want and expect to hear, their background systems of beliefs. This in turn changes with the external environment and pressures they perceive—beliefs are shaped by needs (although it may be that *individuals* do not often change their beliefs, but are simply replaced).

New knowledge of the sort that emerges from research thus may be picked up and amplified or muted and suppressed, depending on whether or not it resonates with the beliefs or perceived needs of the moment. This is not to suggest that only research which will "sell" is worth doing or supporting. Apart from the significance of knowledge for its own sake, if the conventional wisdom has got it wrong, the problems will be back and the audience may be more receptive next time. But the audience or resonance effect raises, as an interesting and important object of study in itself, how knowledge (or ignorance) becomes translated, through the formal and informal political processes, into policies and laws.

Notes

1. U.S. health expenditures data referred to here and subsequently are drawn from tables provided with a press release, "HHS News," issued 29 July 1986 by the Department of Health and Human Services. These contain preliminary 1985 data by expenditure component, and revised total expenditures from 1978. Expenditures by component from 1980 to 1984 are from Table 2 of K. R. Levit et al., "National Health Expenditures, 1984," *Health Care Financing Review* 7 (1985): 1–35; components from 1965 to 1979 and totals from 1965 to 1977 are from Table 2 of R. M. Gibson et al., "National Health Expenditures, 1983," *Health Care Financing Review* 6 (1984): 1–29; earlier data back to 1948 are from B. S. Cooper et al., *Compendium of National Health Expenditures Data* (Washington: U.S. Department of Health, Education, and Welfare, 1973), DHEW Pub. No. (SSA) 73-11903. Revised GNP data are from "Selected National Income and Product Estimates, 1929–85," *Survey of Current Business* (Washington: U.S. Department of Commerce, February 1986) pp. 17–23, with additional minor revisions to the 1983–85 data provided by K. R. Levit of HCFA, as of August 1986. The 1990 projections are from M. S. Freeland and C. E. Schendler, "Health Spending in the 1980s: Integration of Clinical Practice Patterns with Management," *Health Care Financing Review* 5 (1984): 1–68, Tables 1 and 5.
2. E. Kleiman, "The Determinants of National Outlay on Health," in *The Economics of Health and Medical Care*, M. Perlman, editor (London: Macmillan, 1975), pp. 66–81; and J. P. Newhouse, "Medical Care Expenditure: A Cross-National Survey," *Journal of Human Resources* 12 (1977): 115–25.
3. Organization for Economic Cooperation and Development, *Measuring Health Care 1960–1983* (Paris: OECD, 1985), Social Policy Studies No. 2.
4. Sources for U.S. data in Figures 1–3 are in note 1. Canadian data from 1975 to 1985 referred to here and subsequently are prepublication tabulations of recent revisions and updates made available by Health and Welfare Canada, Health Information Division, as of September 1986. Data from 1970 to 1975 are from Health and Welfare Canada, *National Health Expenditures in Canada 1970 to 1982* (Ottawa: HWC, n.d. [1984]). Earlier data are from Health and Welfare Canada, *National Health Expenditures in Canada 1960–75* (Ottawa: HWC, 1979); and R. D. Fraser, "Vital Statistics and Health," in *Historical Statistics of Canada* (2nd edition), F. H. Leacy, editor (Ottawa: Statistics Canada and SSHRC, 1983). Canadian data on national health expenditures (NHE) comparable to those for the U.S. were not compiled prior to 1960; the personal health care (PHC) series shown in Figure 1 from 1948 to 1985 includes only costs of hospitals, services of physicians and dentists, and prescription drugs.
5. Levit et al., "National Health Expenditures, 1984."
6. A selection of the supporting studies is in R. G. Evans, "Illusions of Necessity: Evading Responsibility for Choice in Health Care," *Journal of Health Politics, Policy and Law* 10 (Fall 1985): 439–67.
7. Levit et al., "National Health Expenditures, 1984," Tables 1 and 11.
8. Reported in *Medical Benefits: The Medical-Economic Digest*, 15 May 1986.
9. Levit et al., "National Health Expenditures, 1984," p. 7.
10. Fee increase data are reported in Levit et al. for 1984 and preceding years, in *Medical Benefits* (15 May 1986) for 1985, and for first half 1986 were compiled from Bureau of Labor Statistics data as of mid-August, 1986, and kindly provided by Professor Uwe Reinhardt of Princeton University.

11. The pattern of escalation of U.S. physician fees over time, in the context of a comparison with the Canadian experience of negotiated binding fee schedules, is described in Chapter 3 of M. L. Barer, R. G. Evans, and R. Labelle, "The Frozen North: Controlling Physician Costs Through Controlling Fees—The Canadian Experience," a monograph prepared for the U.S. Office of Technology Assessment project on "Physician Payment and Medical Technology under the Medicare Program," November 1985.

12. A survey of Minnesota physicians in 1982 found that 60 percent reported that they would respond to increased competitive pressures by *raising* their fees; only 4 percent thought they might lower fees, and 11 percent might join an HMO or PPO. See S. S. Foldes and S. McCollor, *Medical Practice in Minnesota: Physician Perceptions of Medical Manpower, Competition, and Other Public Policy Issues in 1982* (Minneapolis: Minneapolis Medical Association, 1983), quoted in H. S. Luft, S. C. Maerki, and J. B. Trauner, "The Competitive Effects of Health Maintenance Organizations: Another Look at the Evidence from Hawaii, Rochester, and Minneapolis/St. Paul," *Journal of Health Politics, Policy and Law* 10 (1986): 625–58. The majority gave the "wrong" answer; increased competition is supposed to cause fees, like any other price, to fall. From this perspective physicians simply do not understand economics, and survey responses do not predict behavior. Subsequent experience suggests the converse. The survey may have correctly indicated how physicians would respond to competition, a "perverse" response implying that many economists do not understand medicine.

13. Levit et al. "National Health Expenditures, 1984," Tables 1 and 11; Barer et al., "The Frozen North," Chapter 3.

14. Comparative U.S. and Canadian data are reported in M. L. Barer and R. G. Evans, "Riding North on a South-bound Horse? Expenditures, Prices, Utilization and Incomes in the Canadian Health Care System," in *Medicare at Maturity: Lessons from the Past, Challenges for the Future*, R. G. Evans and G. L. Stoddart, editors (Calgary: University of Calgary, in press). The detailed analysis of fee schedule changes, and of the negotiation process and its effects, is in Barer et al., "The Frozen North."

15. Average lengths of stay in "public general" hospitals in 1984-85 were 10.86 days (Statistics Canada, *Hospital Statistics Preliminary Annual Report 1984-85* (Ottawa: Statistics Canada, 1985), Cat. No. 83-217A. This average excludes long-term care hospitals, but includes LTUs in short-term hospitals. Changes in the distribution of days over the 1970s for the province of Manitoba are analyzed in more detail in D. J. Roch et al., *Manitoba and Medicare 1971 to the Present* (Winnipeg: Manitoba Health, 1985).

16. Or perhaps the competitive strategy has been misapplied, or subverted, the "revolution" being lost through ignorance, incompetence, or malice. Such an argument easily relapses into comfortable circularity—the strategy *must* have been misapplied, since it is not working . . .

17. J. Merrill and C. McLaughlin, "Competition versus Regulation: Some Empirical Evidence," *Journal of Health Politics, Policy and Law* 10 (Winter 1986): 613–23; Luft et al., "The Competitive Effects of Health Maintenance Organizations"; A. N. Johnson and D. Aquilina, "The Competitive Impact of Health Maintenance Organizations and Competition on Hospitals in Minneapolis/St. Paul," *Journal of Health Politics, Policy and Law* 10 (Winter 1986): 659–74; and R. Feldman et al., "The Competitive Impact of Health Maintenance Organizations on Hospital Finances: An Exploratory Study," *Journal of Health Politics, Policy and Law* 10 (Winter 1986): 675–97.

18. Canadian Medical Association, *Evidence Presented to the Special Committee on the Federal–Provincial Fiscal Arrangements,* House of Commons, Canada, Minutes of Proceedings and Evidence, Issue No. 10, pp. 10-3 to 10-54 and 10A-1 to 10A-44, Tuesday, 12 May 1981, First Session, Thirty-Second Parliament, 1980–81.

19. H. J. Aaron and W. B Schwartz in *The Painful Prescription: Rationing in Health Care* (Washington: The Brookings Institution, 1984) have popularized the phrase, but the general class of argument has had a long and wide currency among defenders of the status quo in health care delivery. At root it is a projection to the policy arena of the ancient threat implicit in "doctor's orders"—"If you do not follow my advice, the consequences for your health will be grave."

20. Evans, "Illusions of Necessity."

21. D. Feeny, G. Guyatt, and P. Tugwell, editors, *Health Care Technology: Effectiveness, Efficiency, and Public Policy* (Halifax: Institute for Research on Public Policy, in press).

22. M. R. Chassin et al., "Variations in the Use of Medical and Surgical Services by the Medicare Population," *New England Journal of Medicine* 314 (1986): 285–90.

23. P. D. Fox, W. B. Goldbeck, and J. J. Spies, *Health Care Cost Management: Private Sector Initiatives* (Ann Arbor, MI: Health Administration Press, 1984), p. 89.

24. A recent comprehensive review of the intellectual and methodological structure underlying physician manpower projections and planning, as part of a critique of a recent exercise, is in J. Lomas, M. L. Barer, and G. L. Stoddart, *Physician Manpower Planning: Lessons from the Macdonald Report* (Toronto: Ontario Economic Council, 1985).

25. Since the physician to population ratio has been rising for decades, and on present projections will continue to rise for more decades, one would expect that analyses based on some augmentation of current utilization levels would inevitably yield a forecast of surplus, if not a current finding. But the future is a big place. It suffices to express concern about future possibilities, while emphasizing not only that there is no present surplus, but that action in the future should of course be based on further study. Such further studies, at a later date, will take as appropriate the new, higher utilization rates which will have been generated by the increase in manpower, so they in their turn will find no surplus. The history of official manpower "planning" in Canada repeats this dismal cycle several times; each new study redefines the target level to ratify the then-current situation. See Lomas, Barer and Stoddart, "Physician Manpower Planning." The U.S. GMENAC report, on the other hand, avoids this inherent circularity by basing its estimates of requirements on an "adjusted needs" concept which is derived from epidemiological data for the population served, and judgments about appropriate clinical practice responses. See *Report of the Graduate Medical Education National Advisory Committee to the Secretary, Health and Human Services* (Washington: Public Health Service, Health Resources Administration, 1980). Appropriate utilization patterns and levels are thus no longer determined, at least not as a matter of definition, by observed practice. The report projects very large physician surpluses in the U.S. in 1990 and 2000.

26. A. R Tarlov, "HMO Enrollment Growth and Physicians," *Health Affairs* 5 (1986): 23–35.

27. The recent reversal, in the summer of 1986, of the AMA's long-held position on the issue, may provide indirect support for this position. After many years of assertion that physician manpower was a matter for the "free" market to deal with, and not a policy problem (e.g., J. F. Boyle [president of the AMA], in "Response to Uwe Reinhardt," *World Medical Journal* 32 [1985]: 14-6, said " . . . there is no evidence at this time of a physician surplus in the United States"), the AMA has now decided that there *is* a surplus, which the market will *not* deal with, though it is of course the government's fault. (*Final Report of the AMA Task Force on Physician Manpower: House of Delegates Handbook, Board of Trustees Report T*, reported in "AMA Backgrounder," June 1986, "There is a surplus of physicians, regardless of specialty, in many areas of the U.S. . . . [and] . . . a surplus or impending surplus . . . in most specialties.") This suggests a loss of confidence in its members' ability to control the "free" market. The AMA task force, however, asserts that the surplus will have negative consequences for the cost and quality of patient care. This is the complete reverse of the view of supporters of the competitive marketplace—not surprisingly—but the weight of evidence on the performance of the "physician market" so far supports the AMA position. The task force is probably right, regardless of its motivations (T. R. Marmor, "The More There Are, The More We Pay," *New York Times*, 29 June 1986). And if organized medicine routinely makes self-serving use of the concept of "quality of care"—and they do—many of the advocates of increased competition simply trivialize it.

28. Lomas, Barer and Stoddart, "Physician Manpower Planning"; the report confirms an aphorism of Stoddart to the effect that nothing is ever wasted—it can always serve as a horrible example.

29. The GMENAC report (see note 25) *does* go back to the epidemiological foundations. It will be interesting to see if, as the methodology is used over time, growth in manpower supply enters into the projection of needs indirectly by modifications to the appropriate patterns of clinical response to particular illnesses.

30. H. S. Luft, *Health Maintenance Organizations: Dimensions of Performance* (New York: Wiley, 1981).

31. J. M. Watt et al., "The Comparative Economic Performance of Investor-Owned Chain and Not-for-Profit Hospitals," *New England Journal of Medicine* 314 (1986): 89–96.

32. A survey of the evidence and analysis underlying debates about the proper role of differently motivated organizational forms in health care is in G. L. Stoddart and R. J. Labelle, *Privatization*

in the Canadian Health Care System: Assertions, Evidence, Ideology and Options (Ottawa: Health and Welfare Canada, 1985).

33. And not only in the hospital sector. R. M. Bailey, *Clinical Laboratories and the Practice of Medicine* (Berkeley, CA: McCutchan, 1979) developed both analysis and evidence for the view that while for-profit motivation might encourage commercial laboratories to lower the unit costs of testing, this was quite consistent with *higher* overall costs of achieving particular therapeutic outcomes in a for-profit environment.

34. Harvard Medicare Project, *Medicare: Coming of Age: A Proposal for Reform* (Cambridge, MA: Kennedy School of Government, Harvard University, 1986).

American Medical Policy and the "Crisis" of the Welfare State: A Comparative Perspective

Theodore R. Marmor, Yale University

Abstract. Health policy debates rarely include broad review of cross-national experiences with related social policies. This article addresses the connection between medical policy concerns and the development of welfare states in the advanced industrial democracies following the oil crisis of 1973–74. After examining the evidence about what actually occurred during the "crisis" years of the welfare state, the article relates the debates about the welfare state's crisis to American concerns about medical care in the 1980s. The distinctive American response to the fiscal strains of stagflation—more severe cuts in social spending than necessary based on the country's economic strength, threats of bankruptcy to produce small adjustments to large programs, and inability to address the problems of medical care as anything other than budgetary strain—is linked to American dissensus about the purposes of the welfare state.

Most policy debates in most countries are parochial affairs. They address national "problems," cite historical and contemporary national developments in a particular domain (e.g., pensions, urban affairs, transportation), and embody conflicting visions of what policies the particular country should adopt. Only rarely are the experiences of other nations seriously considered. When cross-national examples are employed in such parochial struggles, their use is typically part of policy warfare more than of policy understanding.[1]

So it was in the United States during the postwar period that Britain's "socialized medicine" became a familiar epithet in discussions of national health insurance and, later, Medicare. For others, the "advanced" welfare state of Sweden has been a model of how pensions should be structured. In child welfare, the universal child allowances of many European nations have been the exemplary instances—or criticized symbols—of what family policy should include. Historically, the focus is national and programmatic; cross-nationally, the emphasis

---

Support for the research and writing of this paper was provided, in part, by a grant to Professor Marmor and the Institution for Social and Policy Studies by the Henry J. Kaiser Family Foundation of Menlo Park, California.

is on similar problems or policies abroad. Only very rarely in social policy debates has the agenda included a broad review of other national experiences with a set of related, but distinct, policies. Where such review takes place, it more typically occurs in economic policy, where the cross-national treatment of fiscal, monetary, and industrial policy issues is far more developed.[2]

This article takes as its focus the connection between medical policy concerns and the postwar development of welfare states in the advanced industrial democracies. First, I discuss the widespread cross-national questioning of the welfare state in the wake of the stagflation of the post-1973 period. For the past decade and a half, the "crisis" of the welfare state has become a staple of policy discussion in otherwise quite varied regimes. Exactly what is alleged to have occurred? Second, I examine the evidence about what in fact happened during this period—the information crucial to understanding the response of different polities to the common strain of lower growth rates, inflation, increased unemployment, and large welfare state claims on public expenditure. Finally, I explain how the argument about crisis and the facts about adjustment relate to American concerns about medical care in the 1980s.

This paper's agenda is broad and its commentary summary, but its argument is straightforward. Our medical policy disputes have been substantially changed by the fear that our nation cannot afford its present social programs; attention to the broader welfare context is therefore crucial to understanding American medicine and its politics. It is as if our debates have centered on the distribution and character of an area's fires, without much attention to the direction and velocity of the prevailing wind.

The alleged crisis

The claim of crisis in the welfare state that arose in the 1970s and continues to be voiced in the 1980s calls for the radical restructuring of the set of social programs that emerged in the Depression and postwar period. In America, that claim is very much identified with the election of Ronald Reagan in 1980 and the subsequent attacks on federal social spending. In Europe, it is certainly associated with the triumph and continued political victories of Margaret Thatcher in Great Britain and with shifts to the right in a number of other political regimes.[3]

The claim of the welfare state's crisis has been a cliché of political debate over the last fifteen years. That claim is, however, quite ambiguous. Contemporary discussions, relying on unclear and often misunderstood terms, provide a clue to the confusion about exactly what the "troubles of the welfare state" are. Are the social policies of the modern state in crisis, or is the state in crisis because desirable welfare commitments overwhelm fiscal capacity? What exactly is meant by "the welfare state"? Does it refer to the major spending programs of contemporary governments? If so, leaving defense aside, we are talking about pensions, medical care, education, and housing in different mixes in different countries. Or is legitimacy, rather than expenditure, the issue? Measured by popular support, the major spending programs in health and pensions are cross-nationally popular. Is the crisis then one of finding the means to finance crucial and popular commitments? Or does the problem include governmental extension of authority into disputed policy areas such as abortion and busing in the United States, redistribution towards French-speakers in Canada, "guest workers" in Germany and Sweden, and the like? Simply put, there is no agreement about what the topic is.

The impulse to sort out the disagreements is thus understandable. One approach avoids much of the contentiousness by changing the question from an analytical one to an historical one. That is, as Peter Flora and Arnold Heidenheimer write in their introduction to *The Development of Welfare States in Europe and America,*[4] one can easily move from recent troubles to wondering how it is that the conditions of the 1970s emerged. Using this approach the development of welfare states becomes the subject, rather than the character, causes, and implications of contemporary disputes. It may well be that historical understanding of development will illuminate matters, but there is no assurance of this.

Another approach is to assume we know what the crisis is and proceed to ask about its causes and prospects. This alternative was vividly illustrated by the efforts of the Organization for Economic Cooperation and Development (OECD) in the late 1970s and early 1980s. Two years of preparation went into a conference on social policies in the 1980s. But the book that emerged from the conference— *The Welfare State in Crisis*[5]—showed how little consensus there actually was about the topic. The book proceeds from the assumption that the papers address the prospects for improving a clearly worrisome state of affairs that is similarly understood by all analysts. Instead, the papers proceed past one another. Some ask why protest emerges in such a mix of welfare states; others address the tradeoffs between investment and consumption policies of the modern state; still others concentrate on the values of citizens in modern states with extensive social programs. Neither the developmental approach nor the premature presumption of agreement promises an adequate understanding of the contemporary problems of the welfare state. To understand the crisis debate, other starting points are necessary.

The wide body of literature concerning the welfare state falls into three categories. Some analysts regard the welfare state's growth as the main cause of many contemporary political troubles. Most often associated with the apocalyptic right, those who espouse this belief focus on restraining the overreaching state and redeveloping the institutions of the market and the hegemony of individual choice.

Others see the modern state's experience with slowed economic growth as the source of strains *for* social welfare programs. In the middle politically, these center incrementalists are preoccupied with the way in which fiscal strain and stagflation required cutbacks. They view the current crisis as caused by fiscal strains on welfare state programs rather than as a result of any inherent feature of welfare state institutions. They assume that if and when economic growth resumes, the crisis will abate.

A third group stresses the controversies over particular social programs (usually not fiscally important ones) that reach to issues of legitimate governmental purpose. The proponents of this view see the strains on the welfare state as evidence of the contradictions of modern capitalism, and the crisis in the modern welfare state as a portent of future troubles along the way.

There are, of course, overlaps among these three approaches, and the first two can, without heroic effort, be tightly linked. But there are differences, and they make a difference in mapping the subject.

Approach #1: From social welfare programs to the state's crisis. There are two different versions of this approach. Both share the view that social welfare programs played a major role in the poor economic performance of the 1970s. At the theory's simplest level, social programs compete with other budget outlays, preventing the proper balance between investment and consumption. Some critics call this the "bankrupting" of the state; they insist on the importance of budgetary competition and the unfortunate consequences of welfare state expansion.[6] The second form of argument stresses the indirect consequences of many social programs for the mobility of capital and labor. This argument gives us something worth pondering. But it is important to notice that the causal arguments very differently interpret the undeniable growth of spending in this sector during the 1960s and early 1970s. The first argument treats spending as the problem. In the second argument, the rigidities are not centrally involved with the largest spending programs, though unemployment insurance is certainly both important and moderately prominent in budget terms.

The striking thing about these criticisms is their familiarity. They represent the oldest thread of objection to the initial development of social programs. Fiscally, the most substantial expansion of public social welfare took place in the 1960s and early 1970s (see Table 1). This body of criticism became more widely noted only after stagflation strains spread in the wake of the 1973–74 oil shock.

It is also worth noting that the worst scenario of the bankruptcy view was discredited almost as soon as it was generated. The major spending programs of the welfare state did not continue to grow as if uncontrolled by political authorities. Expansion did not continue automatically in the midst of fiscal strain; everywhere review took place, although often without clarification.[7] Finally, it is worth noting that big spenders in the welfare state did not necessarily have the most serious growth problems in the 1970s. The simple connection between the size of the public sector (or social welfare sector) and economic growth problems does not hold up under comparative scrutiny.[8]

Approach #2: From the fiscal crisis of stagflation to welfare state troubles. From this point of view, the problem is that the worldwide recession of

Table 1.   Social Expenditures in Selected OECD Countries: Average Annual Growth Rate of Deflated[a] Social Expenditures,[b] 1960–81

	1960–75	1975–81
Canada	9.3%	3.1%
France	7.3[c]	6.2
Germany	7.0	2.4
Italy	7.7	5.1
Japan	12.8	8.4
Norway	10.1	4.6
United Kingdom	5.9	1.8
United States	8.0	3.2

a. Deflated expenditures are defined as public expenditures measured at constant GDP prices.
b. Defined as education, health care, pensions, and unemployment compensation.
c. Excluding education.
Source: Organization for Economic Cooperation and Development, *Social Expenditure: 1960–1990, Problems of Growth and Control* (Paris: OECD, 1985), Table 1, p. 21.

the mid-1970s critically threatened the welfare state. The combination of lower rates of economic growth, increasing levels of unemployment, and worrisome levels of investment produced strain for the programs that grew rapidly in the earlier decade. In the short run, the welfare state programs appropriately cushioned the effects of recent recession. But because inflation and unemployment increased outlays when recession reduced government revenues, the fiscal strain became quickly apparent.[9] For the longer run, the prospects of unavoidable pressures in medical care and pensions are evident and are sometimes used to prod present action through panic mongering.[10] For the United States, the crucial strains in pensions lie in the twenty-first century, when the baby-boom generation will be old.[11] There is thus ample time to adjust taxes, benefits, and retirement conventions. But it is important to see the difference between the short-term effects of stagflation and the structural-demographic prospects for major spending programs over time. It is difficult to exaggerate the fearfulness of these discussions in the United States, and thus it is important to consider the range of reactions to common stresses.

The relation between welfare state growth and present fiscal strain has another dimension. During the 1960s, when program expansion took place under exceedingly favorable economic circumstances, very little policy discussion considered what would happen under adverse economic conditions. The central ideas of the welfare state were canonized, not analyzed. There was little discussion about alternate means to settled ends. And in the United States, where the least consensus about the original purposes of a welfare state had emerged, rapid growth and uncertain commitment coincided. It is not surprising, from that point of view, that welfare state laggards like the United States and Canada have suffered the most diffuse fearfulness about the future.[12] The rates of growth of social spending in the 1960s could not, in any event, have been sustained forever. But since they rested on optimistic economic assumptions, the reversal in economic fortunes was all the more startling. It is worth reviewing, as we do below, the management of adjustment to worldwide economic downturns, particularly looking at ways of pursuing central objectives with some flexibility but without fears of programmatic betrayal.

Approach #3: Welfare state strains and governmental legitimacy. The two perspectives just outlined need not attack the fundamental purposes of major social welfare programs. The elimination of want, ignorance, squalor, disease, and idleness are aims that are compatible with either the view that remedial programs have grown too costly for economic health or the view that, with less means, more efficient ways to established ends are required. But a third perspective on the social policy strains of the 1970s and 1980s is in one sense more fundamental. It is the view that welfare state programs include some efforts that are wrong— public means that should not be employed even if funds are available or the effects on economic vitality are not worrisome. This is what I mean by criticisms of legitimacy.

The particular items of principled objection vary somewhat from one OECD nation to another, but typically they do not center on the major domestic spending programs we have mentioned. In the United States, Aid to Families With Dependent Children (AFDC), abortion, bilingualism, affirmative action, and school busing have dominated the agenda of the most vitriolic debates.[13] The British counterparts to these controversial but fiscally modest programs are the dole and issues of immigrant workers. Not all critics agree on what the state should forswear. But in general, the claim is that family, custom, and local community should regulate these areas more than governmental decree. In particular, there is serious challenge to politics that emerge from court decisions establishing rights where legislative decision has been hesitant, stalemated, or ambiguous.

The striking fact about AFDC finance, for example, has been its modest role in the overall growth of American social welfare expenditures (see Table 2). AFDC's prominence in our debate arises from racial and moral concerns far more than from fiscal ones.[14] And in the frustrating efforts to reform public assistance over the past fifteen years, sweeping legislative reform has not been achieved. Instead a series of legal and political challenges has, in practice, changed the ways in which some assistance is given—by whom, and to whom. Likewise, school busing policies emerged far more prominently through judicial interepretations of the famous 1954 *Brown* decision of the Supreme Court than through decades of legislative debate and policy making.

In these cases, the argument is less one of retreat from a widely accepted aim than a challenge to the legitimacy of the aim itself. In other nations, analogous challenges to legitimacy have arisen, but not for the same mix of programs. In Sweden and West Germany, both the treatment of ''guest workers'' and the struc-

Table 2. Total Federal Expenditures for Selected Social Programs, 1970–85 (In Billions of Constant 1985 Dollars)

	1970	1975	1980	1985
Social Security (OASDI)	78.3	123.4	153.6	186.4
Medicare	17.9	27.4	44.6	69.6
Unemployment Insurance	8.1	24.8	22.1	16.1
AFDC (Assistant Payments Program)[b]	10.9[a]	9.9	9.1	8.6
Supplemental Security Income	—	8.4	7.5	8.7

a. Includes aid to needy aged, blind, and disabled adults, which became SSI in 1974.
b. Since 1974, most outlays in the "assistant payments" category have been for AFDC.
Source: Congressional Research Service, *1986 Budget Perspective: Federal Spending for the Human Resource Programs,* February 1986, pp. 55 and 81.

ture of public education have prodded fundamental questioning.[15] In Canada, the policies towards French Canadians and bilingualism have prompted widespread objection to governmental authority reaching the redistribution of opportunities to different language groups. My claim is simply that such changes, coincident with the fiscal strains in all OECD welfare states, have confusingly shaped the sense of crisis. The addition of legitimacy concerns to fiscal fears has reduced the degree to which more familiar methods of problem solving seem appropriate to the state's contemporary troubles. How different regimes have treated similar controversies is one subject for cross-national research. Particularly relevant here are studies of broadly similar regimes; the possibility of cross-national learning increases substantially as national differences are, in a sense, "controlled."

What actually happened

The differing views just outlined charge in one way or another that the critical flaws of the welfare state programs and thus of the welfare state itself were part of a general dissatisfaction with the modern institutions of government. These assumptions rest on factual mistakes. Cross-national evidence from the 1970s— a time when government revenues were restrained by stagflation and the burdens on the welfare state increased—supports the notion that the major social spending programs remained quite broadly popular. In the United States the major programs—pensions, medical care, and education—never lacked public or political support. Both public opinion polls and the public reaction to attempted cutbacks by the Reagan administration testify to the popularity of these programs. The most vehement criticism of the welfare state has largely concentrated on its more fiscally trivial programs.

It is quite clear, however, that the future of the welfare state in countries with large, settled programs cannot possibly replicate the extraordinary growth in social spending that marks the postwar experience. It is equally clear that the slowed growth of social spending in the 1970s and 1980s is due to the combination of slower economic growth and the overwhelming fact that large, mature programs simply cannot continue to grow rapidly without imposing steadily increasing opportunity costs.[16] Further sharp increases in already-large government programs would, for instance, impose additional tax burdens on those already at the bottom of the income distribution. The defensible argument for selectivity in program growth and spending arises therefore not from ideological rejection of their earlier purpose but from the reality that these very large, settled programs in pension, health care, and education reduce the margins for continued growth in the future.

Klein and O'Higgins use the most recently published OECD data (1985) on social expenditure trends from 1960 to 1981 to analyze the overall pattern as well as the country-by-country and program-by-program variations.[17] Their analysis yields a number of significant conclusions. First, from 1975 to 1981, all the OECD countries reduced the rate of increase in social spending, but none actually reduced real total social expenditures. They all exhibited the capacity to steer their welfare states to hold down spending increases in response to the adverse economic environment. Second, the reactions of different countries varied both in the extent to which they reduced spending growth and in the priorities accorded different spending programs.

Over the OECD as a whole, the average annual growth rate of real social spending fell between the periods 1960–75 and 1975–81 from 8.4 percent to 4.8 percent. Economic growth during the same time periods fell from 4.6 percent to 2.6 percent. National reductions, however, varied by a factor of eight—from 1.1 percent in France to 8.8 percent in the Netherlands. Klein and O'Higgins speculate that such differences may reflect the degree of maturity reached by different welfare states by the mid-1970s (as reflected in the level of social spending in 1975) or the different degrees of economic difficulty experienced after 1975, as well as different political responses.

Their analysis of the cross-sectional data suggests that the rate of growth of social spending is negatively linked to the 1975 spending share, but positively related to subsequent economic growth rates. Thus the higher a country's level of social spending in 1975, the lower its rate of increase in social spending during 1975–81; and countries with the highest economic growth rates during 1975–81 can be expected to have experienced the highest rate of growth in social spending.[18]

Of particular importance for our purposes, however, are the deviations from this general pattern exhibited by a number of the countries, most notably the United States. Table 3 uses the measure of income elasticity of social spending to illustrate national differences in the relationship between the change in growth rates of social spending and the degree of economic strain experienced by individual countries.[19] Three countries—Norway, Canada, and the United States—show substantial declines in their elasticities between the two periods. In other words, these countries experienced significantly less growth in social spending

Table 3. Income Elasticity[a] of Social Expenditures in Selected OECD Countries, 1960–75 and 1975–81[b]

	1960–75	1975–81
Canada	1.8	0.9
France	2.2	2.2
Germany	0.8	0.8
Italy	1.4	1.6
Japan	3.9	1.8
Norway	2.4	1.1
United Kingdom	2.2	1.8
United States	2.4	1.0

a. The ratio of the growth rate of nominal social expenditures to the growth rate of nominal GDP.
b. Or latest year available.
Source: Organization for Economic Cooperation and Development, *Social Expenditure: 1960– 1990, Problems of Growth and Control* (Paris: OECD, 1985), Table 1, p. 22.

as compared with their overall economic growth during the period 1975–81 than they did during the 1960–75 period. The cases of the United States and Norway are particularly interesting because despite their very different political traditions, they are two of the strongest overreactors. The result in each case reflects a combination of a lower fall in economic growth than the OECD average (0.2 for both countries as against the OECD average of 2.0) and a greater fall in social spending growth (4.6 and 5.5 points respectively, against an average of 3.6). These data suggest that national perceptions and definitions of fiscal crisis are as important as economic performance in understanding welfare state policy making.

Klein and O'Higgins also find significant national variations in spending changes by program for the major welfare state programs—health, pensions, and education. Their analysis showed that many more countries reacted to the crisis by restraining spending growth for education and health care rather than curbing spending for pensions. From 1960 to 1975, spending on health care grew at the fastest rate: in the seven largest OECD economies, real spending grew by an average of 9.0 percent, as compared to 8.2 percent for pensions and 6.2 percent for education. From 1975 to 1981, average annual growth rates for health care and education fell to 3.4 percent and 1.4 percent respectively, while that for pensions only fell to 6.8 percent. Their data suggest that there is some scope—given flexibility and adaptiveness—for accommodating new demands (such as those created by the aging of the population) by holding back the growth rates of other programs and changing public spending priorities.

The experience between 1975 and 1981, as Klein and O'Higgins argue, shows how "a common economic crisis was translated into very different social spending responses by national political systems." This calls for an analysis of the impact of politics and policies on welfare state spending,[20] and raises broad questions about the claim that the crisis of the welfare state reflects "some systematic affliction common to all the advanced capitalist countries, independent of national political ideology or institutions.''[21]

America's distinctive response

The comparative evidence above provides the basis for interpreting the distinctive American responses to stagflation. By the mid-1970s, the United States had moved considerably from its postwar position as the laggard in the scope and financing of social welfare programs toward being a mature welfare state, with a large, fully indexed (after 1972) pension scheme. Our governmental health insurance for the poor and the elderly, although not on the universal scale of other countries, had expanded considerably and contributed to that growth. We had an apparatus of social welfare programs that covered a wide range, and the key spending components—old-age pensions and medical care—were inflating just as in the rest of the world. The predictable result was fiscal stress as stagflation increased program outlays and as lowered economic growth reduced governmental revenues. This much was common across the world of industrial democracies. Where the United States differed was in the more limited degree of acceptance of the welfare state's purposes and clarity about its aims. The growth of the early 1970s had largely come from unexpected inflation and pension indexation, not from a fundamental reexamination of purpose. The result was that the maturing American welfare state had fewer means to cushion the strains macroeconomic developments brought. It was all too easy to confuse economic problems facing the welfare state with problems within the programs of the American welfare state.

The reasons for this mismatch between scale of effort and national understanding have much to do with the structure of American politics and the nature of its typical policy developments. The fragmentation of American politics puts an enormous premium on consensus, on gaining agreement so that the multiple veto points of the polity can be avoided. But agreement on the existence of a problem is far easier to secure than agreement on an appropriate policy response. The result is that American politics moves by fits and starts, with long periods of gestation and sudden bursts of political action when issue majorities are assembled. This also means that as long as the question is whether sufficient support exists for taking action, the political incentives direct reformers to concentrate on problem symptoms and the broad legitimacy of desirable remedies.

So it was that in the long battle over Medicare contending parties debated endlessly whether the medical troubles of America's aged warranted anything like a social insurance response. The debate between 1950 and 1965 centered less on the programmatic details of Medicare proposals than on whether the circumstances and claims of the aged warranted a central government as opposed to a private or a state remedy. The very name of the program—Medicare—misdescribed the limited hospitalization proposals that in fact constituted the legislative agenda in the late 1950s and early 1960s.[22] What the public expected was much broader than what the Medicare legislative battle addressed. And when a broader Medicare program unexpectedly emerged from the bargaining of 1965, there was little public agreement about the program's purposes and the cost-control implications of the program's design. Likewise, the indexation of Social Security in 1972—the result of congressional bargaining in an election year—produced long-run increases in Social Security payments without a glimmer of broad review.

Programmatic innovation thus proceeded without purposive clarity or agreement on strategies of implementation. The Vietnam War meant that expenditures for "guns" accompanied increases in the "butter" programs of the welfare state. The result was predictable, if lamentable. The United States faced the stagflation strains of the mid-1970s with the worst of all combinations: a large, rapidly growing system of social programs and a very incomplete comprehension of where we were coming from and what we were hoping to accomplish.

If I am right about the inability of mature welfare states to continue to grow on the scale of expansion during the first two decades of the postwar period, it follows that altered modes of adjustment will be necessary. In making that adjustment it makes an enormous difference precisely how the welfare state is conceptualized. For most of the OECD countries, the diagnosis was straightforward: the challenge of welfare state adjustments was to determine how to make modest changes in the large spending programs so as to respond to reduced revenues and to open up opportunity for more targeted initiatives. It was not going to be possible to expand on a number of policy fronts. Yet rather modest tinkering with large spending programs would free up substantial financial resources. In the short run, minor adjustments would relieve financial strain. In the longer run, policy flexibility would emerge from the slow adjustment of details in the shape and administration of the medical care, pension, education, and housing programs that make up the bulk of OECD social expenditures. The implication was clear as well. Time spent worrying about how to make marginal adjustments in major programs made sense because the relative benefit of freeing up resources would be very great when the economic constraints were so serious. Tinkering, for the OECD, was sensible and, in the main, forthcoming.[23]

The adjustments in American politics did not closely follow this model. On the one hand, the financial strain of stagflation did produce marginal changes— the Social Security amendments of 1977 and the more substantial adjustments of 1983 in the wake of the Greenspan Commission. It has been more than a decade since any major new social policy initiative has commanded national attention. In this sense, deficit politics have constrained welfare state development sharply. On the other hand, the adjustments we have made have occasioned fundamental debate and prompted great fearfulness. In that sense, the tinkering that actually emerged brought degrees of social insecurity that the scale of adjustments hardly warrants. Two examples illustrate this process.

In Social Security, fiscal strain evoked fears of bankruptcy. The doomsday scenarios, on the other hand, made small adjustments all the more difficult, as partisan opponents traded specters of doom or complacency. Indeed, both a special commission and the most extraordinary use of twenty-first-century forecasts were required to prod the marginal action of the Congress in 1983.[24] In welfare reform, by contrast, the fiscal stakes are far smaller, but there is a similar cycle of crisis mongering and profound questioning. In this instance, no adjustments of public assistance policy are large enough to affect the American welfare state's fiscal stability over the long run. Yet the discussion takes place without this fiscal fact in clear view.

Both these instances illustrate the mismatch of rhetoric and reality as well as the constraints of deficit politics. Politicians get credit for addressing the programs for the poor critically or sympathetically. But changes in the programs for poor people are incapable of affecting the fiscal realities of limits on a large welfare state. On the other hand, Social Security and (to a lesser extent) Medicare are precisely where fiscal strain is apparent. Yet our politics express the appeal of these popular programs in the form of limiting adjustments, making Social Security a sacred cow for fear that poachers will attack the whole herd. The result is a social policy debate full of smoke and mirrors, a world of fantasy where the debate departs greatly from the margin of responsible adjustment—in benefits and taxation—that long-run alterations will require.

Implications for medical care

The concern of this paper is whether the cross-national evidence and the general policy directions illuminate current American medical policy trends as well as the policy directions not taken. What, in short, are the straightforward implications for medical care of the argument about welfare state developments introduced at the outset of this paper?

That argument, simply put, is that the broader politics of America's reaction to stagflation (and later the budget deficit) have dominated American health politics in the past fifteen years. For those who concentrate on disputes within the medical polity, attention has centered on the regulatory disappointments of the 1970s, the emergence of cost containment as a preoccupation (even obsession), and the much-noted disputes over the relative merits of regulatory versus so-called competitive strategies in reforming an expensive, troubled American medical world. These phenomena, undeniable at the surface of discussion, constitute for these purposes the consequences as much as the causes of American health developments.

Macroeconomic events—the inflation of the Vietnam years and the stagflation that worsened after the 1973–74 oil crisis—set the direction of social policy response but did not determine the particular shape. The economy required restraint; that restraint was achieved differently and to varying degrees in the welfare state economies of the OECD. The American political response to the economic strains was one of a widespread sense of crisis in social policy—the "overreaction" to which Klein and O'Higgins refer. The definition of the problem as one of crisis meant that as the low growth of the economy reduced revenues and the tax cuts of 1981 coupled with the arms buildup of the Carter–Reagan years produced very large deficits, new initiatives like national health insurance would become increasingly unthinkable. Deficits, a large defense budget, and the political unwillingness to raise taxes has put medical care policy in a paralytic vise. Only policy proposals that promise reductions in federal expenditure—like the heralded DRG innovation in Medicare hospital reimbursement (1983)—are on the agenda of active discussion. Otherwise social policy energy has concentrated on protecting current programs from further budget cutbacks. And the Gramm–Rudman–Hollings Act of 1985 has institutionalized the politics of constraint, making large-scale programmatic innovation practically unthinkable.

The crisis formulation of the 1970s put medical care reformers on the defensive; the deficit politics of the 1980s have boxed discussion still more tightly. The United States is, by international comparison, well known as a big spender for medical care. The nearly 11 percent of GNP that is expended for medical care results from widespread third-party payments, public and private. This fragmented and expensive system leaves sizable proportions of the society under- or uninsured. Access problems are bound to worsen as state health programs, federal programs, and private employers compete to shift costs to other parties, driving as hard a bargain as they can with beleaguered providers and insurers. Within the federal Medicare program, the debate hovers between those intent on increasing the out-of-pocket expenses and those who favor stricter limits on what medical providers can charge. It is rare to find serious discussion of recasting the program as a whole so as to extract a better bargain for the $70 billion level of expenditures.

I have characterized the welfare state debate in the United States as the triumph of rhetoric over reality. For the world of medical care, that triumph was evident in two of the most common disputes of the past decade: regulation versus competition and the related cost-control debate. In both instances, the broader reaction to the welfare state's troubles conditioned the struggle within medicine.

The competition/regulation dichotomy makes little analytical sense. There is no form of competition that does not rest on rules that enforce price competition as the central way in which suppliers gain customers. Equally, there is no form of state regulation that obliterates competition among providers for customers, advance, favor, and honor. The dispute over competition and regulation is in fact over what form of competitive regulation is desirable and what its consequences would be for equity of access, fairness of finance, and quality of care. In developing this rhetorical dichotomy, American political discourse sets itself apart from the rest of the OECD world. But that divergence in turn resulted from the peculiar American interpretation of the welfare state strains of the stagflation era as a crisis requiring retrenchment and precluding creative or flexible use of resources to meet changing needs.

The American form of cost-control disputes is equally distinctive. It is widely believed that governmental insurance triggered medical care inflation in the 1960s and that only the rigors of competition will restrain this failing industry. Again the broader context of cross-national findings makes one skeptical of the claim. In the rest of the OECD world, medical expenditures were the subject of considerable tinkering and restraint, but nowhere was there a major transformation of the postwar models of universal health coverage under public auspices. In these nations, increased expenditures in public medical programs are of great concern. But since the public programs are near-monopsonistic purchasers of care, the decision to reduce services affects all citizens directly. In the American case, the central state is but one payer (or purchaser). In recent years, it has become a participant in the scramble to spread the inflated costs of medical care to other budgets. In Medicare, for example, the cost-control effort is directed at reducing federal deficits, permitting costs to spill onto other actors whether they are the elderly, the providers, or other payers.

The turbulent world of medical care in the 1980s is, in my view, not the product of forces internal to medicine. Having come late to the welfare state's expansion, and having done so in the context of economic abundance and ideological hesitancy, the American polity was exceedingly ill prepared for the strains of the 1970s. In the 1980s we have been living with the debris.

Notes

1. See T. R. Marmor, A. Bridges, and W. L. Hoffman, "Comparative Politics and Health Policies: Notes on Benefits, Costs, Limits," in *Political Analysis and American Medical Care: Essays,* T. R. Marmor, editor (New York: Cambridge University Press, 1983) for a discussion of the uses of cross-national evidence in health policy. More generally, see D. E. Ashford, editor, *Comparing Public Policies: New Concepts and Methods* (Beverly Hills, CA: Sage Publications, 1978).
2. See, for example, Robert B. Reich, "Bailout: A Comparative Study in Law and Industrial Structure," *Yale Journal on Regulation* 2 (No. 2, 1985): 163–224.
3. Sweden and Australia in the late 1970s, and more recently France, Germany, and Canada.
4. New Brunswick, NJ: Transaction, 1981.
5. Organisation for Economic Cooperation and Development, *The Welfare State in Crisis: An Account of the Conference on Social Policies in the 1980s* (Paris: OECD, 1981). The conference took place in Paris, 20–23 October 1980.
6. Richard Rose and Guy Peters, *Can Government Go Bankrupt?* (New York: Basic Books, 1978).
7. Rudolf Klein and Michael O'Higgins, "Defusing the Crisis of the Welfare State: A New Interpretation," in *Social Security in Contemporary American Politics,* T. Marmor and J. Mashaw, editors (in preparation).
8. For further discussion, see David Cameron, "On the Limits of the Public Economy," *Annals of the American Academy of Political and Social Science* 459 (1982), and Manfred Schmidt, "The Welfare State and the Economy in Periods of Economic Crisis," *European Journal of Political Research* 11 (1983): 1–26.
9. Daniel Tarschys, "Curbing Public Expenditure: Current Trends," *Journal of Public Policy* (No. 7, 1985): 23–67.

10. See, for example, Peter G. Peterson, "Social Security: The Coming Crash," *The New York Review of Books*, 2 December 1982.

11. John Palmer and Barbara Torrey, "Health Care Financing and Pension Programs," in *Federal Budget Policy in the 1980s*, Gregory Mille and John Palmer, editors (Washington, DC: The Urban Institute, 1984).

12. See Robert T. Kudrle and Theodore R. Marmor, "The Development of Welfare States in North America," in *The Development of Welfare States in Europe and America*, P. Flora and A. J. Heidenheimer, editors (New Brunswick, NJ: Transaction Books, 1981), especially pp. 114–16.

13. The celebrated public disputes over Charles Murray's book, *Losing Ground* (New York: Basic Books, 1985) are illustrative. Few such exchanges have addressed Social Security pensions or Medicare, programs that are overwhelmingly more significant fiscally (as Table 2 shows) than the whole nest of poverty and public programs.

14. It is true that some critics of public welfare, such as Murray, also emphasize the consequences for work of public assistance rules and regulations.

15. Flora and Heidenheimer, *The Development of Welfare States in Europe and America*.

16. Klein and O'Higgins, "Defusing the Crisis of the Welfare State."

17. Organization for Economic Cooperation and Development, *Social Expenditure: 1960–1981, Problems of Growth and Control* (Paris: OECD, 1985). Klein and O'Higgins are careful to note the limitations as well as the benefits of using this particular data source. While it does make comparable data conveniently available, it has the disadvantage of ending its time series in 1981, five years ago. Further, by treating the periods 1960–75 and 1975–81 as though each were homogeneous, the study may suggest conclusions that would not hold if the focus of analysis were on trends *within* each of these periods. In addition, the particular form of presentation for these data begs the question of whether, in the words of the OECD report, "the passage of time would probably have seen some automatic moderation as the major social programmes approached maturity" (p. 9). They also note the following additional difficulties with the OECD data: First, social expenditure, defined as spending on education, health care, pensions, and unemployment compensation, ignores spending on means-tested social assistance and also ignores possible substitution effects between different types of programs. Second, the data ignore tax expenditures. And yet, they note, "some of the most significant shifts in public policy, particularly in terms of their distributional effects, have taken the form of tilting the balance between direct and tax spending." Klein and O'Higgins, "Defusing the Crisis of the Welfare State," p. 8.

18. Details of this analysis can be found in Klein and O'Higgins, "Defusing the Crisis of the Welfare State."

19. The income elasticity of social expenditures is defined as the ratio of the growth rate of nominal social expenditures to the growth rate of nominal GDP (Gross Domestic Product). An income elasticity of less than 1.0 indicates that the country's economy grew at a faster rate than its social expenditures. An elasticity of 1.0 indicates that a given percent increase in economic growth was matched by the same percent increase in social expenditures.

20. See Francis G. Castles, editor, *The Impact of Parties* (London: Sage, 1982) and Harold L. Wilensky, Gregory M. Luebbert, Susan R. Hahn, and Adrienne M. Jamieson, *Comparative Social Policy* (Berkeley, CA: Institute of International Studies, 1985).

21. Klein and O'Higgins, "Defusing the Crisis of the Welfare State."

22. T. R. Marmor, *The Politics of Medicare* (Chicago: Aldine, 1973).

23. Klein and O'Higgins, "Defusing the Crisis of the Welfare State."

24. Paul Light, *Artful Work: The Politics of Social Security Reform* (New York: Random House, 1985). The exchange in *The New York Review of Books* between Peter J. Peterson ("Social Security: The Coming Crash," 2 December 1982, "The Salvation of Social Security," 16 December 1982, and "A Reply to Critics," 17 March 1986) and Alicia Munnell ("A Calmer Look at Social Security," 17 March 1983) illustrates the way in which long-term specters—that is, twenty-first-century developments—were centrally at issue in the commentary on Social Security's 1982 troubles.

Prospective Payment in Perspective

Harvey M. Sapolsky, Massachusetts Institute of Technology

Abstract. Prospective payment promises improvement for a health care system plagued by inefficiency and rising costs, but is likely to disappoint. Serious efforts to control costs threaten the system's access and quality objectives and will be resisted. Moreover, serious cost containment, whether the result of all-payer regulation or competition, requires a stronger civil service than America seems capable of providing. A comparison with the experience in defense demonstrates the important limitations in applying incentive-based models in policy areas with conflicting goals. The search for panaceas will go on, but there are none.

The struggle to control health care costs took a dramatic turn with the election of a conservative administration in 1980. Until then, it was liberals who primarily worried about health care costs, realizing that they could not achieve their elusive goal of national health insurance for the United States without first demonstrating that health expenditures could be controlled. The major step to extend the medical franchise taken with the enactment of the Medicare and Medicaid programs in 1965 had set off a spiral of health care inflation that blocked essentially all further initiatives to improve access to care in the United States. A series of ineffective regulatory efforts followed, intended to curtail the growth in costs sufficiently to begin again the legislative march toward national health insurance. Conservatives would occasionally join in these efforts, but most often they helped weaken them because of their ideological distaste for regulation.

What the conservatives wanted was less government and taxes, not more; the free market, not controls. A good part of the welfare state erected in the 1960s seemed vulnerable by 1980 to attack, but not Medicare, which paid for the health care of everyone's elderly father and mother.[1] However, because Medicare expenditures are such a large component of the domestic budget, no meaningful savings could be achieved unless the rate of growth in Medicare spending was brought under control. Any scheme that promised limitations in Medicare payments without directly curtailing its benefits seemed worthy of embrace. When the prospective regulation of Medicare's hospital reimbursements was proposed as a procompetitive, budget-reducing reform, its appeal was irresistible. In 1983,

The author thanks the Robert Wood Johnson Foundation for supporting his work on prospective payment, Caroline Richardson for providing research assistance, and James Maxwell, James Morone, and Sanford Weiner for comments on early drafts of this article.

after only the briefest consideration, Congress approved the adoption of a prospective payment system for the Medicare program.[2]

The hospital industry promoted the shift to prospective payment with both the
American Hospital Association and the Federation of American Health Care Systems claiming credit for persuading the Reagan administration to endorse the
change.[3] The Medicare program brought enormous prosperity to America's hospitals, but also continuing anxiety. Because of Medicare, the federal government
gained a permanent interest in controlling hospital costs. Reclaimable as they
were, the monetary and administrative concessions extracted during the implementation phase of Medicare offered no protection from the potential exercise
of federal controls.[4] Once the inflationary impact of Medicare was recognized,
each budget cycle seemed to bring forward another solution to the health care
crisis.

Most posed no real threat or could easily be evaded, but not the regulations
embodied in the Carter administration's cost-control bill of 1978, which called
for constraints on private as well as public reimbursements for hospitals.[5] So eager
was the industry to defeat the bill that it promised the impossible—self-restraint
in the form of voluntary control of health care cost increases. The clearly ver-
ifiable failure of the "voluntary effort" embarrassed even the industry's closest
political allies.[6] The feared Carter controls were reborn in modified form to apply
only to Medicare reimbursements and passed in 1982 as a section of the Tax
Equalization and Fiscal Reform Act (TEFRA) for implementation in 1983. With
TEFRA the federal government gave up at least temporarily the attempt to deal
with health care costs in general and sought instead a solution to its own health
care cost problem. Both the Congress and the president appeared determined to
prevent hospitals from dictating the future size of federal health care expenditure
through profligate behavior. Not surprisingly, hospitals were now ready to bargain.[7] In exchange for the inflexible expenditure controls that TEFRA was to
impose, they would accept a prospective payment system for Medicare that would
use incentives to improve the efficiency of hospital services—competition, if you
like.

The question to ask is whether or not the new Medicare payment arrangement
will lead to meaningful cost control. I think not. The reimbursement system prospective payment replaces is not inherently inflationary, nor is prospective payment inherently cost-constraining. Much depends on how the systems are managed. Moreover, retrospective payment, the reimbursement system prospective
payment replaced, served well certain societal goals that have not been abandoned
despite the Reagan administration's desire to focus exclusively on expenditure
reduction objectives when addressing health care issues. Americans still want
good access to high-quality health care services as well as control over health
care costs. And most important, the effort needed to achieve control over health
care costs may be beyond the administrative capacity of American government.
Both the competitive and the regulatory paths to cost control require for their

realization an effective civil service. There is nothing in the American political experience that would lead one to believe that such a civil service is likely to be created.

Importance of the level of payment

The consensus among health policy analysts is that retrospective payment spurs hospital cost inflation. Retrospective payment involves the after-the-fact payment of the costs incurred in the treatment of patients. In some versions the reimbursement is made on the basis of charges (essentially a hospital's price list), while in others it is made on the basis of reasonable costs (the list of audited costs), but in all, the incentive is to provide as many services to patients as are needed or thought appropriate. Because in most instances it is not clear what services are needed or appropriate, services tend to proliferate under these arrangements. Moreover, because the audited costs of the services or better will be reimbursed, the providers of care have no incentive to control costs.

But not all charges need be paid nor all costs considered reasonable.[8] It is the choice of the reimbursing agency to accept or reject particular charges. The agency may wish to reimburse for nursing services, but not for the application of unproven technologies. Payment may be provided for the capital costs of a new wing in a hospital, but not for a money-earning parking facility. The details of the arrangement are negotiable with providers or can be dictated by powerful payers. Cost discipline also can be achieved indirectly through cost sharing by patients. Copayments, deductibles, and coinsurance fees can limit the ability of providers to increase costs as well as the costs reimbursement agencies will pay.

Prospective payment is generally considered to be much more cost constraining. It involves the payment of predetermined prices for hospital care rendered or guaranteed. Being predetermined, the prices set limits on reimbursement and give incentive to reduce costs. But the actual effect of prospective payment on hospital costs depends on how the specific prices are determined and how much or little of a hospital's activities they cover. Rates can be based on a single hospital's past costs, the costs of classes of hospitals, regional or national experience, or various combinations. They may or may not include the cost of medical education, hospital capital, and services provided on an outpatient basis. Limits may be placed on volume increases, which left uncontrolled can weaken the impact of prospective payment. Compensation may be made for variations in the intensity of illness hospitals encounter or for difficulties hospitals can have in shifting patients to other care settings.

The difference between prospective and retrospective payment often fades in practice. A reconciliation occurs after the end of a payment period to clear discrepancies between hospital payment requests and agency reimbursement. The final reconciliation for a given fiscal year may be delayed still further by court appeals of reimbursement agency decisions. Substantial amounts may be in dispute for upwards of several years, converting prospective into retrospective payment and blunting cost-containment incentives.

In the end, though, it is the level of payment that should matter most in affecting provider behavior. Payment rates may be stringent or generous irrespective of whether or not they are set prospectively. Medicare's experience with the end stage renal disease (ESRD) program demonstrates the point.

The Social Security Act was amended in 1972 to provide Medicare coverage for victims of end stage renal disease, including thrice weekly dialysis treatments. Because Medicare's practice of using retrospective reimbursement was by that time already severely criticized as being inflationary, the decision was made to use prospective payment for both dialysis and related physician care in order to contain ESRD program costs. But just as in the case of the implementation of Medicare, there was a parallel concern that there would not be a sufficient supply of services to meet the demand for the lifesaving care unless rates were attractive to providers. The expectation was that the initial generous ESRD rates would be subsequently revised downward when the program stabilized.

The program did not stabilize. Rather, it grew rapidly during the next decade as the population of patients treated expanded.[9] The unrevised rates were apparently generous enough to bring forward an increasing supply of dialysis services despite the significant inflation that occurred in overall health care costs. Fixed rates did require dialysis providers eventually to seek efficiency improvement, but little of these cost savings accrued to the government because the rates were not adjusted. When the rates were finally revised downward in the early 1980s, the reductions were minor so as not to force any of the dialysis providers out of business. Congress, which controlled the rate revisions, was more concerned with the balance of competition among providers than with capturing efficiency gains. Although prospective payment did help limit ESRD program expenditures, it did not produce the savings envisioned when the arrangement was selected.[10]

The trade-off among goals

Generous reimbursement not only encourages the supply of health services, but also increased access to care and improved quality. The goals that we have set for the health care system are contradictory. Cost control threatens access and the quality of care. Attempts to improve quality threaten to increase costs. Increased access without increased expenditures is likely to lead to deteriorating quality. Claims of an ability to convert expenditure waste into better access and quality are usually the assertions of policy alchemists who choose to exaggerate the existence of waste and ignore the ability of professions to channel resources to uses that they prefer.

Looking back, we tend to see policy mistakes being made where there were none. The choice of generously structured cost- or charge-based reimbursement was intentional for private insurance and for Medicare.[11] During the first two decades after the Second World War the clear desire was to expand access to health care services. Subsidies for medical research during and after the war stimulated significant advances in therapy. Postwar affluence caused increased demand for this technologically improving health care, which in turn threatened to press a continually expanding supply of health care services.[12] Those who financed care, concerned that promised access would not be met, knowingly accepted reimbursement arrangements that were most favorable to the providers of care.

In 1948 the Supreme Court ruled that unions could bargain for health insurance benefits.[13] The most powerful unions quickly won these benefits for their members, enhancing the appeal of unionization among unorganized workers. Major employers countered by offering similar or better benefits to their nonunionized employees.[14] Competition among firms for scarce labor further expanded the availability of employer-provided health insurance. Favorable tax regulations, previously obtained, eased the financial burden of health insurance on employers and employees alike.[15] So did the large subsidies that government subsequently provided to medical education and hospital construction.[16]

By the mid-1960s health insurance had spread to a substantial portion of the population, but not to all. Millions of people—primarily the elderly and the poor, but also many employed by marginal employers—lacked such protection. The existence of large numbers of uninsured patients helped constrain health care inflation. Although some observers worried about the temptations that cost reimbursement offered the providers of care,[17] health care costs could not exceed the ability of those who had to pay their own bills to gain at least modest access to hospital and physician services.

The enactment of the Medicare and Medicaid programs changed the situation drastically. Suddenly, millions were added to those whose health care needs were to be met by full costs reimbursement. Nearly (though not quite) all of the population had guaranteed access to most health care services. Health care costs began a rapid acceleration that most often exceeded by a large margin the rate of general inflation, itself about to begin an unexpected rise due to the Vietnam War and then the energy crisis. Health care costs became a national problem.[18]

Benefactor of the elderly and the poor, the federal government had the most expensive patients and thus the greatest cost burden. A decade and a half passed before the federal government found a formula that promises relief, the adoption of a prospective payment arrangement for hospital reimbursement utilizing fixed fees based on diagnosis classification—the DRG (diagnosis-related group) system. Several state governments have followed suit by adopting DRGs for Medicaid reimbursement. The freezing of physician fees is more of the same strategy. Because government—state and federal—controls so many patients, the dictated prices have to be accepted.

If cost control is seriously pursued there will be important consequences. The health care system is built on cross-subsidies. The young subsidize the old; the rich, the poor; the well, the sick; the childless, parents; and so on in patterns that sometimes contradict and sometimes reinforce. When government seeks a special advantage for itself, it destroys the network of cross-subsidies, forcing extra costs on others. Some private payers also possess market power, especially large employers with geographically concentrated workforces and insurers with significant localized market penetration. They now are beginning to demand discounts in order not to fall victim to cost shifting by providers. So, too, are health maintenance organizations with growing client bases and local governments with large workforces. The losses providers sustain in turn will have to be shifted ever more onto the smaller employers and insurers who are price takers rather than price makers.

Small employers and insurers are not the only potential victims of this "beggar thy neighbor" strategy. Some hospitals lack a sufficient number of privately insured patients to absorb the losses sustained in meeting government demands for price advantages. Especially vulnerable are inner-city hospitals that serve the uninsured and that often maintain expensive teaching programs.[19]

Discount-seeking payers encourage the skimming of patients from hospitals by entrepreneurial ventures such as those that create chains of day surgery clinics and emergicenters. Marketing becomes medicine's newest and most lucrative specialization. With the growing surplus of physicians, it is easier and easier to promise large payers bargains by providing services in specialized settings unencumbered by the reserve capacity and costly overheads needed to maintain tertiary care facilities. Bargains for some, no doubt, but this pattern of stripping away profitable clients destroys the complex web of cross-subsidies that in large part supports teaching and services for the poor and for those with rare or expensive illnesses.

Worse yet, the methodology for determining the price that hospitals are to receive under the DRG arrangement is based on averages—the average cost of the average hospital in treating the average patient. But average cost and average care is not necessarily good medicine. There is great variability in the cost of health care services because there is great variability among practitioners in the definition of good care. Medicine is not an exact science.

Wasteful care certainly exists, but it is not easy to identify. An extra day of hospitalization can provide reassurance to patients frightened by their own mortality. An extra test can increase the confidence of physicians whose decisions have consequence. Amenities may make dehumanizing situations somewhat more tolerable. The way to guarantee that ineffective or unnecessary care is eliminated is to offer no care at all, a growing temptation of government when it reviews its beneficiary rolls to save money.

The policy dilemma is obvious. Attempts to control health care costs place in jeopardy access to quality health care services, and attempts to improve access to these services stimulate health care inflation. When one goal is emphasized, the others are likely to suffer. Although some seek political advantage in pointing out the trade-offs—providers, for example, are always quick to warn of deteriorating quality as soon as the discussion turns to cost control—trade-offs among the goals are unavoidable and unpleasant. Neither wishful thinking by politicians nor deception by policy advocates can make the contradictions of the health care system disappear.

Another obstacle to cost control

Although it seems unlikely, we may be willing to accept significant limitations in the access to care for some parts of the population in order to achieve cost control. Perhaps also we will be willing to restrict advances in medical technology or limit their use to those who are able to pay a premium for the advantage. We will then discover that there is another, more formidable barrier to cost control—our tradition of limiting the administrative capacity of government.

There are two visions of a cost-contained future, both based on the use of prospective payment. In one, the effects of the tight control of Medicare reimbursements are so disruptive on providers and insurers that an all-payer plan for the regulation of hospital payments is established. Under this concept, we choose a national prospective rate-setting scheme as our salvation. In the other, the federal government and most purchasers of care decide to become prudent buyers, auctioning their beneficiaries to the lowest qualified bidder. Instead of regulation, we choose competition.

However, both the regulatory and the competitive visions require for their realization something that is highly improbable in our society—the maintenance of an effective civil service. Regulation is a contest of skill between government and the regulated.[20] It is unlikely to achieve measurable benefit for the public without government being represented by knowledgeable regulators who are willing to remain committed to the task for their careers. Competitive contracting also requires very competent civil servants, for there are new contracts to structure and old ones to monitor. What some prefer to describe as a ''market mechanism'' is in reality another form of regulation that places no less of a burden on government administration than does rate or capital regulation.[21]

America does not reward its public officials with high salary and much esteem.[22] Hospital administrators, hospital association directors, and hospital lawyers earn much more than do hospital regulators. The administrator of the Veterans Administration and the administrator of the Health Care Financing Administration have five-figure salaries and severe restrictions on their outside incomes. The senior officers of the major health care firms and associations, and their consultants and advisors, can count on six- or seven-figure incomes, plus bonuses and, for many, stock options. *They* ride in the limousines and have the fancy offices, not the government regulators and contract administrators.

Of course, it is possible to fill the available government jobs. At the highest levels, some businessmen tire of making money and seek a charitable outlet.

College professors can take leaves and may want practical experience or the chance to live an ideology. And there are always defeated politicians desperately looking for sinecures. At the upper-middle and middle levels, government provides good training that often leads to high-paying private sector jobs that allow one to work on the same subjects, but for the other side. Minor restrictions notwithstanding, today's official is likely to be tomorrow's lobbyist, industry negotiator, expert witness, or knowledgeable consultant. It is not just business firms that exploit human frailties. Hospitals, universities, and other nonprofit organizations also can find use for those with the right government experience.[23]

This "in and then elsewhere" phenomenon is not conducive to tough regulation or negotiation. To be sure, it is important to do something noticeable while in government service to get the good next job. But it is mostly being there at the right time, knowing the details of something important, and knowing those who will take your place in government. Being the industry or profession's nemesis confines one to a gadfly role and requires either independent wealth or the desire for relative poverty.

We work hard to make government service unattractive. Government purchasing and personnel rules are restrictive. It is difficult for officials to buy pencils, sign a lease, and fire incompetent subordinates. There is never enough travel money, salaries are often frozen, and programs are frequently handicapped by personnel ceilings and budget disputes. The public is encouraged to believe the bureaucracy is more ineffective than it is by the news media which know the factors limiting government performance are too complex to convey and so instead revel in its more easily described blunders. Politicians, sensing the public attitudes, campaign incessantly against the bureaucracy.

Whether the policy choice is regulation or competition, expectations of success cannot be great. Just as the industry's lawyers and lobbyists ground down facility regulation in the 1970s, so too are they likely to blunt national rate regulation. California and Arizona's uneven and, at times, unhappy experience with Medicaid contracting revealed the problems of converting seductive theoretical concepts into practice.[24] Government, as we know it, lacks the required managerial capacity and is prevented form obtaining it.

Learning the comparative lessons

Although they have their limitations, comparisons are useful for analyzing policies. Too often, though, the comparisons for health are with other nations, foreign travel perhaps the lure. But the cultural difference between the United States and most other industrialized nations is substantial. The absence of a parliamentary form of government, a tradition supportive of public service, a strong socialist party, and a large portion of the workforce that is unionized are surely among the important factors affecting policy development that distinguishes the United States from a likely foreign pairing. Add to this our society's size and diversity and the potential benefits from cross-national comparisons fade from sight.

The more appropriate comparison is with another policy area, especially defense. Besides a common culture and jurisdiction, American health and defense share many characteristics. Both are technology-oriented, are dominated by a strong profession, and consume enormous resources (health vastly exceeds defense in GNP percentage, but when government expenditure is the measure they are more equal). Both depend heavily upon private sector organizations in the provision of government-financed services. And as one witty observer has noted, both seek the same goal—the prevention of natural death.

The defense weapons procurement experience is especially instructive for health policy analysts. Cost-based retrospective payment is known in defense as cost-plus contracting and was used routinely for the Cold War buildup of U.S. forces. Under its provisions, contractors are offered full cost reimbursement for the development of new weapons and a predetermined profit (the "plus" in cost-plus contracting). By the early 1960s, the cost-generating problems of the contracting methodology became obvious, as did the failings of reorganizations and regulation to correct them. President Kennedy's secretary of defense, Robert McNamara, instituted a major reform, the most relevant feature of which was a requirement that incentive contracts be used as much as possible instead of cost-reimbursement-type contracts.[25] Incentive contracts resemble the outline of the Medicare prospective payment system in that they offer contractors the opportunity to profit from cost savings but also the risk of absorbing losses when costs exceed predetermined prices. Another element of the reform was increased reliance on competition, with winners awarded fixed-price contracts for weapons procurement.[26]

The results were mixed. Some improvement in cost control has been identified, but it is not clear that this is due to the adoption of any particular measure.[27] Incentive contracts (and fixed-price contracts as well), it turns out, have their own problems. Contractors cannot absorb really large losses, nor can the government tolerate important contractors going out of business. Thus when Lockheed faced a bankruptcy loss in part as a result of problems encountered with its C5A contract, it was provided with a special government loan. Election-year politics, the threat to the California and Georgia economies, and the military's need for Lockheed's services assured the contractor's survival despite inefficiencies and bad luck.

The government also came to realize that there are multiple goals involved in defense contracting. Not only is there a desire to be efficient, but the government also wants high-performance equipment delivered as quickly as possible. In weapons procurement jargon this is called the cost/performance/time trade-off. The parallel goals in health are cost control, quality, and access. More often than not, the demand of the weapons consumers (the military services) is for greater emphasis on performance and early acquisition rather than on cost control. Given that lives can be said to be at stake ("nothing is too good for our boys") this weighting of the goals is hard to resist.[28] Add in the need to protect jobs and local economies and it is not surprising that weapons costs are never fully under control.

Periodically, weapons costs and contractor inefficiency gain public attention. Headlines blare: "Patrol Plane Has $600 Toilet Seat"; "Antiaircraft Gun Can't Hit Targets"; "Air Force Buys $400 Hammer"; "B-1 Plagued With Construction Faults." Congressional hearings are held, blue-ribbon commissions convened, reports written, and new reforms announced. The solutions are always the old ones in different guises. We need greater regulation of contractor behavior and/or more competition. It becomes a repeating cycle of calls for reform, reform adoption, disappointment, and renewed calls for reform.[29]

An inevitable component of reform is reorganization. Contracting responsibility is alternately centralized and decentralized. Czars are designated and later deposed. New training programs for contract negotiators are created as are additional volumes of procurement regulations. The Department of Defense no less than the Department of Health and Human Services has difficulty attracting program managers; many of those who gain sufficient experience join the ranks of the defense contractors or the industry's numerous consultants.[30]

There is no solution as long as there are serious international threats. The nation needs armed forces, and armed forces need weapons. The government is dependent upon contractors for the delivery of weapons. (Direct ownership of the weapons producers would not eliminate a dependency and is not "the American way.") Multiple goals in the weapons acquisition process mean ever-shifting priorities. Too much emphasis on performance improvements and schedule accelerations is likely to lead to cost overrun problems. Too little, and there will be calls for reform because America is falling behind in the arms race. Each new administration faces the same problems, but finds no new truths. Some prefer to call their plan regulation; others call it competition. Having a plan to show to critics is the preoccupation of most administrations.

Conclusions

Producers of vital public services—be they government arsenals, defense contactors, hospitals, or physicians—hold important policy leverage. Government cannot meet its obligations to citizens without accommodating to the interests of those who produce what it needs and what it must finance. This is especially true because of government's necessity to pursue multiple goals. In health, the concern for cost containment must be balanced against access and quality concerns.

The hope is for a panacea, a policy that will painlessly arrange the priorities. Especially appealing are economic theories in which organizations and individuals rationally respond to material incentives arranged to reward desired behavior. Unfortunately, the politics of contentious issues does not disappear because of the creation of specific incentives. The unpleasant reality of goal conflict remains to frustrate the next promising reform.

The switch to prospective payment will not bring satisfactory stability to health policy. Costs can still rise, as can dissatisfaction with health care access and quality of health care services. Even if we were certain of the desired direction for health, the administrative capacity to accomplish governmental objectives is limited. Much talent in the society stands ready to block policies that threaten industry or professional prerogatives. Even the designers of the policy may soon be employed to reveal its inevitable loopholes.

Defense is not precisely analogous to health. In defense, government is a monopsonist and competition among its suppliers is limited because of the scale of weapons projects. These differences notwithstanding, the experience in defense is revealing of the future of prospective payment. The use of incentives has not changed significantly the dynamics of weapons procurement. Politics still shape the process by which we determine how much and what type of defense we buy. The government, we learned in defense, cannot wish away intractable problems by imagining that they have simple and permanent solutions.

Prospective payment may promise improvement, but that promise is unlikely to be fulfilled. Rather, prospective payment should be considered as just another in a series of unsatisfactory reforms. The search for a panacea will go on.

Notes

1. There is, of course, a difference between perceptions of vulnerability and actual vulnerability. Nearly all of the social welfare programs of the 1960s remain in existence, though some have had their budgets trimmed. The failure to eliminate these programs (much of government beyond social security and defense) combined with the large tax cut enacted in 1981 gave us our large budget deficit.

2. Elizabeth Rolph and Phoebe Lindsey, *Medicare's Prospective Payment System: Health Care Community Reactions and Perceptions* (Santa Monica, CA: Rand Corporation, January 1986), pub. no. Rand R-3418-HCFA.

3. Currently they have joined together with more than a hundred other organizations to lobby for more health care funds and claim that prospective payment rates are too stringent. See Michael D. Bromberg, "The Health Budget Coalition," *Federation of American Health Care Systems Review,* March/April 1986, p. 4; and Mark F. Baldwin, "Plan to Increase Medicare Rates 0.5% Spurs Unanimous Industry Opposition,"*Modern Healthcare,* 1 August 1986, p. 28.

4. Judith M. Feder, *Medicare: The Politics of Federal Hospital Insurance* (Lexington, MA: Lexington Books, 1977).

5. Mary Link, "Hospital Costs: Carter Calls for Controls," *Congressional Quarterly,* 30 April 1977, pp. 787–791; David S. Abernathy and David A. Pearson, *Regulatory Hospital Costs: The Development of Public Policy* (Ann Arbor, MI: AUPHA Press, 1979); and Linda E. Demkovich, "No Recess in Hospital Costs Debate," *National Journal,* 18 August 1979, p. 1379.

6. Linda E. Demkovich, "Who Can Do A Better Job of Controlling Hospital Costs?" *National Journal,* 10 February 1979, pp. 219–23.

7. Lawrence D. Brown, "Technocratic Corporatism and Administrative Reform in Medicare," *Journal of Health Politics, Policy and Law* 10 (Fall 1985): 593; Gail R. Wilensky, "Underwriting the Uninsured: Targeting Providers or Individuals," in *Uncompensated Hospital Care,* Frank A. Sloan et al., editors (Baltimore, MD: Johns Hopkins University Press, 1986), p. 151; and Karen Davis, "Research and Policy Formulation," in *Applications of Social Science to Clinical Med-*

icine and Health Policy, David Mechanic and Linda H. Aiken, editors (New Brunswick, NJ: Rutgers University Press, 1986), p. 116.

 8. For a historical perspective on reasonable costs, see John D. Thompson, "On Reasonable Costs of Hospital Services," *Milbank Quarterly* 46 (January 1968): 33–51.

 9. Jeffrey Prottas, Mark Segal, and Harvey M. Sapolsky, "Cross-National Differences in Dialysis Rates," *Health Care Financing Review,* March 1983, pp. 91–103.

10. James Maxwell and Harvey M. Sapolsky, "The First DRG: Lessons of ESRD Payment Arrangements for Prospective Payment," *Inquiry* (forthcoming).

11. Irwin Wolkstein, "The Legislative History of Hospital Cost Reimbursement," in Social Security Administration, *Reimbursement Incentives for Hospital and Medical Care: Objectives and Alternatives* (Washington, DC: Government Printing Office, 1968), pp. 1–15; Robert D. Eilers, *Regulation of Blue Cross and Blue Shield Plans* (Homewood, IL: Richard D. Irwin, 1963); and Wilber J. Cohen, "Reflections on the Enactment of Medicare and Medicaid," *Health Care Financing Review,* 1985 Annual Supplement, pp. 3–11.

12. Too few have recognized the important interaction that has existed between technology and demand subsidies in health care. See John Goddeeris and Burton A. Weisbrod, "What Don't We Know About Why Health Expenditures Have Soared?" Discussion Paper 214, Center for Health Economics and Law, Department of Economics, University of Wisconsin, December 1984.

13. The relevant cases are Inland Steel Co. v. National Labor Relations Board, 170 F.2d 247 (September 23, 1948) and W.W. Cross & Co., Inc. v. National Labor Relations Board, 174 F.2d 875 (May 24, 1949).

14. Harvey M. Sapolsky, Drew Altman, Richard Greene, and Judith D. Moore, "Corporate Attitudes Toward Health Care Costs," *Milbank Quarterly* 59 (Fall 1981): 561–85.

15. John Krizay and Andrew Wilson, *The Patient As Consumer: Health Care Financing in the United States* (Lexington, MA: Lexington Books, 1974).

16. Paul L. Joskow, "Alternative Regulation Mechanisms for Controlling Hospital Costs," in *Health Care—Professional Ethics, Government Regulation or Markets?* Mancur Olson, editor (Washington, DC: American Enterprise Institute, 1981), pp. 219–57; and Brian M. Kinkead, "The Evolution of Policy," *Health Affairs* 3 (Fall 1984): 49–74.

17. Herman M. Somers and Anne R. Somers, *Medicare and the Hospitals: Issues and Prospects* (Washington, DC: Brookings, 1967). Note also Hugh Cabot, *The Patient's Dilemma* (New York: Reynal & Hitchcock, 1940), pp. 202–203.

18. Alicia H. Munnell, "Paying for the Medicare Program," *Journal of Health Politics, Policy and Law* 10 (Fall 1985): 489–512.

19. "Health Insurance and Cross-Subsidization," *Hospitals,* 16 October 1985, pp. 126–30; Karen Davis and Diane Rowland, "Uninsured and Underserved: Inequities in Health Care in the United States," *Milbank Quarterly* 61 (Spring 1983): 149–76; and Charles E. Phelps, "Cross-Subsidies and Change—Shifting in American Hospitals," in *Uncompensated Hospital Care,* Frank A. Sloan et al., editors (Baltimore, MD: Johns Hopkins University Press, 1986), pp. 108–25.

20. Frank A. Sloan, "Government and the Regulation of Hospital Care," *American Economic Review* 72 (May 1982): 196–201.

21. The difficulty in structuring contracts for health care services is noted by Odin W. Anderson, *Blue Cross Since 1929: Accountability and the Public Interest* (Cambridge, MA: Ballinger, 1975), p. 7.

22. Robert H. Davidson, "The Politics of Executive, Legislative, and Judicial Compensation," in *The Rewards of Public Service: Compensating Top Federal Executives,* Robert W. Hartman and Arnold R. Weber, editors (Washington, DC: Brookings, 1980), pp. 53–98. See also Charles H. Levine, *The Unfinshed Agenda for Civil Service Reform* (Washington, DC: Brookings, 1985). Not untypical is the complaint of a senior defense official who bemoans the difficulty of attracting qualified personnel to government positions. See Trish Gilmartin, "Pentagon's Former R&D Czar Looks Back at His Old Shop," *Defense News,* 10 February 1986, pp. 32–33. For a more general analysis of the U.S. Civil Service see Hugh Heclo, "In Search of a Role: America's Higher Civil Service," *Bureaucracy and Policy Making,* Ezra N. Suleiman, editor (New York: Holmes & Meier, 1984), pp. 8–34; and James W. Fesler, "The Higher Civil Service in Europe and the United States," in *The Higher Civil Service in Europe and Canada,* B. L. R. Smith, editor (Washington, DC: Brookings, 1984), pp. 87–92.

23. Harvey M. Sapolsky, James Aisenberg, and James Morone, "The Call to Rome and Other Obstacles to State-Level Innovation," *Public Administration Review* (forthcoming). See also "Government Employees: From White House to Bank," *Economist*, 19 April 1986, p. 28; Haynes Johnson, "Turning Government Jobs Into Gold," *Washington Post National Weekly Edition*, 12 May 1986, pp. 6–7; and Ronald Brownstein, "Credentialing the Right," *National Journal*, 19 July 1986, pp. 1764–69.
24. Lucy Johns, Maren D. Anderson, and Robert Derzon, "Selective Contracting in California: Experience in the Second Year," *Inquiry* 22 (Winter 1985): 335–47; and Jon B. Christianson and Diane G. Hillman, *Health Care for the Indigent and Competitive Contracts: The Arizona Experience* (Ann Arbor, MI: Health Administration Press Perspectives, 1986).
25. Charles Hitch, *Decision Making for Defense* (Berkeley: University of California Press, 1966).
26. Arnold Kanter, *Defense Politics: A Budgetary Perspective* (Chicago: University of Chicago Press, 1979); and Alain C. Enthoven and K. Wayne Smith, *How Much Is Enough?* (New York: Harper & Row, 1972).
27. Robert Perry, "American Styles of Military R&D," in *The Genesis of New Weapons*, Franklin Long and Judith Reppy, editors (Elmsford, NY: Pergamon Press, 1980), pp. 89–112.
28. Robert J. Art, "Restructuring the Military–Industrial Complex: Arms Control in Institutional Perspective," *Public Policy* 22 (Fall 1974): 423–59.
29. The list of studies, reports, and reform proposals is long. A sample for the curious reader would include: F. M. Scherer, *The Weapons Acquisition Process: Economic Incentives* (Boston, MA: Harvard Business School, 1961); Paul Y. Hammond, *Organizing for Defense* (Princeton, NJ: Princeton University Press, 1961); John C. Ries, *The Management of Defense* (Baltimore, MD: Johns Hopkins University Press, 1964); Edward N. Littwak, *The Pentagon and the Art of War* (New York: Simon & Schuster, 1984); Robert J. Art et al., editors, *Reorganizing America's Defense* (Elmsford, NY: Pergamon-Brassey's, 1985); and General Accounting Office, *Strengthening Capabilities of Key Personnel in Systems Acquisitions*, Report to Congress, May 1986.
30. General Accounting Office, *DOD Revolving Door: Many Former Personnel Not Reporting Defense-Related Employment*, Report to the Chairman, Committee on Governmental Affairs, United States Senate, March 1986.

Of course, states may facilitate economic development through some social expenditures. Those who rank states for their business climates weight such variables as vocational education enrollment and greater numbers of high school educated adults as assets in competing for business. However, much more weight tends to be attached to low taxes and limited debt. Welfare expenditure, in contrast, receives treatment as an undesirable factor—as an outlay "viewed by businesses as not directly beneficial to their performance."[7]

While one economic perspective sees interstate competition for financial growth as undermining state commitment to health programs for the poor, another questions whether states have adequate incentives for efficiency. One variation on this theme holds that problems arise when the level of government that raises the money is not the one that implements the program. Federal grant programs provide the states with free or discounted dollars. Therefore, state administrators presumably have weak "structural incentives for efficiency."[8] Another variation on this theme holds that dispersion of financial responsibility for health care weakens the incentive of any one level of government to introduce more efficient delivery systems.[9]

Aside from doubts about state commitment, questions persist about state capacity, i.e., the degree to which states possess the resources to formulate and implement policy effectively, efficiently, lawfully, and with adequate opportunity for public participation. In the past many diagnosed the states as having limited capacity. Their legislatures lacked professional staffs; governors confronted departments over which they had minimal formal authority; relatively low pay and patronage characterized personnel administration; election processes inhibited minority voting. These and other deficiencies prompted many to view state capacity as inferior to that of the federal government.

Tax progressivity also spawned skepticism about the role of the states in subsidizing health care programs. Assessments of progressivity depend on certain basic assumptions about the incidence of the property tax. But whatever the assumptions, state and local tax structures emerge as less progressive than their federal counterpart.[10] Those less able to pay might, therefore, bear "too much" of the costs of expanding state health programs.

To describe these sources of doubt about the states is not to suggest that analysts have written them off as hopeless. Some believe that state capacity has increased to a point that they can play a useful role in a national health insurance system. The Canadian health care program, which heavily emphasizes provincial administration, often serves as an example.[11] Still, considerable suspicion of state discretion persists. These concerns about the states helped fuel opposition to the New Federalism initiatives of the Reagan administration.

Policy evolution under Reagan

The evolution of federalism and health care policy during a given presidential administration revolves primarily around two issues—federal financing and state discretion. Does a president seek to shift the costs of shared programs to the states? Does he propose statutory and other changes that give state officials more freedom to choose who will get what, when and how from the shared program? Developments during the Reagan years reveal certain basic themes in response to these questions, but those seeking perfect thematic consistency face disappointment.

On 23 January 1982 President Reagan pledged in his first State of the Union address to "make our system of federalism work again," promising that "cumbersome administration and spiraling costs at the federal level" would abate, and accountability and responsiveness would be restored.[12] President Reagan's version of the New Federalism came with a special twist. In contrast to the federalism proposals of presidents Nixon and Ford, Reagan paid special attention to enhancing the role of the states rather than localities. Moreover, he went beyond decentralization to noncentralization by proposing a swap: the federal government would assume responsibility for certain programs and functions while leaving others completely to the states.

From the perspective of health policy, the call for a swap produced a bizarre twist. The president endorsed a plan that political liberals had long espoused—Washington's takeover of the Medicaid program. In exchange, the states were to assume complete responsibility for such social programs as Aid to Families with Dependent Children (AFDC) and Food Stamps. The swap proposal generated little political support and quickly exited from center stage. The enduring themes of Reagan's New Federalism for health policy follow a much more predictable course, requiring states to shoulder a greater portion of program costs and enhance state discretion, or at least to pursue economy and efficiency. Proposals for block grants and Medicaid embodied the prime expressions of these themes.

Shifting costs to the states and others. While the president's block grant initiative in part sought to cut federal expenditures, his Medicaid proposals more fully illustrate this thrust. Reagan repeatedly stressed the need to place a cap on the federal government's annual contribution to Medicaid. No longer would the program be an open-ended entitlement whereby the federal government gave the states a blank check. During his first year in office, the president proposed a five percent limit on growth in Washington's Medicaid support for the states for fiscal 1982. Despite congressional rejection, he persisted in espousing caps, albeit with variations on the theme. For example, the White House budget proposal for fiscal 1987 proposed to limit federal increases in its subsidy of state programs to a rate not to exceed increases in the medical component of the Consumer Price Index. The administration also sought to cut subsidies in other ways. Arguing that state administrative capacity had increased sufficiently to curtail the need for a "complicated and disparate set of matching rates" for state administrative costs, the White House proposed to set the match at a uniform 50 percent.[13]

White House attempts to cap Medicaid loom even larger if they are placed against the backdrop of other Reagan initiatives to remove financial props from the states. From 1980 through 1985 federal grants to states and local governments declined as a percentage of total federal outlays, as a percentage of state and local expenditures, and as a percentage of the Gross National Product.[14] In addition, the president's tax reform proposal of 1985 called for abolition of the federal deduction for state and local taxes.

Initiatives to shift Medicaid costs to others made very modest headway in Congress. While failing to cap the program, the Omnibus Budget and Reconciliation Act of 1981 (OBRA) imposed some ephemeral cuts. This statute called for federal Medicaid contributions to be computed as under previous law, but then reduced the federal contribution each year by a steadily increasing percentage—three percent in fiscal 1982, four percent in 1983, and 4.5 percent in 1984. States, however, had various options for dodging the cuts. For instance, they could hold down the overall increase in state Medicaid expenditures, operate hospital rate-setting programs approved by Washington, or demonstrate effective control of fraud and abuse. Moreover, the OBRA cuts expired with fiscal 1984 and were not replaced with other legislation.[15]

Financing initiatives also involved shifting costs to beneficiaries and third parties. The Tax Equity and Fiscal Responsibility Act of 1982 granted the states discretion to require Medicaid beneficiaries to pay nominal fees for medical services. It also permitted states to put liens on the property of permanently institutionalized Medicaid recipients. But the statute removed much of the bite by allowing many exemptions. The White House interest in cost sharing went beyond its ideological commitment to enhancing state discretion. By 1984, the president proposed that states be required to impose nominal fees on Medicaid beneficiaries for hospitalization. Statutory modifications also put new pressure on states to collect from other third parties for services provided to Medicaid patients. The Deficit Reduction Act of 1984 required Medicaid beneficiaries to assign to the states any right they had to other health benefit programs. States could thereby collect from such programs any available payments for medical care of the covered beneficiaries. Prior law had permitted but not required states to take this step. Some policy makers hoped that the change would allow Medicaid to recover $500 million to $1 billion in claims from private insurance companies.[16]

Selective enhancement of state discretion. While attempting to shift costs to the states, the Reagan administration also launched initiatives to bolster state discretion. Soon after taking office, the president sought to lump 25 categorical health programs into two major block grants—one for general health services and the other for preventive health measures. These block grants would presumably enable state officials to tailor federal programs to their particular priorities and would reduce overlapping reporting requirements.

Table 1. Consolidation of Health Policy Categorical Programs,[a] 1981–1985

Preventive Health and Health Services (Appropriation in Fiscal 1985 = $89,496,000)	Alcohol, Drug Abuse and Mental Health (Appropriation in Fiscal 1985 = $490,000,000)	Primary Care (Appropriation in Fiscal 1985 = $382,954,000)	Maternal and Child Health (Appropriation in Fiscal 1985 = $477,986,000)
Emergency medical services Health incentive grants Hypertension control Rodent control Fluoridation Health education and risk reduction Home health services Rape crisis centers	Community mental health centers Alcoholism grants and contracts Drug abuse grants and contracts	Community health centers	Maternal and child health and crippled children grants Supplemental security income, disabled children Lead paint poisoning Sudden infant death syndrome Hemophilia Genetic disease control Adolescent health services

Not Consolidated: Childhood immunization, venereal disease control, migrant health centers, black lung services, family planning, rape crisis centers.

a. Definitions of programs vary. Other descriptions of consolidation may therefore show slightly different numbers and configurations of programs.

Sources: Congressional Quarterly Almanac, 1981 (Washington: Congressional Quarterly Inc., 1982); *Appendix, Budget of the United States Government Fiscal Year 1987* (Washington: Government Printing Office, 1986).

Congress responded in 1981 by placing 19 categoricals into four major block grants: (a) Preventive Health and Health Services, (b) Alcohol, Drug Abuse, and Mental Health, (c) Primary Care, and (d) Maternal and Child Health. The specific programs under each block grant as well as those that preserved their categorical status appear in Table 1.

As is evident, one of the block grants amounts to little more than a name change. The Primary Care Block Grant essentially gave the states the option of receiving block funds in lieu of direct federal financing of community health centers. But the law gave the states almost no incentive to prefer the block grant as opposed to continued categorical aid. If they opted for the block grant, states had to put up matching funds in order to receive federal support. If they did not participate in the block grant, states faced no such requirement. The Reagan administration continued to call for movement toward consolidation. Reagan's budget proposal for fiscal 1987, for instance, sought to expand the Primary Care Block Grant to include categorical programs for black lung clinics, migrant health, and family planning. After 1981, however, Congress persistently rebuffed him. In March 1986, the House of Representatives went so far as to approve a bill that repealed the Primary Care Block Grant.

In spite of the block grant initiative, the legacy of the Reagan administration should not be read as an unrelenting quest to give states more formal discretion in implementing federal health programs. The White House displayed the most interest in granting states more latitude when it seemed to promise cost reductions. The evolution of Medicaid policy in the early 1980s, especially provisions related to client eligibility, provider eligibility and provider payment, illustrates this proclivity.

Those who control the gates to AFDC and Supplemental Security Income (SSI) eligibility de facto control access to Medicaid. In addition, Washington subsidizes states that extend Medicaid coverage to certain medically needy individuals who do not qualify for these welfare programs but cannot afford to cover their health care expenses. The Reagan years featured a degree of legislative ambivalence about eligibility. OBRA contained several provisions that made it more difficult for the working poor in particular to become eligible for AFDC. For example, the law required the states to limit expenses counted against income in determining eligibility for AFDC. It also reduced the total income any family could receive and still qualify for welfare. OBRA also permitted the states to assess income and asset levels differently for specific groups seeking Medicaid coverage as medically needy. States with programs for the medically needy thereby acquired more freedom to target certain groups (e.g., the aged versus the disabled) for eligibility.

While the 1981 initiative to prune AFDC rosters set the dominant tone for the first five years of the Reagan administration, spurts of legislative activity to ease eligibility also surfaced. As part of the Deficit Reduction Act of 1984, for instance, Congress required states to set up a new child health assurance plan. In essence, the statute required them to broaden their Medicaid coverage to include more low-income women during their first pregnancy, pregnant women in two-parent families in which the principal breadwinner was unemployed, and poor children up to age 5 in two-parent families. The law also took some of the sting out of original AFDC cuts by allowing up to 15 months of additional Medicaid coverage to those who lost AFDC eligibility because they had taken low-paying jobs. The Deficit Reduction Act also expanded AFDC eligibility to families with slightly higher incomes than previously allowed.

In terms of provider eligibility, OBRA authorized formal retreat from the principle of free choice of mainstream providers for Medicaid recipients. (Informally, low payment rates in many states had already reduced the number of medical providers willing to treat Medicaid beneficiaries.) OBRA allowed the states to buy laboratory services and medical devices via competitive bidding; they could require physicians and patients to use these outlets. In addition, the law gave the Department of Health and Human Services greater authority to grant waivers to states to implement systems that required Medicaid enrollees to use certain providers. Other statutory changes made it easier to use new kinds of providers—particularly HMOs. Prior law had prevented the states from entering contractual arrangements with an HMO when Medicare and Medicaid enrollees would comprise more than 50 percent of its membership. OBRA raised this figure to 75 percent. OBRA also permitted the states to apply for waivers to cover home and community-based services for persons who would otherwise require care in skilled or intermediate nursing facilities. States that obtained waivers could rely more heavily on such personnel as homemakers and home health aides.

Provider payment, according to some observers, amounted to the "single most important change" introduced by OBRA.[17] Ironically, federal policy makers uncoupled states from requirements to pay hospitals in a way comparable to Medicare during the very period when Washington adopted a new and increasingly tightfisted prospective payment system based on diagnosis related groups. States ostensibly need to pay only "reasonable and adequate" rates designed to assure sufficient access to medical care. OBRA took a small step toward enhancing the already substantial discretion states enjoyed in setting physician fees. The law removed Medicare payment levels to physicians as an upper limit on Medicaid fees. This change emanated from a concern among some lawmakers that the Medicare limit discouraged states from using uniform statewide fee schedules that could foster greater economy in health care delivery.

General assessments of Reagan's New Federalism vary. One observer concludes that the President won "surprisingly little."[18] Others, however, predict that Reagan's New Federalism will prove to be the "major sleeper" of his administration.[19] Viewing changes in the law with respect to health block grants and Medicaid, the president appears to have won a quarter of a loaf. While the modifications that occurred did not inevitably boost state discretion, the Reagan years provided states with new authority as implementing agents. The degree to which Reagan's New Federalism proves to be a sleeper or insignificant depends largely on what states do with that discretion.

Commitment, capacity, and progressivity revisited

How did state governments respond to the statutory changes enacted under Reagan? What are the implications of their behavior for such critical medical system outcomes as access to care for particular groups, the quality of that care, and its price? What do these outcomes portend for the health of the populace in different states? Haze shrouds the answers. Insufficient time has elapsed to render a definitive judgment. Moreover, the perennial social science problems of definition, measurement, and the disentanglement of one causal force from another loom large.

Beyond this, however, data on basic state activities frequently remain difficult to obtain. For instance, valid information on the numbers eligible for Medicaid are unavailable for many states.[20] State practices in defining, computing and documenting administrative costs vary so widely that calibrating any gains in efficiency and economy resulting from health block grants may well prove unfeasible.[21] The difficulties of obtaining basic information about state programs point to a paradox. The devolution of authority implicit in the New Federalism heightens prospects for greater state variation in approaches to health care problems; in the abstract, this would seem to enhance opportunities for learning about what works, what does not, and why. However, to the degree that the New Federalism perpetuates and heightens permissiveness with respect to state data gathering and reporting requirements, prospects for learning plummet. One cannot acquire enough comparable information from the states to take advantage of the learning experience born of variation.

While information shortages constrain analysis, sufficient evidence exists to foster informed speculation about the posture states will assume in implementing health care policies. Contemplation of possible scenarios suggests the importance of reconsidering state commitment, capacity, and progressivity from the vantage point of the 1980s. To what degree do states appear to have moved forward on the three dimensions? Have they increasingly become more equal in these respects? Has the gap between the state and federal government on the three criteria narrowed?

State commitment: half empty, half full. As implementation authority devolves, state politics becomes more pivotal. In very general terms, these politics have produced modest increases in state commitment to spending for public programs. State spending in constant 1972 dollars per capita (after intergovernmental transfers) rose by 4.3 percent during the Carter years and 3.6 percent during the first term of the Reagan administration. As a proportion of GNP, state outlays declined from 5.4 percent in 1976 to 5.2 in 1980 to 5.0 in 1984. State spending increases clearly outpaced those of local government but lagged behind the increase at the federal level.[22]

Dynamics of state health politics. General observations about state commitment to spending do not, of course, cast much light on state health politics in particular. What internal political groups and forces seem likely to push state officials toward greater commitment to efficient and comprehensive health programs? What forces will militate against these developments?

Local governments comprise a major lobby for generosity. More generous Medicaid eligibility and payments can ease the amount of free or "underpaid" care they must deliver in public hospitals. As it becomes more difficult to shift costs to other payers, their incentive to support more bountiful Medicaid programs increases. The local government lobby can be potent. In Arizona, for example, the counties emerged as the foremost group urging state participation in Medicaid.[23]

But local governments do not inevitably prevail. In California, for instance, officials eliminated a program for the medically indigent that the state had covered with its own funds.[24] Instead, it gave block grants to the counties to provide medical services to this group. The grants amounted to about 70 percent of the funds the state would have otherwise spent to provide service to this cohort. States can also impose costs on localities via regulatory policy, i.e., requiring them to serve indigents. In general, local governments have not succeeded in persuading states to pay a steadily higher percentage of their combined costs for health and hospitals (excluding Medicaid). From 1975 to 1983, the percentage of state and local expenditures for health and hospitals subsidized by the states from their own revenue sources increased only slightly from 49 to 50 percent (roughly the same share states paid in 1942). Twenty-five states decreased the percentage they paid, 21 boosted their share, and 4 remained the same.[25]

Other groups also have a stake in state commitment to more bountiful health programs. Hospitals, physicians, nursing homes and other providers comprise a significant lobby for generosity especially with respect to payment and eligibility. In this regard, the projected increases in the number of doctors may prove significant. While the causal dynamics remain fuzzy, larger numbers of physicians per capita appear to fuel greater Medicaid expenditures by a state. Aside from local governments and some providers, the program beneficiaries themselves may exert some pressure for more comprehensive access to care. Medicaid beneficiaries typically lack political clout, but in some states groups in the liberal coalition, such as unions, lend a helping hand.

Public attitudes also comprise a modestly positive force for more comprehensive health programs. Opinion surveys generally reveal support for the proposition that the poor should have adequate health care services. However, this support is fragile. Welfare remains an area where most Americans want no additional spending.[26] To the extent that the public views Medicaid as a welfare program, this attitude could undermine state commitment. Moreover, this sentiment could fuel further erosion in eligibility for Medicaid's feeder program, AFDC.

In considering the constellation of pressures for more generous health programs, it deserves emphasis that these groups do not necessarily support efficiency initiatives as well. For instance, state efforts to get more services delivered at reduced costs hardly receive warm welcomes from providers. Efficiency concerns typically loom larger to business and those segments of the public more strongly opposed to tax boosts. In the case of these groups, however, the desire to see the state government economize often assumes a higher priority than an improved efficiency ratio.

The interests and lobbying of business provide a major counterweight against state commitment to more comprehensive health programs. The imperative of the economic development model—sustaining policies that will retain and attract firms and the affluent—helps assure that state policy makers will pay attention to business interests even if corporate leaders fail to lobby energetically.[27] Beyond this potent dynamic business lobbies often pursue more specific agendas. To the extent that Medicaid (and Medicare) become more stringent in their payment practices, hospitals attempt to shift costs to the private insurance plans employers subsidize. At times, this cost shift may lead these firms to support rate regulation of all third-party payors—an innovation that may allow states to subsidize more care for the poor at a lower price.[28] But as the case of California suggests, the mobilization of business interests can also lead to an explicit rejection of rate regulation. In California, the chamber of commerce backed legislation (ultimately approved) that featured copayments, restrictions in Medicaid eligibility, reductions in funding for indigent care, and a shift in health care responsibilities to the counties.[29]

State officials do not, of course, simply react to external pressures; they also have preferences of their own. At times, they behave in ways that defy predictions of the economic development model.[30] Altruism as well as a desire to win support from certain constituencies can prompt policy makers to back more bountiful health care programs independent of economic development concerns. The degree to which the creation of an attractive business climate motivates officials no doubt varies from one state to the next. Officials in wealthier states probably feel less pressure to attach a high priority to it. Businesses and affluent individuals have some incentive to avoid relocation costs. State officials can therefore impose modest tax increases with little fear of driving them out. The economic development model tends to play a more potent role in poorer states where policy makers must provide enough incentives (e.g., lower taxes) to persuade businesses to move into the state.

While recognizing the substantial variation among states, it seems likely that pressures for more comprehensive health programs will meet stiff countervailing forces. Some of the evidence concerning block grants and Medicaid suggests the limits of expansionist tendencies.

State commitment to block grants. Economists generally hold that block grants tend to stimulate less state spending than categorical programs.[31] While far from definitive, preliminary evidence from the health arena is not inconsistent with this view. Separate analyses of the Maternal and Child Health as well as the Preventive Health Block Grants followed program expenditure levels in the same eleven states from 1981 through 1983. In the case of the Maternal and Child Health grant, total expenditures in constant dollars increased in only four states. State funding from their own sources for this grant rose in only five cases when one controls for inflation. The trend also emerges in the case of the Preventive Health and Health Services Block Grant. In real terms, only two of the eleven states witnessed an increase in expenditures. Using constant dollars, the expenditure of state funds for the block increased in five of eleven cases.[32]

Aside from any dampening effect on funding levels of the move toward blocks, the shift raises the issue of winners and losers among the programs that previously enjoyed categorical status. Bovbjerg and Davis suggest that, other things being equal, categorical programs with the following characteristics tend to do better in the competition for funds when merged into a block: (a) geographic dispersion of program beneficiaries throughout the entire state; (b) larger numbers of individuals eligible for services; (c) services that directly benefit the middle as well as working and lower classes; (d) an emphasis on medical treatment rather than prevention; (e) services for many types of diseases rather than one or a few; and (f) a history of substantial state funding for the program (presumably, an indicator that the program possesses a vigorous constituency in state politics).[33]

Which of these qualities are more important in shaping state commitment to particular programs? Answers must await research. If the most potent predictor proves to be the degree to which program benefits cross class lines, the finding would be consistent with the economic development model's assumptions about state aversion to redistributive policies. In this regard certain preliminary patterns deserve note.[34] In the Maternal and Child Health Block Grant,the crippled children program appears to have fared well in the competition. In the preventive health block, the flouridation program seems to have done relatively well. Aside from the fact that the two programs extend geographically to all corners of a state, they both bestow relatively direct benefits to all social classes.

State commitment to Medicaid. Data pertaining to Medicaid eligibility and expenditures provide further evidence concerning the limits to state commitment to more comprehensive programs. State generosity with respect to eligibility is a function of both the formal policy adopted and the degree to which officials leniently implement it (e.g., by easing the burden of proof on applicants who seek to qualify for Medicaid or by promptly expediting their applications). The proportion of a state's poverty population enrolled in Medicaid serves as a rough proxy for program generosity. While valid data on the number of Medicaid eligibles, or enrollees, are not consistently available, recipient data are accessible. A recipient is an individual who received at least one Medicaid service during the year. Recipient numbers probably underestimate enrollment by 20 to 30 percent.[35]

Table 2 indicates that the total number of Medicaid recipients declined by five percent from President Ford's last year of office to the final year of the Carter administration. During the same time frame, the total number of Medicaid recipients as a percentage of those below poverty fell by 17 percentage points. This erosion appears to have continued under Reagan, although at a reduced rate. Medicaid recipients in 1984 amounted to one percent fewer than in 1980. Total Medicaid recipients as a proportion of those below poverty declined by 11 percentage points between the two years. These general trends mask differences among categories. The number of recipients eligible because of their status as adults in AFDC families increased, as did disabled recipients covered by SSI. The "other" category, consisting largely of the medically needy, dropped substantially.

Failure of AFDC income eligibility criteria to keep pace with inflation probably accounts for much of the decline in the recipients/poverty population ratio.

Table 2.   Medicaid Recipients by Basis of Eligibility, 1976, 1980, 1984

Program	1976	1980	1984	Percent Change 1976–80	Percent Change 1980–84
		(in thousands)			
AFDC					
Dependent children under 21	9,924	9,333	9,771	−6	+5
Adults in families with dependent children	4,773	4,877	5,598	+2	+15
SSI					
Age 65 or over	3,612	3,440	3,166	−5	−8
Blind	97	92	80	−5	−13
Disabled	2,572	2,819	2,870	+10	+2
Other	1,836	1,499	1,184	−18	−21
Total	22,815	21,605	21,365	−5	−1
Total Medicaid recipients as a percentage of those below poverty	91%	74%	63%		

Source: Marian Gornick et al., ''Twenty Years of Medicare and Medicaid: Covered Populations, Use of Benefits, and Program Expenditures,'' *Health Care Financing Review* 6 (1985 Annual Supplement): 28; and *Statistical Abstract of the United States, 1986* (Washington: Government Printing Office, 1985), p. 457.

Changes introduced by OBRA probably had much less effect. A significant number of states took steps to soften the impact of OBRA eligibility restrictions. Sixteen states adjusted their needs standards for eligibility to allow more people to qualify, and others chose to cover families where both parents were unemployed.[36]

While recipients declined, expenditures rose, but at a shrinking rate. Table 3 shows that Medicaid outlays both in the aggregate and per recipient rose less rapidly during the first term of the Reagan administration than during the Carter years. When controls for increases in the medical care component of the Consumer Price Index are introduced, the same picture emerges. Whereas the Carter years featured real growth in Medicaid expenditures of 33 percent, the Reagan years experienced an increase of 2 percent. One must be cautious about imputing changes in outlays under Reagan to legislation such as OBRA. One analysis found that Medicaid expenditure growth fell substantially in the year after passage of this statute. However, when controls for shifts in state income and other variables are imposed, it appears that OBRA had relatively little effect on Medicaid outlays.[37]

Aside from trends in aggregate expenditures, the percentage of state budgets allocated to Medicaid casts some light on commitment. From 1975 through 1981, Medicaid increased its share of total expenditures from 5.6 to 7.7 percent; other

Table 3.   Medicaid Expenditures, 1976, 1980, 1984

	1976	1980	1984	Percent Change 1976– 1980	Percent Change 1980– 1984
Expenditures (in millions of dollars)	$14,245	$25,200	$34,262	+77	+36
Expenditures in constant 1976 medical dollars[a] (in millions of dollars)	14,245	18,932	19,362	+33	+2
Expenditures per recipient (in dollars)	624	1,166	1,604	+87	+38

a. Adjusted for increases in the medical care component of the Consumer Price Index.
Sources: U.S. Public Health Service, *Health, United States, 1978* (Washington: DHEW No. 78132, 1978), p. 394; U.S. Public Health Service, *Health, United States, 1984* (Washington: DHHS 85-1232), pp. 141, 158; Marian Gornick et al., "Twenty Years of Medicare and Medicaid: Covered Populations, Use of Benefits, and Program Expenditures," *Health Care Financing Review* 6 (1985 Annual Supplement): 28, 47.

state health outlays rose from 8.2 to 8.9 percent. In contrast, the percentage of state expenditures going to education, highways, and welfare declined.[38] But state officials face considerable pressure to resist allocation of an ever-larger budget share to health care. Competing claims to upgrade education and infrastructure (expenditures more consonant with the economic development model) gained strength in the 1980s.

Efficiency more than comprehensiveness? While preliminary evidence concerning block grants and Medicaid suggests limited state commitment to expanding program comprehensiveness, will states use their new discretion to pursue greater efficiency? Innovations in competitive bidding by providers for Medicaid contracts, capitation payment strategies, and all-payor rate regulation may increasingly surface in the states.[39] For states committed to doing more, efficiency offers an opportunity to get more medical "bang for the buck." Of course, efficiency may also accompany the status quo or reductions in services to beneficiaries. Furthermore, some state innovations may be exercises more in cost cutting than in efficiency enhancement.

Some analysts express skepticism that state officials have adequate incentive to pursue major reforms aimed at efficiency. While significant and growing, the proportion of state expenditures consumed by health care programs may nonetheless be too small to motivate state policy makers to pursue changes opposed by medical providers. The payoffs of reform may be too uncertain and distant for policy makers; the short-term political costs of taking on medical providers may seem much larger. Yet several states, including California, New Jersey, and New York, have initiated significant new policies. Ideas have a momentum of their own and often find advocates among the professionals who staff state health bureaucracies. At times medical providers (e.g., public hospitals) support significant reform because it promises to ease their financial problems over the short term.[40] On balance, it seems more likely that states will pursue efficiency measures rather than reforms which would make their health care programs more comprehensive.

State homogenization in commitment? Discussions of general proclivities among the states beg the issue of equality. Are states becoming increasingly similar in their commitment to certain policies in the health arena, or less so? A thorough answer to this question would require trend analyses of a host of indicators. For present purposes, such exensive analyses are not feasible. However, glimmerings of insight can be obtained from an examination of state tax effort and certain measures of Medicaid expenditures.

Tax effort serves as a rough proxy for state willingness to spend resources for public purposes. A tax effort index can be computed for a state by dividing its tax collections by its estimated tax capacity and multiplying by 100. Drawing on these computations, the standard deviation for the 50 states on this index serves as a rough measure of their homogeneity. In 1982, the standard deviation for tax effort scores of the 50 states amounted to 21.5 (with a mean score of 97.4). The comparable standard deviation for the states in 1975 was 17.1. Hence from the mid-1970s to the early 1980s tax efforts among the states appear to have become slightly less similar.[41]

Turning to the health arena, a similar trend can be noted when one examines standard deviations for 1971 and 1981 for two different measures of state Medicaid expenditures: Medicaid outlays as a percentage of total state expenditures, and Medicaid expenditures as a percentage of state budgets exclusive of intergovernmental transfers. In the case of both indicators, the magnitude of the standard deviation rose during the decade.[42]

What accounts for persistent state variations in commitment to Medicaid? Table 4 presents a brief overview of the results of three studies. Diversity in the dependent and independent variables as well as disparate methodologies make direct comparisons difficult. In general, however, the following propositions receive support: (a) Wealthier states tend to spend more per capita on Medicaid and score higher on an index of program comprehensiveness; in effect, states that have to pay a higher percentage of program costs out of their own coffers adopt more comprehensive programs. (b) The greater presence of certain medical providers (as measured by physicians, dentists or nursing home beds per capita) appears to trigger greater Medicaid expenditures per capita. But these indicators have uncertain effects on other aspects of program comprehensiveness. (See the somewhat conflicting findings of Davidson and Hanson.) (c) A traditionalistic, as distinct from a moralistic, political culture tends to retard commitment to expanding Medicaid eligibility and services.[43] Thus state responses to enhanced discretion over Medicaid may well depend on their wealth, provider density, and political culture. Clearly, however, researchers need to push beyond this hy-

Table 4.   Correlates of Variations in State Medicaid Programs

Major Dependent Variables	Major Explanatory Variables	Study
Expenditures		
Average Medicaid cost per recipient, 1977	Major predictor is greater state share of Medicaid outlays. Adjusted r^2 = .64.	Hanson
Medicaid expenditures per capita, 1979–82	Income per taxpayer, physicians per capita, nursing home beds per capita, region (with the South less supportive). r^2 = .63	Holahan
Other characteristics		
Medicaid caseload, 1977	State population. Adjusted r^2 = .92.	Hanson
Medicaid eligibility, 1977	Moralistic as opposed to traditionalistic political culture, more doctors and dentists per capita. Adjusted r^2 = .41.	Hanson
Scope of professional services factor score, 1977	Moralistic as opposed to traditionalistic political culture, greater state share of Medicaid outlays. Adjusted r^2 = .23.	Hanson
Scope of institutional services factor score, 1977	Moralistic as opposed to traditionalistic political culture, domination of state by Democratic party. Adjusted r^2 = .16.	Hanson
Medicaid program index based on adding scores of four dimensions: coverage of the medically indigent, optional services covered, limitations on service, and reimbursement procedures, 1970, 1975	Per capita income, fewer physicians per capita, low percentage of black population, lower percentage of the population in manufacturing. r^2 = .66.	Davidson

Sources: Stephen M. Davidson, "Variations in State Medicaid Programs," *Journal of Health Politics, Policy and Law* 3 (Spring, 1978) : 54–70; Russell L. Hanson, "Medicaid and the Politics of Redistribution," *American Journal of Political Science* 28 (May 1984): 313–19; John Holahan, *The Effects of the 1981 Omnibus Budget Reconciliation Act on Medicaid* (Washington: Urban Institute, 1985 Progress Report).

pothesis to an examination of other variables and a more in-depth understanding of the precise dynamics involved.

State versus federal commitment. On balance, the "old perspective" on the limits to state commitment continues to be applicable. The evidence provides little support for the view that most states have taken or will take bold new strides toward assuring adequate access to health care for the poor or medically needy.

In certain respects, however, matters have changed. The gap between federal and state commitment has narrowed. In the period from the mid-1970s to the mid-1980s deficit politics began to replace technical politics in Washington. Technical, or "rationalizing," politics have several distinguishing characteristics. Debates tend to be couched in terms of economy, efficiency, and adjustment rather than in ideological rhetoric that distinguishes the left from the right in the political system. The issues it addresses pose complexities that the media and the populace cannot readily grasp. Instead, groups of "experts" (particularly economists) representing different values and priorities engage in policy debate. In this regard, the bureaucracy frequently becomes the home of major decisions not only in shaping the options Congress considers but in implementation processes. While technical politics can profoundly shape who gets what from government, the language of this politics emphasizes efficiency rather than bold breakthroughs toward expanded coverage.[44]

With the coming of the Reagan administration, deficit politics has in many respects replaced the technical version. In effect, economy triumphs over efficiency. Expert analysis and the bureaucracy become less relevant. Instead, the political question of where program costs can be cut with the least resistance assumes center stage. Freezes on increases in DRG rates or physician fees become staples of health politics. As the deficit mounts, thoughts of major program expansion fade even further from the political agenda.

Willingness to raise federal taxes could prompt a return to a more balanced technical politics in Washington. A major economic downturn might even fuel federal commitment to more comprehensive health programs. But other forces could apply brakes on any such movement. Large segments of the public continue to believe that federal taxes are too high. Moreover, the 1980s witnessed a substantial increase in identification with the Republican party among the electorate. Many analysts believe that this shift will not be ephemeral.[45] Cost cutting as well as the devolution of authority and funding responsibility to lower levels of government comprise an intrinsic part of the Republican agenda.

Beyond these factors, economic development theory has reared its head at the national level. Paul Peterson observes "that the economies of industrialized nations are becoming so interdependent that significant changes in the international economy seem imminent . . . If these trends continue, nation-states may come to look increasingly like local governments."[46] Hence, Washington policy makers may come to perceive a sharper trade-off between initiating redistributive policies for the poor and fostering economic growth.

Gains in capacity. Judgments about the states in the health care arena also depend on views of their capacity. The conventional wisdom holds that state capacity has increased markedly. For instance, a recent 406-page report of the U.S. Advisory Commission on Intergovernmental Relations points to a "profound restructuring of the state governmental landscape" in the 1960s and 1970s.

The report finds state governments to be "more representative, more responsive, more activist, and more professional in their operations than they ever have been."[47] The volume draws this conclusion after reviewing developments with respect to a host of indicators pertaining to state constitutions, legislatures, governorships, executive branch organization, personnel systems, financial administration, open government laws and more. While the report synthesizes vast amounts of pertinent information, two impressions stand out. First, basic data about state practices (e.g., personnel procedures) are limited. Second, the relationship between specific state structures (e.g., large legislative staffs) and efficiency or effectiveness remains the subject of informed speculation rather than empirical verification.

Uncertainty opens the door to conflicting interpretations. Some hold less sanguine views about state capacity. To be sure, most everyone agrees that the introduction of "one person, one vote" and greater protection of minority rights represent important steps forward. But beyond this, some analysts express doubts that a "new era" has surfaced in state politics. Among other things, they note that the governor's office continues to be weak in many states and that amateurs with little staff assistance fill many state legislatures.[48] Still others believe that the reforms designed to modernize and democratize state governments have worked, but that this success spawns new quandaries. Greater openness and capability have presumably fueled a dispersion of power, the rise of single-issue politics, and government overload. Ironically, the problem-solving capacity of the states may be no stronger than before.[49]

While the available evidence does not permit definitive judgments, states do appear to have bolstered their administrative capacity. Of greater significance, any gap between their administrative capacity and that of the federal government has probably diminished since the mid-1970s. Faced with negligible pay increases and antibureaucracy rhetoric from the White House, turnover among top career officials of the Senior Executive Service has been unusually high.[50] These and other developments, such as reductions in force, have probably weakened Washington's administrative capacity.

To the extent that states have suffered blows to their capacity in the last decade, it probably stems from the tendency of electorates to restrict state discretion to tax and spend. In the period from 1976 through 1981, 19 states, including larger ones such as California and Michigan, enacted such restrictions. These legal restrictions vary greatly in their stringency and the degree to which they contain escape clauses.[51] In some instances, they may well inhibit expanded support for health programs.

As with commitment, states vary greatly in capacity. Nor can one assume they are converging along all pertinent dimensions. For instance, some analysts have suggested that "the growing economic equality among the states" may make it more appropriate for states to play an enhanced role in dealing with social policy.[52] If one examines state tax capacity, however, doubts arise about any movement toward economic equality. Tax capacity refers to the amount of money each state would raise if it applied a nationally uniform set of tax rates to specified revenue sources. A tax capacity index can be computed by dividing a state's per capita tax capacity by the average for all states with the value for the mean set at 100. To gauge the degree of heterogeneity among the states, one can examine the standard deviation from the mean of state tax capacity indices in a given year. The standard deviation was 37.0 in 1982 as opposed to 16.7 in 1975.[53] This comparison suggests a growing disparity among the states in their revenue capacity, rather than the hypothesized movement toward economic equality.

Shrinking of the progressivity gap. Little evidence exists that state tax structures have become more progressive in their incidence. Hence, to the degree that states increase taxes to support health programs, citizens most able to pay may well escape much of the tax burden. Much of the public appears to prefer taxes notorious for their regressivity. When asked to choose between a sales tax hike and an income tax boost in the event state taxes had to be raised, 57 percent indicated that the former "would be a better way to do it"; 23 percent preferred the income tax.[54] As if these pressures were not sufficient, some evidence suggests that greater tax progressivity tends to retard the net migration of higher income households into a state.[55] Whether pressures such as these yield increased convergence among states in the progressivity of their tax structures awaits systematic research.

Whatever the limits to state progressivity, the extent to which the federal government surpasses them may well be diminishing. Since 1966, the progressivity of the tax system in general has declined. This diminution appears to be accounted for entirely by changes in the federal tax system. The rise in the payroll tax as well as revenue policy modifications in 1981 contributed to this trend.[56] Furthermore, if pushed to endorse some form of federal tax increase, most of the public prefers a national sales tax to a hike in the federal income tax.[57] Hence, any claims for federal superiority in the health arena based on the progressivity of its funding may increasingly come to rest on shaky foundations.

Conclusion

The increased discretion granted to state implementing agents in the health policy arena makes the perennial issues of state commitment, capacity, and progressivity all the more pertinent. While hard evidence remains elusive, a plausible case exists that any gap on these dimensions between state governments and Washington has declined. State capacity in particular has probably increased. The continued presence of substantial variation among the states needs to be underscored, however. While states may be converging, they emerge as increasingly dissimilar on such important dimensions as revenue capacity and tax effort. Furthermore, the relentless imperative of the economic development model sets genuine limits on how far states can feasibly go in making their programs more comprehensive. In all likelihood, the most optimistic and plausible scenario one can muster, given current federal laws, would envision the rise of a technical politics of efficiency in the states. Responding to competing values of cost containment and generosity, state officials would modestly expand benefits via gains in efficiency.

The role of state governments in the health care arena deserves continued scrutiny by those seeking change. Conservatives have had the clearest vision in this regard, one that involves devolution of authority and financial responsibility back to the states with little concern for such outcomes as adequate access to medical care for all segments of society. Liberals have belatedly become aware of the states, seeing a role for them in the implementation of national health insurance. While important, this liberal vision lacks immediate relevance in an era of deficit or, at best, technical politics. In such an era, liberals need to develop proposals that involve the states in expanding coverage to the poor and medically indigent without requiring so major a reform as national health insurance. In this regard, significant technical changes in programs may, as Lawrence Brown has observed, be the best stimulus to open debate about the larger purposes of the health care system.[58]

The Report of the Committee on Federalism and National Purpose, a group chaired by former governor of Virginia Charles Robb and U.S. Senator Daniel Evans of Washington, comes close to being a step in the right direction. Among other things, the committee recommends that Washington set eligibility standards for Medicaid and fund 90 percent of the program's costs.[59]

Alternatively, those favoring expanded programs for the poor and medically indigent might push for a floating federal match rate for Medicaid. Under current law, a state's share of its Medicaid program costs largely depends on its per capita income relative to that of the entire country. A financially strapped state in the throes of a recession cannot count on Washington to pay a higher percentage of program expenses unless other states tend to be simultaneously gaining in affluence. The reluctance of state officials to expand their programs during good times in part reflects a concern about how they will pay for them in bad. A funding formula more sensitive to economic cycles might reduce state inhibitions. For instance, the basic federal match for a state (as determined by the current formula) might increase from 50 to 60 percent if unemployment rates rose and GNP declined. A floating federal match rate would allow state officials to expand Medicaid when state treasuries were flush without worrying so much about the possible need for cutbacks or tax boosts when revenues shrink. It would acknowledge Washington's traditional role as a refuge and stimulator during economic downturns but would reduce demands on the federal budget during more prosperous periods.

. No doubt other technical "sleepers" might also lead to a better set of problems or improved discussion of more comprehensive health care reform. Whatever the specifics, the role of the states requires continued examination. Political scientists have struggled with issues of federalism for years, only to conclude that they have yet to develop an adequate theory that specifies appropriate activities for the central government vis-à-vis its state and local counterparts and accounts empirically for persistent patterns of conflict and cooperation among these levels.[60] Within their province, students of health policy confront a similar challenge.

Notes

1. Lawrence Brown traces the phrase back to the New Deal. "The Politics of Devolution in Nixon's New Federalism," in *The Changing Politics of Federal Grants*, Lawrence D. Brown, James W. Fossett and Kenneth T. Palmer, editors (Washington, DC: Brookings Institution, 1984), pp. 54–55.

2. Theodore J. Lowi, "Why Is There No Socialism in the United States? A Federal Analysis," in *The Costs of Federalism*, Robert T. Golembiewski and Aaron Wildavsky, editors (New Brunswick, NJ: Transaction Books, 1984), pp. 38, 49–50.

3. See, for instance, Helen Ingram, "Policy Implementation Through Bargaining: The Case of Federal Grants-in-Aid," *Public Policy* 75 (Fall 1977): 499–526; and Paul Sabatier and Daniel Mazmanian, "The Conditions of Effective Implementation: A Guide To Accomplishing Policy Objectives," *Policy Analysis* 5 (Fall 1979): 481–504.

4. Brown, "The Politics of Devolution," p. 64.

5. See Bruce Vladeck, "The Design of Failure: Health Policy and the Structure of Federalism," *Journal of Health Politics, Policy and Law* 4 (Fall 1979): 528.

6. See Paul E. Peterson, *City Limits* (Chicago: University of Chicago Press, 1981); and Edward M. Gramlich, "An Econometric Examination of the New Federalism," *Brookings Papers on Economic Activity* 2 (1982): 327–60.

7. Alexander Grant & Company, *1983 General Manufacturing Business Climates* (Chicago: Grant Thorton International, 1984), p. 9.

8. James E. Swiss, "Intergovernmental Program Delivery: Structuring Incentives for Efficiency," in *The Cost of Federalism*, p. 272.

9. Theodore R. Marmor, Donald A. Wittman, and Thomas C. Heagy, "The Politics of Medical Inflation," in *Political Analysis and American Medical Care*, Theodore R. Marmor, editor (Cambridge: Cambridge University Press, 1983), pp. 61–75.

10. Joseph A. Pechman, *Who Paid The Taxes, 1966–85* (Washington, DC: Brookings Institution, 1985), pp. 61–62.

11. See, for instance, Judith Feder and John Holahan, "Administrative Choices," in *National Health Insurance's Conflicting Goals and Policy Choices*, Judith Feder, John Holahan and Theodore Marmor, editors (Washington, DC: The Urban Institute, 1980), pp. 21–71.

12. *Congressional Quarterly Weekly Report* 40 (30 January 1982): 178.

13. U.S. Office of Management Budget, *Budget of the United States Government, Fiscal Year 1987* (Washington, DC: Government Printing Office, 1986), p. 5-102.

14. U.S. Office of Management and Budget, *Special Analyses: Budget of the United States Government, Fiscal Year 1987* (Washington, DC: Government Printing Office, 1986), p. H-20.

15. The Gramm-Rudman-Hollings law of 1985 semed unlikely to pick up the slack. Among other things, the legislation exempted Medicaid and its feeder programs, AFDC and SSI, from automatic cuts.

16. U.S. House Committee on Appropriations, *Departments of Labor, Health and Human Services, Education, And Related Agencies Appropriations For 1986, Part 5* (Washington, DC: Government Printing Office, 1985), pp. 109, 247.

17. Randall R. Bovbjerg and John Holahan, *Medicaid In The Reagan Era: Federal Policy And State Choices* (Washington, DC: Urban Institute, 1982), p. 41.

18. Brown, "The Politics of Devolution," p. 104.

19. Richard P. Nathan and Fred C. Doolittle, "The Untold Story of Reagan's 'New Federalisms'," *The Public Interest* 77 (1984): 96–105.

20. John Holahan, *The Effects of the 1981 Omnibus Budget Reconciliation Act On Medicaid* (Washington, DC: Urban Institute, 1985).

21. U.S. General Accounting Office, *States Use Added Flexibility Offered By The Preventive Health And Health Services Block Grant* (Washington, DC: GAO/HRD-84-41, 1984), pp. 60–62.
22. Local government expenditures dropped 1.8 percent during the Carter years and rose by only half of one percentage point under Reagan. This represented a decline from 9.2 percent of GNP in 1976 to 8.3 in 1980 to 7.8 in 1984. During the Carter and Reagan years, federal expenditures climbed by 12.5 and 17.8 percent, respectively. Federal outlays rose from 18.8 percent of the GNP to 19.5 in 1980 to 21.5 in 1984. U.S. Advisory Commission on Intergovernmental Relations, *Significant Features of Fiscal Federalism, 1984 Edition* (Washington, DC: Government Printing Office, 1985), p. 10.
23. Charles Brecher, "Medicaid Comes to Arizona: A First-Year Report on AHCCS," *Journal of Health Politics, Policy and Law* 9 (Fall 1984): 411–25.
24. Linda Bergthold, "Crabs in a Bucket: The Politics of Health Care Reform in California," *Journal of Health Politics, Policy and Law* 9 (Summer 1984): 203–22.
25. U.S. Advisory Commission on Intergovernmental Relations, *Significant Features of Fiscal Federalism*, p. 41.
26. Robert J. Blendon and Drew A. Altman, "Public Attitudes About Health-Care Costs," *New England Journal of Medicine* 311 (30 August 1984): 613–16.
27. See, for instance, Gramlich, "An Econometric Examination of the New Federalism," as well as Paul G. Althaus and Joseph Schacter, "Interstate Migration and the New Federalism," *Social Science Quarterly* 64 (March 1983): 35–45.
28. Andrew B. Dunham and James A. Morone, *The Politics of Innovation: The Evolution of DRG Rate Regulation in New Jersey* (Princeton, NJ: Health Research and Educational Trust, 1983).
29. Bergthold, "Crabs in a Bucket."
30. While not focused specifically on the economic development model, John E. Chubb provides evidence of the limits to economic explanations of policy processes. See his "The Political Economy of Federalism," *American Political Science Review* 79 (December 1985): 994–1015.
31. Wallace E. Oates, "The New Federalism: An Economist's View," *Cato Journal* 2 (Fall 1982): 482.
32. U.S. General Accounting Office, *States Use Added Flexibility Offered By The Preventive Health And Health Services Block Grant, and Maternal And Child Health Block Grant: Program Changes Emerging Under State Administration* (Washington, DC: GAO/HRD-84-35, 1984).
33. Randall R. Bovbjerg and Barbara A. Davis, "States' Responses to Federal Health Care Block Grants: The First Year," *Milbank Memorial Fund Quarterly/Health and Society* 61 (Fall 1983): 523–60.
34. U.S. General Accounting Office, *States Use Added Flexibility* and *Maternal And Child Health Block Grant*.
35. Marian Gornick et al., "Twenty Years of Medicare and Medicaid: Covered Populations, Use of Benefits, and Program Expenditures," *Health Care Financing Review* 6 (Annual Supplement 1985): 25.
36. Ibid., p. 26.
37. Holahan, *The Effects of the 1981 Omnibus Budget Reconicliation Act On Medicaid*.
38. Gornick et al., "Twenty Years of Medicare and Medicaid," p. 49. Drawing on different data sources, another analysis presents slightly different percentages. But these data also point to relative gains by Medicaid as well as by health and hospitals. See Stephen M. Davidson, Jerry Cromwell, and Rachel Schurman, "Medicaid Myths: Trends in Medicaid Expenditures And The Prospects For Reform," *Journal of Health Politics, Policy and Law* 10 (Winter 1986): 703.
39. Arizona, California, and New Jersey serve as examples of states that have initiated one or the other of these measures. For a general assesment of rate regulation, see Frank A. Sloan, "Rate Regulation as a Strategy for Hospital Cost Control: Evidence From The Last Decade," *Milbank Memorial Fund Quarterly/Health and Society* 61 (Spring 1983): 195–221.
40. Dunham and Morone, *The Politics of Innovation*.
41. U.S. Advisory Commission on Intergovernmental Relations, *1982 Tax Capacity of the Fifty States* (Washington, DC: Government Printing Office, 1985).
42. In the case of the former measure, the standard deviation increased from 2.9 to 3.8; in the case of the latter, the standard deviation rose from 2.3 to 3.2. Data are from Davidson et al., "Medicaid Myths," pp. 704–707.

43. These cultural distinctions derive from the work of Daniel Elazar, *American Federalism: A View From The States* (New York: Harper & Row, 1984), pp. 109–49. Very briefly, an individualistic political culture emphasizes the conception of democracy as a market place where government is instituted for strictly utilitarian reasons to respond to demands from society. In a moralistic culture, politics is seen as a contest between various forces in the quest for a good society. A traditionalist political culture accepts government as a forum for assuring the continued maintenance of the existing social order.

44. This description of technical politics borrows heavily from Lawrence D. Brown, *Politics And Health Care Organization: HMOs As Federal Policy* (Washington, DC: Brookings, 1983), pp. 10–11.

45. John E. Chubb and Paul E. Peterson, "Realignment and Institutionalization," in *The New Direction In American Politics*, John E. Chubb and Paul E. Peterson, editors (Washington, DC: Brookings Institution, 1983), pp. 1–32.

46. Peterson, *City Limits*, pp. 27–28.

47. U.S. Advisory Commission on Intergovernmental Relations, *The Question of State Government Capability* (Washington, DC: Government Printing Office, 1985), p. 364.

48. See, for instance, John E. Chubb, "Federalism and the Bias for Centralization," in *The New Direction In American Politics*, pp. 273–306.

49. Jerome T. Murphy, "The Paradox of State Government Reform," *The Public Interest* 64 (Summer 1981): 124–39.

50. U.S. General Accounting Office, *Testimony of the Comptroller General On The Impact of Senior Executive Service* (Washington, DC: GAO/GGD-84-32, 1983), p. 11.

51. New Jersey's limitation expired in 1983, leaving 18 states. U.S. Advisory Commission On Intergovernmental Relations, *Significant Features of Fiscal Federalism*, pp. 148–51.

52. Nathan Glaser, "The Social Policy Of The Reagan Administration," in *The Social Contract Revisited*, D. Lee Bawden, editor (Washington, DC: Urban Institute Press, 1984), p. 235.

53. U.S. Advisory Commission On Intergovernmental Relations, *1982 Tax Capacity of The Fifty States.*

54. U.S. Advisory Commission On Intergovernmental Relations, *1983 Changing Public Attitudes On Governments And Taxes* (Washington, DC: Government Printing Office, 1983), p. 11.

55. Althaus and Schachter, "Interstate Migration And The New Federalism," p. 41.

56. Pechman, *Who Paid The Taxes*, pp. 70, 75.

57. U.S. Advisory Commission On Intergovernmental Relations, *1983 Changing Public Attitudes*, p. 9.

58. Lawrence D. Brown, "Technocratic Corporatism And Administrative Reform in Medicare," *Journal of Health Politics, Policy and Law* 10 (Fall 1985): 595.

59. Committee on Federalism and National Purpose, *To Form A More Perfect Union* (Washington, DC: National Conference on Social Welfare, 1985).

60. Peterson, *City Limits*, p. 67.

The Resistible Rise of Preventive Medicine

Deborah A. Stone, Brandeis University

Abstract. The politics of preventive health care have changed dramatically in the last fifteen years. In the late 1960s and early 1970s, prevention was the motherhood issue of health care reform. With only the slightest glimmer of controversy, vaccination, promotion of lifestyle changes, mass screening, and safety regulation all became widely accepted strategies for improving health and reducing medical expenditures. By the mid-1980s, the dark side of each strategy became visible. Vaccinations can cause serious and permanent injuries; lifestyle factors are being used to raise insurance premiums, to deny eligibility for disability insurance benefits, and to deny employment. Screening is similarly used to deny employment, and new technologies for prenatal screening have raised fears of stigma and selective abortion among racial, handicapped, and antiabortion groups. Occupational safety regulation is increasingly focused on excluding the "high-risk" individual from jobs. In the absence of social protections from these economic and social harms, citizens have used tort and civil rights litigation to resist preventive health measures.

Prevention has always had an ambiguous status in health care politics. It is at once the darling of health care reformers and the stepchild of health care professionals and politicians. Everyone is in favor of the *idea* of prevention—stopping disease and injury before they happen—but few want to stake a career on such an uncertain business or invest public funds in preventive measures.

Although this discrepancy between ideology and practical politics has been a historical constant in preventive health policy, there has been tremendous change in the politics of prevention since the early 1970s. The political coalitions are different. The rhetoric and substantive issues of prevention have changed. And the political strategies of those favoring and opposing preventive measures have shifted.

What I will call the "old politics" involved a liberal, "do-good" reform coalition of public health researchers, physicians, labor, and advocates of the poor and children which was aligned against business and industry and the bogey of public ignorance. The rhetoric was missionary: the purpose of prevention programs was to bring better health to the poor, the uneducated, and the untreated. Through better health would come better performance in schools, better job opportunities, and even upward social mobility. All this was to happen through the classic techniques of prevention: immunization against contagious diseases, mass screening to detect diseases in early stages, public education about lifestyle habits and health, and reduction of occupational health and safety hazards.

If the old politics could be described as missionary, the new politics might well be described as a colonial uprising. The new political line-up often has labor, women's groups, parents' groups, advocates for women and children, and a new breed of "ethics watchers" pitted against medical researchers, public health advocates, and industry. The new rhetoric emphasizes the paternalism of prevention measures, the dangers of coercion in the name of better health, and the protection of individual rights. The resistance uses the strategies of civil rights politics: identifying groups as minorities or victims of discrimination and oppression, mobilizing around these identities, and pursuing political objectives through the courts.

This article traces the transformation from the old politics to the new politics by examining each of the four classic strategies of prevention—immunization, promotion of lifestyle changes, screening, and occupational safety. I also seek to map out the new politics in some detail and make some predictions about the directions of prevention politics and policy in the next two decades.

One aspect of change in prevention politics occurs throughout the four areas, so it deserves a brief mention here: the backlash against prevention as not being "worth the cost." Prevention has always been health reformers' version of a "free lunch." It has been touted by advocates as making economic sense because, so the theory goes, it is cheaper to prevent diseases or treat them early than to treat full-blown cases and sustain the associated economic losses.

Of course, any prevention program has its own costs. A program that detects and treats diseases among the poor is especially likely to generate costs that would otherwise have remained invisible, because poor people do not receive much treatment and what treatment they do get is often covered by charity arrangements rather than "real" dollars. Moreover, the availability of third-party payment stimulates utilization of services; physicians are more likely to prescribe further diagnostic tests and more expensive remedies under a program where these things are paid for. Thus, prevention usually turns out to be more expensive than anticipated. If the alleged savings ever came, they would not show up for a long time. In the cost-containment mania of the 1970s and 1980s, it is no surprise that prevention should be rejected as a false prophet of economy.[1]

Immunization

In a well-known essay published in 1974, Lewis Thomas declared vaccines the most exemplary of what he called "high technology" in medicine. Vaccines were the pinnacle of modern medicine, most of which he saw as still stuck in "halfway technology." He concluded by saying, "If I were a policy-maker, interested in saving money for health care over the long haul, I would regard it as an act of high prudence to give high priority to a lot of basic research in biologic science."[2] But in 1986, discussing development of an AIDS vaccine, David Sencer, M.D., former director of the Centers for Disease Control, told a reporter, "It may be that the lab work will be the quickest part of developing a vaccine. . . . The sociological problems are going to be horrendous."[3] In a similar vein, J. Michael McGinnis, head of the HHS Office of Disease Prevention and Health Promotion, believes that the problems of structuring appropriate clinical trials for a vaccine, finding a manufacturer, liability, indemnification, and victim compensation may well be far more difficult than the research problem of finding a vaccine.[4] What happened in between 1974 and 1986 to entangle the quintessential technological "fix" in a web of political, sociological and legal problems?

The development of the Salk polio vaccine in the mid-1950s led to a wave of optimism about the possibilities of disease prevention through immunization. A polio vaccination campaign began in 1955, accompanied by the Poliomyelitis Assistance Act of 1955 (P.L. 84-377). Between 1961 and 1968, 20 states made polio immunization a requirement for school attendance; by 1976, 47 states required at least one type of immunization as a condition for school entry.[5]

Meanwhile, high technology turned out to have its flaws. In rare cases (probably fewer than one in a million), the vaccine actually *caused* polio. Vaccine-induced polio could happen in three ways. First, the original Salk vaccine was made with killed (inactivated) virus cells. If all the cells were not killed, vaccine recipients would be inoculated with live virus, as happened when 207 people contracted polio from a vaccine manufactured by Cutter Laboratories. Second, the killed vaccine did not protect the recipient's intestinal tract against infection, so the virus could be passed to nonimmune persons—for example, it could be passed by mothers changing their babies' diapers. Third, the newer oral vaccine, based on attenuated live virus cells, had the advantage of providing intestinal immunity, but apparently caused paralytic polio in over 100 people between 1969 and 1982, a ratio calculated at about 1 per 11 million doses.[6] (Since standard practice calls for three doses per person, the risk of any individual contracting polio from the vaccine is obviously higher.)

These anomalies, coupled with a general climate of expanding products liability, led to a number of successful suits against drug manufacturers. From the manufacturers' viewpoint, the most significant cases were *Davis v. Wyeth Laboratories* (1968) and *Reyes v. Wyeth Laboratories* (1974).[7] These decisions held that although it is not negligent for a manufacturer to put a vaccine on the market with such a small risk/benefit ratio, the manufacturer does have a duty to warn the recipient of the dangers of an "unavoidably unsafe product." The lack of a warning that would enable a person to make a truly informed choice is tantamount to putting an "unreasonably dangerous product" on the market, and manufacturers could be held strictly liable for the damages.

The manufacturers were left in an awkward position. They claimed they had provided adequate information to the state medical societies and to physicians, and they had relied on physicians to inform their patients of the dangers. But because of the government's polio campaign, the vaccine was generally dispensed in mass clinics and immunization centers, where there was little (if any) individualized discussion between vaccinees and physicians. The maufacturers wondered how they could possibly provide adequate warnings to all vaccinees in such a distribution system.

Thus, when the Department of Health, Education and Welfare (HEW) in 1976 announced its intention to mount a mass immunization campaign against swine flu, both manufacturers and their insurors were wary. The insurors feared a huge number of claims for which they would have to pay the legal defense costs, even if the manufacturers ultimately won. They cancelled manufacturers' liability coverage for the vaccine. Manufacturers, cancellation notices in hand, told HEW they would not produce swine flu vaccine without coverage or some form of indemnification. And having committed itself publicly to a mass immunization program, the Ford administration pushed Congress to appease the manufacturers. Under the Swine Flu Act, which was passed in two weeks from start to finish, the federal government assumed the duty to warn vaccinees of risks; injured victims were allowed to sue the government under the Federal Tort Claims Act; and manufacturers could not be sued for harms arising from the vaccine unless they were negligent in producing the vaccine.[8]

Since the swine flu affair, the politics of immunization have changed irreversibly. First, there is a greater public consciousness of the dangers of vaccines. After the experience with polio vaccine came the widely publicized (and heavily litigated) cases of Guillain-Barre syndrome associated with the swine flu vaccine, neurological damage and retardation associated with the whooping cough or pertussis vaccine, and encephalitis, retardation and death associated with the measles vaccine.[9]

Second, victim groups, mostly parents of injured children, have mobilized. With the precedents of the polio cases and numerous other holdings against vaccine manufacturers, they are able to impose enormous financial threats, if not losses, on manufacturers. And some parent groups, such as Dissatisfied Parents Together (DPT), are fighting state mandatory vaccination laws.[10] Immunization is no longer seen as an unmitigated benefit to individuals, and potential victims are less willing to sacrifice their well-being for the common good. In fact, the *Davis* case is notable for its rejection of aggregate cost-benefit reasoning, or what the court called "a purely statistical point of view." It said drug companies were not entitled to assume that "common sense" would lead every individual to accept a one-in-a-million risk of contracting polio from the vaccine, even if the risk seems "so trifling in comparison with the advantage to be gained."[11] The individual must be given a real choice whether to underake a potentially devastating risk for the collective good.

The third major change in vaccination politics is that the Swine Flu Act set a precedent for the federal government to indemnify manufacturers. From that experience, vaccine manufacturers learned the strength of their own bargaining position. In the face of epidemics, the public holds the federal government responsible. If manufacturers pull out of the market (as they have done recently with whooping cough vaccine), the federal government is still expected to control the epidemic. Immunizations, for all their potential dangers, are also seen as urgent and essential, and government is under pressure to ensure that they are available. With the AIDS epidemic upon us, the pressure for the federal government to create a victim compensation program and guarantee the supply of vaccines will mount.[12]

Lifestyle

In the 1970s, the prevention establishment discovered and embraced "lifestyle" factors. In 1972, Belloc and Breslow published the first results from their Alameda County study, showing that the things your mother always said were good for you did indeed lead to greater health and longevity.[13] The "good health habits" included sleeping at least seven hours a day, eating breakfast, not snacking between meals, maintaining a reasonable weight, exercising, drinking alcohol in moderation, and not smoking.

In 1974, Victor Fuchs began his highly acclaimed health economics book *Who Shall Live?* with a parable of two states, in which mortality and morbidity for Nevada and Utah were compared, and the lesson was clear: clean living leads to better health.[14] Also in 1974, Canadian health minister Marc LaLonde issued "A New Perspective on the Health of Canadians."[15] The report's message was that contemporary lifestyles are major contributors to health and disease. Boston's commissioner of health proclaimed in the *New England Journal of Medicine* that "the health crisis of today is a lifestyle crisis."[16]

By 1979, the American surgeon general had embraced the lifestyle theory in his report, *Healthy People.*[17] Although the report was careful to give equal billing to conventional preventive techniques such as immunization and environmental measures, it devoted far more space and moral fervor to "the matter of individual discipline and will"[18] and was widely read as the "American Lalonde report." It emphasized throughout the "actions individuals can take for themselves," which included elimination of smoking, reduction of alcohol misuse, dietary changes, exercise, periodic screening for cancer and high blood pressure, and adherence to speed laws and use of seat belts.[19]

The lifestyle approach, or, as it was often called, the New Perspective, trumpeted individual behavior as the most important influence on health and the factor in disease causation most amenable to change. The surgeon general's report said that perhaps as much as half of U.S. mortality in 1976 was "due to unhealthy behavior or lifestyle," and that only about 20 percent was attributable to environmental factors, 20 percent to human biological factors, and 10 percent to inadequate health care.[20] Moreover, changing citizens' lifestyles could be a way to reduce health care expenditures and other economic losses from disease and death. Thus, the New Perspective was another version of the "free lunch."

The lifestyle approach was immediately attacked in some academic quarters. On one front, political scientists, sociologists, and some physicians saw it as another instance of victim-blaming. Public education campaigns to reform individual behavior diverted atention from more effective prevention strategies that would challenge industry and business. The individualism of the lifestyle approach was criticized as a standard liberal response to social problems, as an attempt by industry to avoid safety and environmental reforms and to escape financial responsibility for the health consequences of dangerous working conditions and pollution, and as the inevitable response of a capitalist government dominated by business interests.[21]

On another front, the lifestyle approach was attacked as scientifically invalid, or at least unproven. One by one, the supposed correlations between health and patterns of exercise, diet, alcohol consumption, and high blood pressure were challenged.[22] Critics usually questioned the methodology of the studies, but a few turned the argument on its head and claimed that the supposedly healthy behaviors actually cause diseases or injuries. Exercise causes injuries and perhaps even heart attacks, low cholesterol levels are associated with cancer, smoking has a protective effect against some kinds of cancer, and seat belts kill more pedestrians (because belts make drivers more confident and they drive more recklessly).[23]

But for all the criticism from social scientists and parts of the medical community, almost everyone agreed that there was nothing wrong with promoting "healthy behaviors" so long as the scientific evidence was good and other occupational and environmental reforms were carried out. Now even that consensus is unravelling as the health promotion strategy takes concrete forms.

On the one side are commercial insurance companies, public insurance programs, and employers, who want to use the new evidence about lifestyle and health (however questionable) to lower their costs. They want to design financial incentives and eligibility requirements to alter people's behavior. On the other side are the individuals to whom these policies are directed—primarily employees, insurance policy holders, and potential recipients of public insurance benefits. They and their advocates see economic and political harms caused by the use of lifestyle factors in employment and insurance. Because of this conflict, three policy battles are likely to loom large in the next decade.

The first is whether lifestyle factors can and should be used as actuarial risk factors in setting insurance premiums. In 1976, Robert Veatch proposed that smokers should pay more for health insurance in any national health insurance scheme, since their behavior generates excess health care costs for the community of insureds.[24] Because all insurance distributes the costs of illness over a pool of contributors, shifting them from the sick to the well, the logic applies to any kind of health insurance, not simply national health insurance. Indeed, the surgeon general's report picked up this theme and advocated that insurance companies should offer "preferential rates on life and health insurance to groups engaged in health promotion programs at the worksite."[25] A more recent proposal would rate life and health insurance premiums by "modifiable risk factors," such as alcohol abuse, smoking, cholesterol levels, and hypertension, and would monitor these factors with "objective measures": blood serum level of hepatic enzymes for alcohol abuse, questionnaires and carbon monoxide content of expired air for smoking, blood serum level of lipids for cholesterol, and blood pressure measurement for hypertension.[26]

Actuarial use of lifestyle factors—especially smoking, obesity, exercise, blood pressure, and alcohol consumption—is likely to be challenged under antidiscrimination statutues, notably Section 504 of the 1973 Rehabilitation Act and various state laws prohibiting employment discrimination on the basis of handicap. (As of 1983, 41 states and the District of Columbia had such laws.) The use of gender as an actuarial risk factor in health and retirement insurance has already been curtailed by the Supreme Court.[27] Although the gender cases were decided under Title VII of the Civil Rights Act, which makes gender but not handicap a protected class, the court's rationale is pertinent to the use of lifestyle and other "risk factors" in insurance rating. The first major gender case in this area concerned an employer-operated pension program which (like virtually all pension plans) levied higher premiums from women than from men, because women as a group live longer than men and so draw more in pension benefits. The court noted that Title VII's focus on the individual is "unambiguous":

> Even a true generalization about the class is an insufficient reason for disqualifying an individual to whom the generalization does not apply. That proposition is of critical importance in this case because there is no assurance that any individual woman working for the Department will actually fit the generalization on which the Department's policy is based.[28]

Interestingly, the court used the common insurance practice of *not* rating people by lifestyle factors as part of its justification for eliminating gender:

> . . . when insurance risks are grouped, the better risks always subsidize the poorer risks. Healthy persons subsidize medical benefits for the less healthy . . . *persons who eat, drink or smoke to excess may subsidize pension benefits for persons whose habits are more temperate.* Treating different classes of risk as though they were the same for purposes of group insurance is a common practice that has never been considered inherently unfair. *To insure the flabby and the fit as though they were equivalent risks* may be more common than treating men and women alike; but nothing more than habit makes one "subsidy" seem less fair than the other. (Emphasis added.)[29]

Since the focus of the Rehabilitation Act and state fair employment statutes is undeniably on the individual, and since the associations between lifestyle factors and illness are statistical generalizations, the arguments against permitting actuarial use of lifestyle factors are strong. Moreover, obesity, hypertension, alcoholism, and smoking have already achieved some recognition as handicaps under either the federal Rehabilitation Act or state fair employment statutes.[30]

The dangers of being labeled "high risk" are not lost on victims, and handicapped rights groups have been extremely active in promoting state legislation to prohibit underwriting discrimination on the basis of physical and mental impairments or other medical risk factors. Within one year of the Food and Drug Administration's licensing of the AIDS antibody test, gay rights groups in California obtained a statutory prohibition on its use in life and health insurance applications. Twenty-six states now have some limits on the use of physical or mental impairment in actuarial rating.[31] As litigation under the Rehabilitation Act and fair employment statutes moves more conditions under the protective umbrella of "handicap," insurors will have to justify their rating practices with better statistical data, and may be prohibitied from using some categories at all.

The second battle over lifestyle factors will be whether people can be denied eligibility for disability insurance benefits because they have contributed to their own disabilities through unhealthy behaviors. Disability pension programs usually exclude coverage for conditions which an individual has "willfully" brought on or which are remediable by medical treatment that the person refuses. At the same time, a major tenet of the lifestyle approach is that many of the causal factors of illness are within the control of the individual.

In the aftermath of the rise in Social Security disability pensions during the 1970s and the general political climate for "cutting back the rolls," lifestyle factors could be a convenient lever for reducing expenditures of disability programs. The rationale of the lifestyle approach has already been used by the Social Security Administration to deny disability benefits in cases where a claimant "refuses to stop" smoking or drinking, "fails" to lose weight, "fails to control" diabetes with diet, or "fails to control" hypertension with medication.[32] Very little is known about the extent to which disability insurance programs use these factors to disqualify people, but this dark side of the lifestyle approach is apt to become more prominent as budget deficit worries mount.

Finally, the third battle over lifestyle factors will be whether people who engage in the so-called unhealthy behaviors will be treated punitively or protectively in the labor market. The lifestyle approach's attribution of individual responsibility and application of deterrence is directly at odds with the new civil rights approach embodied in Section 504 of the Rehabilitation Act and state fair employment statutes. Conditions that are seen as behavioral choices in the lifestyle approach are viewed in the civil rights approach as handicaps beyond individual control, and therefore meriting special protection.

Historically, employers have often refused to hire people who are hypertensive, obese, diabetic, or alcoholic.[33] In the last ten years, there has been extensive litigation over this issue, primarily under state fair employment laws but also under Section 504 of the Rehabilitation Act. Increasingly, employers have been barred from excluding job applicants on the basis of hypertension, uncontrolled diabetes, obesity, alcoholism, and drug addiciton, although these conditions are not always treated as handicaps.[34]

In general, once a condition is recognized as a handicap (by applicable law), an employer cannot exclude an affected employee unless the condition actually prevents him or her from safely doing the job.[35] Thus, a city which employed diabetics was not allowed to fire a worker with "uncontrolled" blood sugar levels without showing that uncontrolled diabetics were more susceptible to injury on the job than controlled diabetics.[36] Courts seem to be carefully scrutinizing firings and refusals to hire based on an employer's fear of higher insurance costs, and are generally requiring a tighter connection between a medical condition and ability to perform a job in the near future.[37]

Academic fears about the victim-blaming entailed in the lifestyle approach have proved to be well founded. A great deal of punitive, deterrent, and cost-saving policy is carried out through discrimination in insurance premiums and coverage, denial of disability benefits, and denial of employment. But the lifestyle approach has not been implemented without a fight. Through litigation and the protections of new handicap discrimination laws, the victims of these policies are staging a resistance.

Screening

Screening was the clarion call of health reformers of the 1960s. More than any other aspect of preventive medicine, it was peddled as a "free lunch." It would simultaneously broaden access to health care (because mass screening programs would reach out to populations who do not routinely use medical services) and lower the nation's health care expenditures (because screening would detect diseases at early stages, when they are less costly to treat). Like so many health reforms, large-scale screening was supported by a coalition of fiscal conservatives and social services liberals.[38]

There was support for making screening both more intensive and more extensive. The code word for intensive screening was "multiphasic." Touted by public health advocates such as Lester Breslow and Sidney Garfield,[39] multiphasic screening was an extensive physical examination that included a battery of urine and blood tests (aided by the new automated analyzers), x-rays, an electrocardiogram, and hearing and vision tests. The results were conveniently summarized for the physician in a computer printout, complete with normal ranges for each test. Multiphasic screening, it was claimed, would reduce morbidity and mortality and educate people about proper use of the health care system. Under closer scrutiny, the only thing it accomplished for sure was an increase in testing and hospitalization.[40]

The demand for extensive screening found its expression in Congress. Senate and House committee reports emphasized the need to create awareness of existing

United States.[50] But screening has not always been welcomed with open arms by the Jewish community. There has been an intense debate among rabbis and scholars of Jewish law as to whether screening and/or abortion of fetuses with Tay-Sachs disease should be permitted. The stringent branch of the Orthodox tradition—also the dominant and most influential strand of Jewish legal thought—allows screening only of unmarried and not-yet-engaged persons to aid them in their choice of spouse, but strenuously objects to mass screening programs, screening aimed at married or engaged couples, and selective abortion.[51]

Some Jewish public health advocates oppose Tay-Sachs education programs as well as screening. They fear that the stigma associated with genetic disorders may give "apparent confirmation to age-old prejudices about racial debility," and that the information given to individuals about their carrier status may discourage intermarriage in a "population where fertility is already well below replacement, outmarriage is approaching 40 percent, and cultural continuity has depended on reproductive continuity."[52] In several communities, initial plans for a screening program have been curtailed or abandoned.

Screening for sickle-cell anemia has raised similar issues. People identified as carriers in early screening programs often believed themselves to be sick and were sometimes denied life insurance or employment because of the trait. This phenomenon came to be called "nondisease," and it has been identified in other genetic screening programs as well.[53]

Stimulated by this experience of sickle-cell programs, the biomedical ethics think tanks (such as the Hastings Center and Georgetown's Institute for Biomedical Ethics) have generally acted as a restraining force in the adoption of new genetic screening programs. They have developed criteria for morally acceptable genetic screening programs—criteria which put a higher burden of justification on programs that disproportionately affect racially discrete groups and/or groups that have suffered historical discrimination.[54]

Screening has also been linked with the issue of handicapped rights. In the case of spina bifida and other neural tube defects, for example, the possibility of prenatal detection is seen as a mixed blessing by advocacy groups (mostly composed of parents of children with spina bifida). Testing and selective abortion, they fear, may encourage a cult of "perfect children," devalue the satisfying lives of people with disabilities, and deny the genuine strengths and joys of families with disabled children. They also fear that a general social policy of trying to eliminate a disease will only exacerbate discriminatory attitudes towards disabled people. These advocacy groups monitor new developments in testing, provide their input to the Food and Drug Administration as it licenses new tests, and try to ensure that states make testing and neutral information available to prospective parents but do not make screening mandatory. In general, they are a force for caution and restraint in prenatal screening.[55]

Perhaps even more explosive than prenatal diagnosis is the variety of new tests aimed at identifying a "predisposition" to a disease rather than the disease itself.

Some of these tests involve identifying genes or genetic markers. For example, serum alpha-1 antitrypsin deficiency (SAT) has been associated with increased sensitivity to pulmonary irritants; G-6-PD deficiency is associated with increased sensitivity to hemolytic (blood-destroying) chemicals; and HLA-B-26 is associated with ankylosing spondylitis, an arthritic back disorder. Cancer-disposing genes have been identified for retinoblastoma, Fanconi's anemia, and xeroderma pigmentosum. Some screening tests involve far more common disorders, notably, lower back x-rays to identify people with a high risk of back injury. Other risk screens involve the application of epidemiologic evidence to an individual, so that, for example, an overweight smoker with severe high blood pressure is deemed to be at high risk for cardiovascular disease.[56]

These tests and the reasoning behind them have created a new medical status somewhere between health and disease—the status of being "at risk" or "hypersusceptible." Within clinical medicine, the high-risk status usually entails additional medical scrutiny and attention, more intensive examination, and greater follow-up care. But outside the clinical setting, in the less forgiving arena of the competitive labor market, the new medical status is a political and economic liability.

Employers want to use medical screening for risk factors as a way of controlling their costs. They hope that by eliminating high-risk or hypersusceptible workers from their workforce, they will reduce absenteeism, long-term health problems, health and disability insurance costs, worker's compensation payments, and potential liability for occupational accidents. There is very little information on how many companies actually use medical screening for purposes of employee selection and cost saving. Information is hard to obtain because of adverse publicity about screening as well as fear of litigation under handicap discrimination statutes. But it is clear that medical screening is widespread: according to an HEW survey, preplacement exams are required for 19.2 percent of employees in small firms (8–249 workers), 48.9 percent of employees in medium-size firms (250–500 workers) and 83.3 percent of employees in large firms (over 500 workers). In certain industries, including petroleum and coal products, primary metals, and transportation, required preplacement exams cover over 90 percent of employees.[57]

Medical screening of employees to improve work efficiency and to save money on insurance is by no means a new idea. Employer-sponsored medical examinations began around 1910; by 1917, more than 10 percent of the 300 largest corporations conducted employee exams. At that time, unions already feared "blacklisting" of workers with health defects.[58] The prospect of disability insurance payments led insurors—whether they were employers, commercial companies, or public programs—to seek screening of potential claimants. Thus, it is no accident that employer-sponsored medical examinations were begun as worker's compensation programs were started, that insurance companies were among the promoters of annual physical examinations, and that mandatory chest x-rays for World War II military recruits were billed as a way to save money on veterans' disability pensions.[59]

But what *is* new in contemporary labor policy discussions is the idea of identifying people who are *likely to develop* a disease rather than those who actually have a current medical problem. Moreover, this new version of the "prevention equals savings" equation amounts to a party line within the profession of occupational medicine. The idea that medical screening of high-risk employees can save money is a virtually unchallenged assumption in the pages of the *Journal of Occupational Medicine,* the organ of the American Occupational Medicine Association. One example will give the flavor of this oft-repeated conventional wisdom:

> The physical examination, as part of a risk assessment, is an appropriate and defensible tool for employers to use in evaluating applicants for employment, particularly handicapped persons or disabled veterans. . . . In terms of business economy, this method fosters sound practices since it can reduce the rate of injuries or illnesses due to inappropriate placements. Optimally this can lead to reduced absenteeism, increased productivity, and decreased expenditures for workers' compensation and group health insurance. In addition, it may also reduce the potential for litigation brought against organizations for knowingly and negligently placing uniquely sensitive individuals in environments that may cause harm.[60]

Medical screening, a broad term covering preemployment medical examinations, screening of new hires for specific job assignments (often called "preplacement" as opposed to preemployment exams), and periodic medical surveillance of a workforce, will become a preeminent issue for labor. The issue has already attracted extensive congressional hearings, an Office of Technology Assessment study, a National Research Council Report, and a *Newsweek* cover story.[61] As medical screening becomes a way of allocating jobs, particularly high-paying jobs involving risks to health, workers' interests in obtaining and holding jobs will conflict with their interests in their own health as well as with employers' interests in health and disability cost control.

So far resistance to medical screening has been staged mainly in the courts using the tools of civil rights, primarily Title VII of the Civil Rights Act and Section 504 of the Rehabilitation Act. Title VII comes into play when a test has a disparate impact on a racial or ethnic group. Most of the genetic characteristics allegedly predictive of hypersusceptibility to toxic chemicals are differentially distributed by race and national origin. Sickle-cell trait and anemia are found primarily among blacks (7 to 13 percent have the trait), and only rarely among whites. SAT deficiency is most common among people of Northern European origin (of whom perhaps 5 to 10 percent have the trait). G-6-PD deficiency was found in one study to affect 16 percent of black American males but only 0.1 percent of white American males.[62]

The experience with sickle-cell screening foreshadows what may well develop with other genetic tests for hypersusceptibility. By the late 1970s, sickle-cell trait had been associated with over forty pathological clinical conditions, at least two of which were used to deny jobs to sickle-cell carriers. The armed forces and Air Force Academy would not allow carriers of the trait into flying and diving occupations because of an alleged increased risk in deficient oxygenation of blood. And at least one chemical company (Dow) kept carriers out of jobs involving exposure to hemolytic agents, on the theory that they are more susceptible than noncarriers. Both the Air Force and Dow Chemical backed down on using sickle-cell trait as a preemployment screen in the face of media publicity. At least one Equal Employment Opportunity Council decision has disallowed a blanket policy of rejecting all applicants on the basis of sickle-cell anemia, and several states moved to prohibit employment and insurance discrimination based on sickle-cell trait.[63]

Medical screening faces an even tougher challenge under handicap discrimination laws. Even though the Rehabilitation Act of 1973 applies only to employers having federal contracts or receiving federal assistance (Title VII applies to all employers), its definition of ''handicap'' is broad enough to cover virtually any form of hypersusceptibility, regardless of its distribution among racial and ethnic groups. A person is handicapped for purposes of this law if he or she has a physical or mental impairment that substantially limits a major life activity, has a record of such an impairment, or is regarded as having such an impairment.[64] Whether this law applies to the new status of ''high risk''—i.e., the employee is at risk of future harm and therefore is not hired because an employer fears future costs—is still an open question. But a substantial body of legal scholarship suggests that protection should and will be afforded the high-risk employee.[65] State fair employment statutes offer protection as well. And with those windows of legal opportunity open, it is sure that medical screening for purposes of employee selection and placement will be resisted by labor, especially when and where unemployment remains high.

Occupational safety and health

The Occupational Safety and Health Act of 1970 is one of the most controversial pieces of regulation ever passed. Throughout the 1970s, it stood at the center of a raging debate on the scope and effectiveness of government. The issues were cast as ''government versus the private sector'' and ''safety versus cost.'' Can government effectively regulate millions of management decisions in hundreds of thousands of locations? Is it better to use mandated standards or economic incentives to promote change? How strict should safety standards be? How safe is safe enough? How should cost concerns be balanced with health and safety concerns?

Labor and industry fought for the program's soul—the design requirements and exposure levels incorporated in its standards. Labor played the role of tough cop, watching the Occupational Safety and Health Administration (OSHA) for any signs of giving in to the more lax standards desired by industry. Labor leaders saw red whenever industry purported to trade off worker well-being for cost saving or the promise of general economic prosperity. For labor, any risk with workers' bodily health was too much risk. Companies and trade associations watched OSHA with equal attentiveness. They formed the American Industrial Health Council to promote the idea that risk is a "fact of industrial life" and therefore "socially acceptable." And they went straight to the White House to plead their case, whence they obtained restraints on OSHA in the form of required "economic impact analyses" and new layers of regulatory review controlled by the White House and the Office of Management and Budget.[66] In short, occupational safety and health was an area of prevention policy where all the political actors behaved true to character, no matter whether one viewed the drama from a pluralist or a Marxist perspective.

The concept of hypersusceptibility challenges the underlying premise of the legislation—namely, that it is possible to set a standard for exposure to a hazard which will protect all workers from dangers to their health. The premise of hypersusceptibility is that there are some people whose inner defenses are weakened or compromised, so that only a lower level or no exposure would protect them. On the question of exposure levels, traditional politics still hold: labor would like to see standards set to a level protective of the most vulnerable worker, while industry would like to have standards protective of the average worker combined with screening to exclude more susceptible workers.

But labor—from the staunchest leaders to the men and women on the shop floor—knows that exclusion of unhealthy or weaker workers is a longstanding reality in the labor market. As Anthony Mazzocchi testified in hearings on the lead standard, "Job security is foremost in mind to the people we represent. It probably is foremost in the minds of most workers. Their experience demonstrates adequately that if they suffer abnormality on the job, they are removed."[67] Nor are workers with even mild health problems likely to be hired in the first place.[68]

The "prevention equals job loss" equation was chalked on the national blackboard in 1979 when the *New York Times* broke a story about American Cyanamid's policy of excluding fertile women from its pigment department because of exposure to lead dust that could be harmful to fetuses.[69] Five women underwent sterilization to avoid transfer to lower-paying jobs. It soon became known that many companies barred fertile women from certain jobs involving toxic exposure.[70]

The issue of "reproductive hazards," as it is politely called, brought home to labor, women, and civil rights groups that a policy of exclusion of "high-risk" workers could adversely affect an enormous number of people. In the case of lead, industry leaders insisted on excluding not only pregnant women but all fertile women, because lead builds up in the body and could damage a fetus before a woman knew she was pregnant. If that kind of reasoning were applied to other toxic hazards, millions of women in the labor force could be affected, since well over two-thirds are of child-bearing age. About 20 million jobs involve exposure to potentially fetotoxic chemicals. And more and more evidence suggests that reproductive and fetal harms occur through male exposure as well as female.[71]

OSHA spearheaded an investigation into these exclusionary practices, joined by the Equal Employment Opportunity Commission and the Office of Federal Contract Compliance. The broad-based Coalition for Reproductive Rights of Workers attracted the major unions (United Steelworkers, United Auto Workers, United Rubber Workers, Oil, Chemical and Atomic Workers Union, and many others), women's organizations (e.g., National Organization of Women, League of Women Voters, and Women's Legal Defense Fund), civil rights organizations (American Civil Liberties Union and National Lawyers Guild), and reproductive rights groups (Planned Parenthood, the Alan Guttmacher Institute, and the Committee for Abortion Rights and Against Sterilization Abuse).

The coalition sought some kind of ban on exclusionary policies. In general, members adopted the traditional labor view that employers should provide a safe workplace, but given the realities of many unsafe jobs, they supported the right of the individual woman, rather than her employer, to choose whether to accept the risks of exposure in a particular job. They also sought to borrow a new remedy from the area of toxic substance regulation, something quite different from the traditional OSHA tool of engineering redesign or the traditional industry policy of exclusion. The new remedy was called "medical removal protection with rate retention" and it involved transfer of a susceptible worker out of the dangerous situation while protecting his or her pay level, seniority rights, and fringe benefits.

The coalition failed in its immediate goals. The EEOC issued some proposed guidelines which generally frowned on exclusion of women without solid evidence that paternal exposure does not contribute to fetal harm, and in any case allowed exclusion only of pregnant women, not all fertile women. But they did not provide medical removal protection. The guidelines were attacked by industry, labor, and women's groups alike, and in the end were withdrawn by the Reagan administration as part of a general undoing of the Occupational Safety and Health machinery.

Nevertheless, the reproductive rights controversy shaped the terms of the debate over occupational safety and health for years to come. Most of all, it highlighted the way the high-risk worker concept forces a choice between job security and high pay on the one hand and future health on the other. It dramatized the potential for the concept to be applied to almost any worker, not merely a few workers in esoteric jobs. It revealed how the focus of the debate had shifted from the safety of the workplace to the weakness of the individual worker. And it exposed the struggle for power implicit in the question of whether employers or employees would get to decide how health risks and job benefits should be balanced.

It is in this respect that the politics of occupational safety and health have changed. In the earlier debate, health and safety were pitted against job security only in an abstract way; industry argued that the high costs of safety provisions would force some businesses to close. The concept of the hypersusceptible worker brought the conflict between health and job security down to the level of the individual.

Forced to choose between job and health, workers and their representatives will fight to preserve jobs. Lloyd McBride, president of United Steelworkers, stated the case poignantly at the 1977 hearings on the lead standard and medical removal protection:

> It is kind of a human equation, perhaps, but I think it is one that most of us would identify with. If we were confronted as the breadwinner of a family, of tolerating a health hazard, perhaps, in order to continue to provide for our families, most of us, absent from some other way to do it, and the high unemployment economy, there is very little other opportunity for the person in the lead plant to go out and get other employment—faced with that combination of circumstances, I think most of us would put up with the continued health hazard.[72]

Labor and its allies are now often in the position of advocating less caution in job safety and the right of individuals to work in unhealthy environments. During the lead hearings, a women's advocacy group submitted testimony that pregnant women should be allowed to decide whether to work in environments dangerous to the fetus; in the 1940s, by contrast, the Women's Bureau of the Department of Labor sought automatic transfer of all women exposed to substances harmful to the fetus.[73] In 1981, workers at risk in an Idaho lead smelter requested that the plant be exempt from OSHA standards, the very standards labor had sought to tighten during the hearings.[74]

OSHA has promulgated 21 toxic substance standards that require employers to monitor their employees' health. These standards, covering asbestos, lead, benzene, vinyl chloride, cotton dust, coke oven emissions, and several carcinogens, generally require employers to conduct preplacement medical examinations, use the information to match employees to "suitable" jobs, and conduct periodic medical examinations ("medical surveillance") with a specified set of tests on all workers exposed to concentrations above a defined "action level."[75] But for the most part, the standards do not say what an employer should do if an applicant is found unsuitable for a proposed assignment or if an employee is found unable to bear continued exposure. Only three of the standards (lead, vinyl chloride, and asbestos) include medical removal protection (that is, transfer to another job), and only one (lead) also provides for rate retention.[76]

The hypersusceptible worker is thus in a no-man's land of social policy. He or she may be medically unemployable by informal company policy or by OSHA standards, but ineligible for any of the available forms of disability insurance— company plans, Worker's Compensation, or Social Security Disability Insurance. These insurance progams typically require that a claimant be physically or mentally unable to work (the Social Security definition requires total and permanent disability) or have sustained an actual injury caused by work (Worker's Compensation). The hypersusceptible worker is quite capable of working but is deemed by company medical personnel or OSHA standards to be at high risk of becoming disabled.[77]

If the occupational safety and health issue during the 1970s and early 1980s was cast as a struggle over the proper cost-benefit balance, the struggle of the next decade will surely be over medical removal protection and rate retention, or other ways of providing for the medically unemployable but nondisabled worker. In a larger sense, the struggle is over access to jobs and job security. It is a bitter irony that precisely when some politicians are bemoaning the growth of disability rolls and the decline of the work ethic, workers are fighting to stay in their jobs, resisting medical examinations and transfers, in the face of private and public policy that would render them unemployable "for their own good."

Conclusion

A review of prevention policy over the last two decades reveals a striking pattern. In each of the major areas of preventive medicine, enthusiasm for large-scale adoption of public health techniques ran into resistance by the very people prevention was supposed to help. In each area, the resistance was triggered by the "beneficiaries'" discovery that they had been harmed by a preventive measure. The harms might be physical (the disease and disability caused by vaccines), psychological (the stigma and anguish associated with genetic screening), economic (the inability to get a job, keep a job, or obtain insurance because of being classified as "high risk"), or social (the setbacks for women and blacks in the labor market as they were found to be at risk and potentially costly to their employers; the subtle harms to the sense of community caused by genetic and prenatal screening).

The politics of preventive medicine described here manifest the strong individualism so deeply ingrained in American politics in general. Philosophically, the whole idea of identifying high-risk individuals and high-risk individual behaviors locates the source of misfortune in the individual rather than in social structure and economic opportunity. Practically, the idea undermines social insurance, the very keystone of the modern welfare state.

Social insurance is based on risk pooling, cross-subsidization, and what the Germans call "the solidarity principle": individuals may pay for more or less than what they actually get back from social insurance, but those transfers are what make a group a community and not just a collection of strangers. In a community, individual misfortunes are a group problem.

Collective responsibility does not sit comfortably in the American political ideology. The United States has always been a laggard in social insurance, whether for industrial accidents, old age pensions, health care, or family needs. The concept of the high-risk individual is a subtle way of dismantling protective insurance. With it, we shuck off people one by one, throwing them out of the risk pool for health insurance, disability pensions, or life insurance, and out of the applicant pool for jobs.

Thus cast off, individuals resort to the one sort of protection American society finds legitimate and acceptable—civil rights. That is the one form consistent with individualism. Civil rights policy is based on the principle that one stands or falls on one's own merits. A person may not be treated according to, or have his life chances determined by, group characteristics that have no relation to individual achievement—race, gender, age, and now physical health. With the tools of civil rights, citizens fight the harms of group classification inherent in the lifestyle, screening, and occupational safety approaches to prevention.

Even in the area of immunization, individuals fight with private, civil tort actions. And when they win, they win not on the principle that society should compensate them for undertaking risk to benefit the community, but rather on the principle that an individual is entitled to decide for himself. Vaccination is just another frontier where the individual pits his wits against the unknown. (In the wake of the initial polio vaccine suits, preventive medicine advocates developed informed consent procedures for children, so even six-year-olds could stake their fortunes on an experimental trial of swine flu vaccine.[78])

That prevention should be resisted is thus entirely understandable. If it is ever to be widely accepted, prevention must take into account the kinds of harms detailed here and include appropriately designed compensation policies, so that already-disadvantaged individuals do not have to bear the brunt of social progress.

Notes

1. See especially Louise Russell, *Is Prevention Better Than Cure?* (Washington, DC: Brookings Institution, 1986), a comprehensive review of cost-benefit studies of prevention. Russell's major message is that the claims being made for prevention as a way to cut medical costs are generally untrue. Russell is careful to note that prevention "can be a worthwhile investment in better health, and this—not cost saving—is the criterion on which it should be judged" (p. 5). But the burden of the book is certainly to show that prevention does not save money.
2. Lewis Thomas, "Halfway Technology," in *Lives of a Cell* (New York: Viking, 1974), p. 34.
3. Michael Waldholz and Jerry E. Bishop, "Testing an AIDS Vaccine in People May Be Tougher Than Creating It," *Wall Street Journal*, 14 April 1986, p. 31.
4. Interview with author, 16 April 1986.
5. Morgenstern, "The Role of the Federal Government in Protecting Citizens from Communicable Diseases," *Cincinnati Law Review* 47 (1978): 545, cited in William David Hardin, "Poliomyelitis Vaccine—History, Regulations, and Recommendations," *Food Drug Cosmetic Law Journal* 40 (1985): 145–71, at p. 151, note 49.
6. See Hardin, "Poliomyelitis Vaccine," pp. 147–51; and Institute of Medicine, *Vaccine Supply and Innovation* (Washington, DC: National Academy Press, 1985), p. 74.
7. Davis v. Wyeth Laboratories, Inc., 399 F.2d 121 (9th Cir. 1968), and Reyes v. Wyeth Laboratories, 498 F.2d 1264 (5th Cir. 1974). For extensive discussion of these cases, see Hardin, "Poliomyelitis Vaccine"; Institute of Medicine, "Vaccine Supply and Innovation," chapter 7; and Mary Elizabeth Mann, "Mass Immunization Cases: Drug Manufacturers' Liability for Failure to Warn," *Vanderbilt Law Review* 29 (1976): 235–66.

8. Richard E. Neustadt and Harvey Fineberg, *The Epidemic That Never Was: Policy-Making and the Swine Flu Affair* (New York: Vintage Books/Random House, 1983).

9. For a review of vaccine complications and estimates of their likelihood, see Institute of Medicine, "Vaccine Supply and Innovation," chapter 5. Chapter 7 reviews vaccine litigation.

10. D. Hitts, "Should Your Child Be Given DPT Shots?" *Redbook* 159 (August 1982): 79; D. Franklin, "Litigation a Threat to Vaccine Supply," *Science News*, 15 September 1984, p. 167.

11. Davis v. Wyeth Laboratories, Inc., 399 F.2d 121, 129.

12. The Institute of Medicine report "Vaccine Supply and Innovation" calls for some kind of national victim compensation system and a resolution of the unstable liability situation in order to assure a continued supply of vaccines. The report offers several options.

13. Nedra Belloc and Lester Breslow, "The Relationship of Physical Health Status and Health Practices," *Preventive Medicine* 1 (1972): 409–21.

14. Victor Fuchs, *Who Shall Live?* (New York: Basic Books, 1974).

15. Marc Lalonde, *A New Perspective on the Health of Canadians* (Ottawa, ON: Information Canada, 1975).

16. Leon S. White, "How to Improve the Public's Health," *New England Journal of Medicine* 293 (9 October 1975): 773–74.

17. Department of Health, Education and Welfare, *Healthy People: The Surgeon General's Report on Health Promotion and Disease Prevention,* DHEW (PHS) publication no. 79-55071 (Washington, DC: Government Printing Office, 1979).

18. Ibid., p. viii.

19. Ibid., p. 10.

20. Ibid., p. 9.

21. See Rob Crawford, "Individual Responsibility and Health Politics in the 1970s," in *Health Care in America,* ed. Susan Reverby and David Rosner (Philadelphia: Temple University Press, 1979), pp. 247–68; Deane Neubauer and Richard Pratt, "The Second Public Health Revolution: A Critical Appraisal," *Journal of Health Politics, Policy and Law* 6 (1981): 205–28; Neil Holtzman, "Prevention: Rhetoric and Reality," *International Journal of Health Services* 9 (1979): 25–39; Marc Renaud, "On the Structural Constraints to State Intervention in Health," *International Journal of Health Services* 5 (1975): 559–70; and J. P. Allegrante and L. W. Green, "When Health Policy Becomes Victim Blaming," *New England Journal of Medicine* 305 (December 1981): 1528–29. For an excellent analysis of the different intellectual strands of this criticism, see Rosemary C. R. Taylor, "The Politics of Prevention," *Social Policy,* Summer 1982, pp. 32–41.

22. In general, see Robert F. Meenan, "Improving the Public's Health: Some Further Reflections," *New England Journal of Medicine* 294 (1 January 1976): 45–47. On exercise, see Nancy A. Rigotti, Gregory Thomas, and Alexander Leaf, "Exercise and Coronary Heart Disease," *Annual Review of Medicine* 34 (1983): 391–412; and Muriel Gillick, "Health Promotion, Jogging, and the Pursuit of the Moral Life," *Journal of Health Politics, Policy and Law* 9 (Fall 1984): 369–87. On diet, see S. Epstein and Joel Swartz, "Fallacies of Lifestyle Cancer Theories," *Nature* 289 (15 January 1981): 126–30; Lenn E. Goodman and Madeleine J. Goodman, "Prevention—How Misuse of a Concept Undercuts Its Worth," *Hastings Center Report,* April 1986, pp. 26–38; and "The Latest on Diet and Your Heart," *Consumer Reports,* July 1985, pp. 423–27. On alcohol consumption, see A. S. St. Leger et al., "Factors Associated with Cardiac Mortality in Developed Countries with Particular Reference to the Consumption of Wine," *Lancet,* 12 May 1979, pp. 1017–20. On high blood pressure, see Louise Russell, *Is Prevention Better Than Cure?* pp. 51–57.

23. On the dangers of exercise, see, for example, David Siscovick et al., "The Incidence of Primary Cardiac Arrest During Vigorous Exercise," *New England Journal of Medicine* 311 (4 October 1984): 874–77; and Jeffrey Koplan et al., "An Epidemiologic Study of the Benefits and Risks of Running," *Journal of the American Medical Association* 248 (17 December 1982): 3118–21. On diet, see "Mass Strategies of Prevention—The Swings and Roundabouts," *Lancet* (4 December 1982): 1257 (which finds an association between low levels of cholesterol and greater risk of cancer). On smoking, see S. M. Lesko, L. Rosenberg, and D. W. Kaufman, "Cigarette Smoking and the Risk of Endometrial Cancer," *New England Journal of Medicine* 313 (1985): 593–96 (finding a correlation between smoking and endometrial cancer in post-menopausal women); and N. E. Weiss, "Can *Not* Smoking Be Hazardous to Your Health?" *New England*

Journal of Medicine 313 (1985): 632–33. On seat belts, see Sam Pelzman, "The Effects of Automobile Safety Regulation," *Journal of Political Economy* 83 (August 1975): 677–725.

24. Robert Veatch and Peter Steinfels, "Who Should Pay for Smokers' Medical Care?" *Hastings Center Report* 4 (November 1974): 8–10.

25. Department of Health, Education and Welfare, *Healthy People*, p. 143.

26. Joseph Stokes, "Why Not Rate Health and Life Insurance Premiums By Risks?" *New England Journal of Medicine* 308 (17 February 1983): 393–95. Such proposals are not rare. Anne Somers proposed that smokers be required to pay an additional premium for Medicare coverage in "Why Not Try Preventing Illness as a Way of Controlling Medicare Costs?" *New England Journal of Medicine* 311 (27 September 1984): 853–56. The state of Delaware is (in August 1986) on the verge of passing legislation that would require rating health insurance premiums according to lifestyle factors. See "Insurance Bill in Delaware Aims to 'Motivate' Health," *New York Times*, 24 August 1986, p. 46.

27. City of Los Angeles, Dept. of Water and Power v. Manhart, 435 U.S. 702 (1978), prohibited gender differentials in premiums in employer-operated plans. Arizona Governing Committee for Tax Deferred Annuity and Deferred Compensation Plan v. Norris 103 S.Ct. 3492 (1983) (per curiam) prohibited gender differentials in payouts (the size of annuities) and also included in its reach private insurance plans sponsored by employers.

28. City of Los Angeles, Dept. of Water and Power v. Manhart, 435 U.S. 702, 708 (1978).

29. Ibid., p. 710.

30. See note 35 below.

31. Based on compilation of relevant statutes by the American Council of Life Insurance, "Discrimination in Insurance" (Washington, DC, unpublished manuscript, March 1985).

32. See Jackson v. Sec. of Health, Education and Welfare, 319 F. Supp. 385 (1970) (continued drinking and smoking); Stone v. Harris, 657 F.2d 210 (failure to lose weight); Plank v. Sec. of Health and Human Services, 734 F.2d 1174 (1984) (refusal to undergo psychotherapy for emotional problems); Tome v. Schweiker, 724 F.2d 711 (1984) (failure to control diabetes with diet); Caprin v. Harris, 511 F. Supp. 589 (1981) (failure to stop smoking); Gordon v. Schweiker, 725 F.2d 231 (1984) (refusal to stop smoking and drinking); Brown v. Heckler, 767 F.2d 451 (1985) (failure to control hypertension and headaches with medication); And Harris v. Heckler, 756 F.2d 431 (1985) (claimant "aggravated" her condition by smoking and overeating).

33. Mark Rothstein, "Employee Selection Based on Susceptibility to Occupational Illness," *Michigan Law Review* 81 (May 1983): 1379–96, at pp. 1421–22. Also refer to the cases cited in note 35 below. Employers feel strongly enough about excluding people with hypertension that when a California court ruled hypertension a handicap within the meaning of the state's Fair Employment and Housing Act, employers immediately sponsored a bill to exclude it from the definition of handicap. See Deborah Kaplan, "California Disability Coalition Pushes for Legislative Change," *Mental and Physical Disability Law Reporter* 8 (January/February 1984): 72–75.

34. For hypertension, see American National Insurance v. Fair Employment and Housing Commission, 32 Cal. 3d 603, 651 P.2d 1151, 186 Cal. Rptr. 345 (1982), p. 1451; and Bey v. Bolger, 540 F. Supp. 910 (E.D. Pa. 1982). For uncontrolled diabetes, see Bentivegna v. United States Department of Labor, 694 F.2d 619 (9th Cir. 1982). For obesity see State Division of Human Rights v. Xerox Corporation, 491 N.Y.S. 2d 106 (Ct. App. 1985). For alcoholism, see Connecticut General Life Insurance Co. v. Dept. of Industry Labor and Human Relations, 18 Fair Empl. Prac. Cas. (BNA) 1811 (Wis. Cir. Ct. 1976), cited in Rothstein, "Employee Selection," p. 1451. For drug addiction, see Davis v. Bucher, 451 F. Supp. 791 (E.D. Pa. 1978). Needless to say, these conditions have not always been regarded by courts as handicaps, and some states explicitly exclude alcoholism and drug addiction from protection under their fair employment statutes. See Rothstein, "Employee Selection," p. 1451, note 469. See also Theresa Johnson, "Laws Prohibiting Discrimination Against the Alcoholic and the Drug Addict," *Labor Law Journal*, September 1985, pp. 702–706.

35. This is a broad summary. See Rothstein, "Employee Selection," pp. 1445–51; and Thomas O. McGarrity and Eleanor P. Schroeder, "Risk Oriented Employment Screening," *Texas Law Review* 59 (August 1981): 996–1076.

36. Bentivegna v. U.S. Dept. of Labor, 694 F.2d 619.

37. But the issue is by no means settled. See McGarrity and Schroeder, "Risk Oriented Employment Screening," p. 1053; and Rothstein, "Employee Selection," pp. 1444–49.

38. This "have your cake and eat it, too" logic is the key to the coalitions behind many health reforms, not merely prevention. HMOs were going to increase access and lower costs by organizing delivery more efficiently. See Paul Starr, "The Undelivered Health System," *The Public Interest* 42 (Winter 1976): 66–85. DRGs were going to do the same by cutting out "unnecessary" hospital services. See James Morone and Andrew Dunham, "Slouching Toward National Health Insurance," *Yale Journal of Regulation* 2 (Winter 1985): 263–91. Health planning would work its magic by cutting out unnecessary facilities. Professional standards review organizations (PSROs) would simultaneously increase quality of care and lower expenditures by eliminating unnecessary services.
39. See Lester Breslow, "Multiphasic Screening Examinations—An Extension of the Mass Screening Technique," *American Journal of Public Health* 40 (1950): 274–78; and Sidney R. Garfield, "The Delivery of Medical Care," *Scientific American* 222 (1970): 15–23.
40. Donnal Olsen, Robert Kane and Paul Proctor, "A Controlled Trial of Multiphasic Screening," *New England Journal of Medicine* 294 (22 April 1976): 925–30.
41. President Lyndon Johnson, "Welfare of the Children," H.R. Doc. No. 54, 90th Cong., 1st sess., 8 February 1967; cited in Donna Wilson Kircheimer, "The Politics of Preventive Services for Disadvantaged Populations," paper presented at the 1985 Annual Meeting of the American Political Science Association, p. 8.
42. Anne Marie Foltz, *An Ounce of Prevention* (Cambridge, MA: MIT Press, 1982).
43. For an excellent description of this campaign, see Russell, *Is Prevention Better Than Cure?* chapter 3. I rely on her book for my account.
44. Department of Health, Education and Welfare, *Healthy People*, p. 10.
45. For a review of this literature, see Russell, *Is Prevention Better Than Cure?* pp. 49–56.
46. R. Brian Hayes et al., "Increased Absenteeism from Work After Detection and Labeling of Hypertensive Patients," *New England Journal of Medicine* 299 (1978): 741–44.
47. Milton C. Weinstein and William B. Stason, *Hypertension: A Policy Perspective* (Cambridge, MA: Harvard University Press, 1976).
48. But see Anne Somers, "Why Not Try Preventing Illness as a Way of Controlling Medicare Costs?" *New England Journal of Medicine* 311 (27 September 1984): 853–56.
49. See Anne Marie Foltz and Jennifer L. Kelsey, "The Annual Pap Test: A Dubious Policy Success," *Milbank Memorial Fund Quarterly* 56 (Fall 1978): 426–62; Samuel O. Thier, "Breast Cancer Screening: A View from Outside the Controversy," *New England Journal of Medicine* 297 (10 November 1977): 1063–65; F. M. Hall, "Screening Mammography—Potential Problems on the Horizon," *New England Journal of Medicine* 314 (January 1986): 53–55; and related correspondence, *New England Journal of Medicine* 314 (May 1986): 1451–53.
50. Madeleine J. Goodman and Lenn E. Goodman, "The Overselling of Genetic Anxiety," *Hastings Center Report* 12 (October 1982): 20–27.
51. For my summary of this debate in Jewish law, I rely on Ronald M. Green, "Genetic Medicine in the Perspective of Orthodox Halakhah," *Judaism* 34 (Summer 1985): 263–77.
52. Goodman and Goodman, "The Overselling of Genetic Anxiety," p. 24.
53. M. L. Hampton, "Sickle Cell 'Nondisease': A Potentially Serious Public Health Problem," *American Journal of Diseases of Childhood* 128 (1974): 58–61. See also R. H. Denan and R. M. Schmidt, "Stigmatization of Carrier Status: Social Implications of Heterozygote Genetic Screening Programs," *American Journal of Public Health* 68 (1978): 1116–20; and Barton Childs et al., "Tay-Sachs Screening: Social and Psychological Impact," *American Journal of Human Genetics* 28 (1976): 550–58.
54. See especially Thomas H. Murray, "Genetic Screening in the Workplace: Ethical Issues," *Journal of Occupational Medicine* 25 (June 1983): 451–54; Marc Lappé, "Ethical Issues in Testing for Differential Sensitivity to Occupational Hazards," *Journal of Occupational Medicine* 25 (November 1983): 797–808; and Marc Lappé, "The Predictive Power of New Genetics," *Hastings Center Report* 14 (October 1984): 18–21.
55. A very sensitive and balanced advocacy group position statement is Betsy Anderson, "Massachusetts Spina Bifida Association: An Advocacy Group's Perspective on MSAFP Screening," *The Genetic Resource* (published by the Massachusett Department of Public Health), Autumn 1985/Winter 1986, pp. 13–19.
56. Most of these tests are the subject of scientific controversy, and there is a substantial degree of opinion that they are not suitable for use as preemployment screening devices, either because

they are not very accurate or not very good predictors of the alleged disease. For a review of the skeptical position on genetic screening, see Cooper, "Indicators of Susceptibility to Industrial Chemicals," *Journal of Occupational Medicine* 15 (1973): 355–59; and Edith Canter, "Employment Discrimination Implications of Genetic Screening in the Workplace under Title VII and the Rehabilitation Act," *American Journal of Law and Medicine* 10 (Fall 1984): 324–47, at pp. 325–26. For the strongest pro-screening position for five genetic tests, see H. E. Stokinger and L. D. Scheel, "Hypersusceptibility and Genetic Problems in Occupational Medicine—A Consensus Report," *Journal of Occupational Medicine* 15 (July 1973): 564–73. There is now an extensive literature discrediting the use of low back x-rays to predict injuries. See especially M. Laurens Rowe, "Are Routine Spine Films on Workers in Industry Cost- or Risk-Benefit Effective?" *Journal of Occupational Medicine* 24 (January 1982): 41–43; E. S. Gibson et al., "Incidence of Low Back Pain and Pre-placement X-Ray Screening," *Journal of Occupational Medicine* 22 (August 1980): 515–19; and Paul H. Rockey, Jane Fantel and Gilbert S. Omenn, "Discriminatory Aspects of Pre-employment Screening: Low-Back X-Ray Examinations in the Railroad Industry," *American Journal of Law and Medicine* 5 (Winter 1979): 197–214. An example of employee screening (though not necessarily hiring or job assignment) based on lifestyle factors is P. F. D. Van Peenen et al., "Cardiovascular Risk Factors in Employees of a Petrochemical Company," *Journal of Occupational Medicine* 27 (March 1985): 217–19.

57. See Department of Health, Education and Welfare, *National Occupational Hazard Survey* (Washington, DC: Government Printing Office, 1977), pp. 77–78, cited in Rothstein, "Employee Selection," p. 1412, note 25. The only figures on employer use of genetic screening come from an Office of Technology survey published in 1983. Of the companies surveyed (the 500 largest industrial companies, the 50 largest private utilities, and 11 unions), 5 respondents said they currently used genetic screening, 12 said they had used it in the past, and 54 said they would consider using it in the future. See Office of Technology Assessment, *The Role of Genetic Testing in the Prevention of Occupational Disease* (Washington DC: Government Printing Office, 1983). These figures probably underestimate the prevalence of genetic testing, because adverse publicity has made corporate management reluctant to discuss medical screening. See Michael Severo, "Screening of Blacks by Dupont Sharpens Debate on Gene Tests," *New York Times*, 4 February 1980, pp. A1 and A13. On corporate reluctance to participate in the OTA survey, see Michael Severo, "59 Top U.S. Companies Plan Genetic Screening," *New York Times*, 23 June 1982, p. A9.

58. W. I. Clark, "Physical Examination and Medical Supervision of Factory Employees," *Boston Medical and Surgical Journal* 176 (1917): 239–44.

59. See R. Buck, "The Physical Examination of Groups," *New England Journal of Medicine* 221 (1939): 883–87; and R. Spillman, "The Value of Radiography in Detecting Tuberculosis in Recruits," *Journal of the American Medical Association* 115 (1940): 1371–79. On the general history of screening see Stanley J. Reiser, "The Emergence of the Concept of Screening for Disease," *Milbank Memorial Fund Quarterly* 56 (Fall 1978): 403–25.

60. Joyce C. Hogan and Edward J. Bernacki, "Developing Job-Related Preplacement Medical Examinations," *Journal of Occupational Medicine* 23 (July 1981): 469–75, quote on p. 474.

61. *Hearings on Genetic Screening of Workers*, Subcommittee on Investigations and Oversight of the House Committee on Science and Technology, 97th Cong., 1st and 2d sess., 1981–1982; Office of Technology Assessment, *The Role of Genetic Testing*; National Research Council, *Hazards, Technology and Fairness* (Washington, DC: National Academy of Sciences Press, 1986); and "Can You Pass the Job Test?" *Newsweek*, 5 May 1986, pp. 46–53.

62. Rothstein, "Employee Selection," pp. 1391 and 1454.

63. Ibid., p. 1385; Canter, "Employment Discrimination," pp. 326–27; and EEOC Decision No. 81-8, 2 Empl. Prac. Guide (CCH) §6764 (1980), cited in Rothstein, "Employee Selection," p. 1457. New Jersey, Louisiana, Florida and North Carolina prohibit employment discrimination on the basis of sickle-cell trait (Rothstein, "Employee Selection," pp. 1444–45, note 434). Florida, Maryland and North Carolina prohibit insurance discrimination based on sickle-cell trait, and California and Maryland prohibit insurance discrimination based on any genetic trait not itself a disease. See American Council of Life Insurers, "Discrimination in Insurance."

64. Rehabilitation Act of 1973, 29 U.S.C. §706(7)(B) (1976 and Supp. II 1978).

65. Rothstein, "Employee Selection," pp. 1442–51; Canter, "Employment Discrimination," pp. 333–34; Caren Sigel, "Legal Recourse for the Cancer Patient Returnee: The Rehabilitation Act

of 1973," *American Journal of Law and Medicine* 10 (Fall 1984): 309–21, at pp. 317–20; and David J. Mahoney, Jr., and Jeffrey D. Kendall, "OSHA's Medical Surveillance and Removal Programs: Implications and Validity," *University of Pittsburgh Law Review* 42 (Summer 1981): 779–821, at pp. 790–94. For a contrary view, see Frances H. Miller, "Biological Monitoring: The Employer's Dilemma," *American Journal of Law and Medicine* 9 (Winter 1984): 387–426, at pp. 414–15. For a view that federal courts have been fairly permissive towards employer exclusion of high-risk individuals, but that state antidiscrimination statutes could provide greater protection, see Thomas O. McGarrity and Eleanor P. Schroeder, "Risk-Oriented Employment Screening," *Texas Law Review* 59 (August 1981): 999–1076; and Rothstein, "Employee Selection," p. 1444, note 434.

66. Insightful discussions of OSHA politics can be found in Frank J. Thompson, *Health Policy and the Bureaucracy: Politics and Implementation* (Cambridge, MA: MIT Press, 1981), chapter 7; and Charles Noble, *Liberalism at Work: The Rise and Fall of OSHA* (Philadelphia: Temple University Press, 1986).

67. Testimony of Anthony Mazzochi, vice president of Oil, Chemical and Atomic Workers Union, in *Federal Register*, 21 November 1978, p. 54442.

68. Murray Weinstock and Jacob I. Haft, "The Effect of Illness on Employment Opportunities," *Archives of Environmental Health* 29 (August 1974): 79–83; T. Schussler et al., "The Preplacement Examination," *Journal of Occupational Medicine* 17 (1975): 254–57 (documenting a 13.5 percent medical rejection rate); Seymour Lusterman, *Industry Roles in Health Care* (New York: The Conference Board, 1974), pp. 31–32 (a survey of one thousand executives found increases in the number of companies using preemployment exams and the proportion of employees screened, and an increase in tests included in exams between 1964 and 1974); and Cornelius Peck, "Employment Problems of the Handicapped: Would Title VII Remedies Be Effective?" *Journal of Law Reform*, Winter 1983, pp. 348–52.

69. "Company and Union in Dispute as Women Undergo Sterilization," *New York Times*, 4 January 1979, p. 7; see also Gail Bronson, "Allied Chemical Compensates 5 Women Laid Off to Protect Childbearing Ability," *Wall Street Journal*, 5 January 1979, p. 1.

70. Company rules were usually worded so that women of childbearing age were excluded unless they could offer medical proof of sterilization or infertility. Companies known to have had such policies include American Cyanamid, Union Carbide, Eastman Kodak, Celanese, Dupont, Allied Chemical, Monsanto, St. Joe's Mineral Corporation (lead smelter), General Motors (battery plant), B. F. Goodrich, Olin, Sun Oil, and Gulf Oil. Donald R. Crowell and David A. Copus, "Safety and Equality at Odds: OSHA and Title VII Clash over Health Hazards in the Workplace," *Industrial Relations Law Journal* 2 (Spring 1977): 567–95, at pp. 570 and 592; and Ronald Bayer, "Women, Work and Reproductive Hazards," *Hastings Center Report* 12 (August 1982): 14–19, at p. 15.

71. 72.4 percent of the female labor force is between the ages of 16 and 44 (Bureau of the Census, *Statistical Abstract of the United States, 1984,* Table 672, p. 407). The estimate of 20 million jobs is from Equal Employment Opportunity Commission and Office of Federal Contract Compliance Programs, "Interpretive Guidelines on Employment Discrimination and Reproductive Hazards," *Federal Register*, 1 February 1980, p. 7514, cited in Bayer, "Women, Work, and Reproductive Hazards," p. 15. A list of chemicals causing reproductive and fetal harms through paternal exposure is in Jeanette M. Valentine and Alonzo Plough, "Protecting the Reproductive Health of Workers: Problems in Science and Public Policy," *Journal of Health Politics, Policy and Law* 8 (Spring 1983): 144–63, at p. 149.

72. *Federal Register*, 21 November 1978, p. 54442.

73. Crowell and Copus, "Safety and Equality at Odds," p. 588.

74. "Settlement Agreement Reached in Effort to Save Bunker Hill," *Occupational Safety and Health Reporter* 11 (1 October 1981): 340.

75. Rothstein, "Employee Selection," pp. 1414–16, provides a listing of all the standards and their medical surveillance requirements.

76. Rate retention was initially provided in the cotton dust standard, but that part of the standard was invalidated in American Textile Manufacturers Institute, Inc. v. Donovan, 452 U.S. 490 (1981). The court said OSHA had not given sufficient reasons why medical removal protection and rate retention were necessary to protect worker safety and health.

77. Collective bargaining agreements do not provide much protection for the hypersusceptible worker, either. See Rothstein, "Employee Selection," pp. 1422–23; and Mahoney and Kendall, "OSHA's Medical Surveillance," pp. 794–97.
78. Charles E. Lewis, Mary Ann Lewis, and Muriel Ifekwunigue, "Informed Consent by Children and Participation in an Influenza Vaccine Trial," *American Journal of Public Health* 68 (no. 11, 1978): 1079–82.

The Changing Locus of Decision Making in the Health Care Sector

Clark C. Havighurst, Duke University

Abstract. In the 1970s, the health policy debate focused on whether government or the medical profession should control the health care system. This article asserts that that struggle between two forms of centralized control was both less promising and less consequential than the devolution of decision-making authority upon consumers and their agents that is occurring today and that seems likely to continue as competitive forces become stronger and opportunities for meaningful consumer choice increase. What we are witnessing is the simultaneous deprofessionalization and depoliticization of important decisions affecting health care, a decentralization and diversification of the system that is opening new possibilities for translating diverse consumer desires into provider performance. Although covering much familiar ground, this article links a variety of seemingly discrete issues under the decentralization theme. Its object in developing this theme is to escape some of the sterility of the competition-versus-regulation debate and to show the historical and ethical significance of the major changes that are under way in the health care sector today.

Decentralization: The emergence of consumer choice

The last decade of health politics, policy, and law has seen the idea that the U. S. health care system can be driven by consumer choice emerge from obscurity to become perhaps the dominant precept guiding health policy development. This idea remains controversial, however. Although the nation is generally content to have other goods and services supplied through competitive markets, many observers balk at using market forces—even with public subsidies to assist those who cannot pay—to allocate resources to personal health care. Indeed, even while dramatic progress is being made toward establishing a health care marketplace in which consumer preferences are effectively translated into provider performance, those who object to any policy that seems to treat health care as just another commodity do not accept the fait accompli.[1] In the absence of a

Work on this article was supported by Grant No. HS 04089 from the National Center for Health Services Research and Health Care Technology Assessment, Department of Health and Human Services. An earlier version was presented at a Liberty Fund conference, Houston, Texas, December 1984.

clearer consensus that the market-oriented system that is emerging is basically the system we want—subject to adjustment and supplementation—the debate over fundamentals continues.

Instead of focusing specifically, as do most discussions of basic health policy, on the relative merits of "competition" or "the market" and "regulation," this article seeks to put the issues in a somewhat different light by observing the decentralization of decision making on health care issues that has occurred in the health care sector in the 1980s as a result of policy changes that began in the late 1970s. Although this period has seen the federal government cede important health policy and financing responsibilities to the states, the decentralization to be stressed here involves much more than a shift in the locus of governmental authority. Likewise, more is involved than privatization—that is, a government turnover of power to private interests. The decentralization to which attention is called here is the devolution of decisions affecting the provision of medical care upon consumers themselves and their newly responsible and accountable corporate and other agents. The current era is seeing both a significant shift of power from public to private hands and a notable decline in the power of private professional interests to control industry developments. Just as the strength of a federal system of government lies in diversity in assessing and solving problems, the simultaneous depoliticization and deprofessionalization of the governance of the health care system holds promise of public benefit.

Emphasizing the decentralization theme serves two particular purposes here. First, it minimizes the distinction—which is extremely important for many other purposes—between government regulatory control and control of the industry by professional interests through codes of ethics, accrediting and credentialing programs, and coercive actions in support of professional objectives. Government regulation and professional self-regulation were the only alternatives generally recognized in health policy debates until late in the 1970s. By calling attention to their similarity in centralizing authority over health care issues, the discussion here seeks to dramatize the more fundamental distinction between a centrally controlled "system" and a decentralized, competitive "industry," in which the various players are accountable directly or indirectly to consumers in the marketplace rather than through political processes. The emergence of the market alternative as a respectable option in health policy was an especially striking event because it contradicted the earlier assumption that central control, in one form or another, was inevitable. This article's discussion of the industry's legal and policy environment in these terms will help to reveal the implications of the many public and private controls that continue to limit, duly or unduly, the range of consumer choice.

A second way in which the decentralization theme is conceptually helpful is in highlighting both the reality that there is often more than one defensible way to meet a health need and the possibility that some consumers might rationally prefer alternatives that professional or political overseers of the system would deny them. Not only is health care fraught with symbolism and intensely personal, value-laden choices, but its nature and content are often less subject to scientific determination than they are represented as being. It may therefore be appropriate to widen the range of permissible private choice and to acknowledge that many of the issues that arise are more ideological than technical, and that even technical issues may not be resolvable with the available data or on technical grounds alone. Once the health care sector is recognized as being in significant part a marketplace of competing technical and nontechnical ideas, the democratic virtues of private choice over professional or governmental fiat begin to appear. Although there are good reasons for society to limit private choice in some respects, this article's review of the health care industry's legal and policy framework will suggest that the diversity fostered by decentralization can be beneficial and could be carried further in the interest of consumer welfare.

For the most part, this article adopts a historical focus, arguing that, long before the debates over regulation in the 1970s, health care was already centrally controlled, not so much by government as by professional interests. In the 1970s, in order to overcome the costly inefficiencies tolerated by the dominant system of regulation, the nation experimented with government regulation as a substitute for the control systems already in place. But the government never quite got its regulatory program organized, as legislatures—particularly a Congress in an increasingly deregulatory mood—refused to adopt comprehensive cost controls applicable to the private sector as well as to public programs. One reason for legislative inaction was the appearance on the horizon of the market alternative, symbolized by health maintenance organizations (HMOs). A crucial event in establishing a market-oriented policy and making it credible was the Supreme Court's *Goldfarb* decision in 1975;[2] by interpreting the federal antitrust laws to mandate competition in the provision of professional services, the court changed de facto federal policy toward the health care sector and undermined numerous industry-sponsored barriers to competition. Since about 1979, as a result of government's refusal to accept an encompassing regulatory role and its pressing of the antitrust attack, decision-making power has begun to devolve upon consumers and private entities accountable to them in the competitive marketplace. Even though it could be carried much further and remains subject to reversal by new policy choices, this decentralization of decision making is already a development of historic proportions.

This article documents both the suppression and later emergence of private choice in health care markets, concluding with some general advocacy of policies and legal doctrine explicitly fostering choice. The article's main purpose is to show the coherence and fundamental significance of the developments of the past decade and to supply a conceptual framework for future legal and policy thinking. The article also argues that, compared to the alternatives, the re-enfranchisement of the consumer of health care is both practically advantageous and ethically satisfying.

The old arrangement: Health care as a privately regulated industry

Although no single governmental agency presided over it—as the Interstate Commerce Commission and the Civil Aeronautics Board presided over surface and air transport, respectively—the health care sector was subject to a network of governmental and extragovernmental controls and influences that made it a "regulated industry" well before the 1970s. A review of the various controls that operated to limit the range of consumer choice and to curb price competition will reveal some of the things at stake in the current deregulation movement, the potential of this movement for bringing about fundamental change in the industry, and some of the ethical significance of shifting to consumers the decision-making authority previously exercised by others. It will appear that public acquiescence in the medical profession's domination of vital decision making gave rise to a system of governance nearly as restrictive of consumer options as a socialistic national health service would be. The discussion will confirm Paul Starr's characterization of medicine as a "sovereign" profession.[3] Granted, in Starr's words, "cultural authority, economic power, and political influence,"[4] the medical profession long exercised one-party control that effectively preempted consumer choice on virtually all important questions affecting the delivery of medical care.

Limiting consumer choice of health care personnel. Professional licensure laws have long made the provision of most personal health services the exclusive province of physicians. Obviously, such regulation limits consumers' options by forcing them to use highly trained, expensive personnel when other types might serve quite well. But exclusionary state licensure also allowed the organized medical profession to make many crucial decisions affecting the nature and employment of health care personnel, thus limiting consumer choice still further. In particular, the medical profession's power to specify the training required and other criteria for public or private recognition as a qualified practitioner or technician was practically equivalent to the state's power to define desirable characteristics and to exclude those not possessing them.

By incorporating by reference organized medicine's own system for accrediting medical schools and graduate training programs, state licensing requirements enabled the profession both to influence the number of physicians trained and to standardize medical education so that its products were highly homogeneous. The result was a prosperous, tightly knit profession sharing a great deal of common experience and a common ideology of medical care. Consumers had no choice but to accept what was offered, and no idea of the diversity and desirable alternatives that they were denied. The same tendency toward uniformity that has been evident in the medical profession's attempts to absorb osteopathy[5] and suppress chiropractic[6] was also present in the accrediting system's homogenization of allopathic training.[7]

One result of the states' delegation of power over medical education to organized medicine was that nonstandard medical training was available only in foreign countries. Despite their lack of approved training, however, foreign medical graduates (FMGs) were allowed, with the profession's consent, to immigrate in startlingly large numbers to the United States and to obtain medical licenses.[8] Indeed, their ability to fill many professional jobs that U.S. graduates were too few, overqualified, or unwilling to fill proved that a large demand existed for a different type of physician than organized medicine and the U.S. educational establishment saw fit to provide. Rather than permit greater variety in and expanded output of U.S. schools, however, the profession chose to import substandard physicians, perhaps counting on racial and ethnic differences to minimize the competitive impact of the immigrants. Consumers willing to patronize a cheaper physician or to obtain care in a nontraditional practice setting frequently encountered language or cultural barriers.

The power to limit both the output of U.S. medical schools (through exercise of accrediting powers) and the influx of FMGs (through control of access to postgraduate training and eligibility for licensure[9]) was a crucial feature of professional self-regulation for several decades between the famous Flexner Report of 1910[10] and the federal government's subsidization of medical school expansion in the 1960s. Although government reclaimed its authority over the physician supply in this latter era, its manpower planning seems to have been no more on target than the profession's own planning had been. Government erred, however, on the side of overproduction,[11] with the fortuitous effect that competition is now much more feasible in health care markets than it would have been had supply restrictions continued. There is an irony here to the extent that the federal government's initiative was undertaken as a central planning move aimed not at facilitating a shift to a truly free market but at providing the manpower needed to operate a centrally controlled system. Public subsidies to state medical schools continue at high and unjustified levels today, threatening an oversupply that could prove harmful to professionalism and the quality of care. Past public policies toward medical education and the manpower supply do not inspire confidence that consumers have much to gain from having the public's need for physicians signalled by government rather than by consumer choice.

The medical profession has used other means besides medical school accreditation to standardize physicians, thus limiting further the range of consumer choice. When increasing specialization by physicians first began to impress upon consumers that all physicians were not necessarily alike in skill, the profession sponsored the creation of medical specialty boards to standardize each field, thus reestablishing within each specialty the homogeneity previously fostered for the profession as a whole.[12] These boards, now twenty-three in number, prescribe postgraduate training and certification requirements in their respective fields, the boundaries of which are carefully negotiated to avoid interspecialty competition.

Although such standardization can be efficient, it can also be carried too far, to the point where desirable diversity and experimentation are suppressed.[13]

At the same time that they promote uniformity in specialty training, the medical specialty boards, despite their pretense of quality assurance, make little effort to ensure that those who became board-certified at an earlier date have kept up with the state of the art. Indeed, by periodically lengthening the period of training required by new applicants and "grandfathering" those certified under earlier standards, the boards not only increase the costs of market entry to new practitioners but also create an appearance of greater homogeneity within the board-certified ranks than in fact exists.[14] Consumers are thus induced to underestimate the differences between physicians, and physicians are limited in the ways they can differentiate themselves from their competitors.

Until the Federal Trade Commission intervened, the profession barred professional advertising under ethical codes,[15] thus ensuring that consumers would not learn of qualitative or other differences among specialists directly from the physicians themselves. Even today, advertising claims of particular skill are infrequent and would probably be challenged as deceptive and unethical. The common thread that linked advertising restrictions with the profession's domination of specialty certification was their cumulative stifling effect on the flow of information concerning relevant differences among physicians.[16] Once again, the profession found ways to limit the ability of consumers to make relatively informed choices—even among the very limited options available.

The medical profession's dominant influence was also felt in the other health care occupations. A number of these occupations are referred to as "allied" professions—an explicit recognition that they have entered into accommodations with organized medicine. (Others, most notably chiropractors, have remained at war with physicians.) Most state licensure laws proceed by creating an exclusive province for physicians and then carving out narrow enclaves within that province for various other licensed occupations. This legal recognition of the medical profession's sovereign sphere gives rise to serious jurisdictional struggles that state legislatures must referee. Because of the political sensitivity of such "turf" battles, legislators usually prefer to ratify peace treaties worked out between state medical societies and the non-M.D. professionals who are seeking to expand their scope of practice. Thus, private negotiation is often the rule, and the consumer interest in having wider choice or in being protected against real danger is frequently overwhelmed by the political exertions of the competing provider groups. Although some nonphysician groups have won political battles for recognition, consumer interests are not always well served by such victories. Thus, many so-called "freedom of choice" statutes, which require private health insurers to cover the services of nonphysicians,[17] require that nonphysicians be paid the same fees that physicians receive; such legislation undercuts the idea that prices should be negotiable and that consumers might choose for themselves which providers' services they want covered in their insurance plans.

Organized medicine has dominated the allied professions in other ways besides its influence over legislation. The American Medical Association (AMA) collaborates with most other health care occupations in accrediting training programs and certifying the personnel produced.[18] Under these arrangements, nonphysicians are trained to fill particular niches in the system; more specifically, they are taught their place vis-à-vis physicians and are in turn accorded a place of their own. Physician influence over hospitals[19] and various payment systems[20] has created additional barriers to nonphysicians seeking to expand their scope of practice and to escape physician control.

Among the cumulative results of occupational licensure and industry self-regulation are a rigid division of labor throughout the entire health care industry, suppression of experimentation with alternative types and uses of manpower, and severe limitations on the range of consumer choice. To a much greater extent than personnel licensure alone requires, there has been a centralization of authority over how health care is organized and delivered. That a few occupational groups remained recalcitrant—for example, the chiropractors, with whom the profession has never come to terms, and the physical therapists, who have refused in recent years to let the AMA prescribe the nature and limits of their training— seems simply to demonstrate, as exceptions that prove the rule, the pervasiveness of professional influence. Competition and consumer choice have had only a very limited role in determining the nature of health care personnel, the allocation of tasks among different varieties of provider, and the configuration of the system that consumers were forced to patronize.

Limiting consumer access to corporate agents. The medical profession has long exerted a powerful influence over the various corporate participants in health care markets. In particular, hospitals and health insurers, both of which occupy strategic positions from which they might have exerted substantial influence over physicians, were prevented from acting as agents of consumers in organizing the delivery of care and imposing appropriate constraints on health care spending. If these market intermediaries had been willing and able to act competitively to please consumers, they would have given the industry a very different look. In addition to neutralizing hospitals and health insurers, the medical profession was also successful, for a long time, in suppressing the development of new types of financing and delivery organizations, particularly prepaid group practices. The various measures by which the profession prescribed how care would be delivered and financed added up to a regulatory regime that narrowed consumers' decision-making role to the extent of effectively preempting it.

The potential independence of hospitals was curbed at an early date by professional advocacy of legal, and enforcement of ethical, bans on contract practice by physicians and the corporate practice of medicine, which effectively discouraged hospitals from employing physicians and retailing their services. Nonprofit hospitals were generally preferred as less likely to assert economic interests opposed to physicians, and the convention of separately billing for hospital and physician services was forcefully maintained to prevent hospitals from assuming a dominant role. Most important, the physician-dominated Joint Commission on Accreditation of Hospitals (JCAH) specified the details of hospital organization and operation. Under JCAH standards, to which nearly all reputable hospitals adhered, self-governing medical staffs were able to control a great deal of hospital behavior and to inhibit unilateral hospital efforts to serve those interests of consumers (in lower costs, for example) that physicians had no interest in serving. Finally, prevailing restrictions on the supply of physicians, which forced hospitals to obtain staff physicians in a seller's market, made hospitals particularly sensitive to threats by physicians—both collectively and individually—to take their patients elsewhere; as was often noted later as part of the rationale for regulation, hospitals were thus forced to engage in costly nonprice competition for the patronage of physicians. In general, hospitals were long bound, by both threats and circumstances, to do their doctors' and the JCAH's bidding and not to act independently as procurers of physician services on terms giving consumers attractive alternatives.[21]

Hospitals were willing to submit to physician dominance only because of the system that emerged for paying the bills for hospital care. In the absence of a reimbursement system that freely underwrote nearly all hospital costs, it would probably have been impossible to induce hospitals to serve physician interests. By the same token, hospitals were quite content with the liberal and essentially passive financing system that developed and, indeed, participated actively in its design and in enforcing adherence to it. Without question, of all the industry activities that characterized the era of self-regulation, those that affected the nature of health insurance and prepayment plans were by far the most important in shaping industry performance. By the influence they exercised over the entities that paid for health services, providers spared themselves from having to compete among themselves on the basis of price. Ultimately, the conditions they created for themselves proved too favorable to last and caused the cost problem that finally destabilized the system, bringing major changes in its wake.

Hospitals collectively developed Blue Cross plans in the 1930s as a way of expanding demand for their services in hard times and ensuring collection of their bills; they quickly hit upon restrospective cost reimbursement as the method of paying hospitals that best insulated patients from having to consider cost when choosing a hospital, thus enhancing hospitals' pricing and spending freedom. For similar reasons, physicians developed Blue Shield plans for medical services shortly thereafter; in addition to refusing to pay nonphysicians for services that physicians wished to provide, these profession-sponsored plans developed methods of payment—most commonly a commitment to pay physicians or indemnify patients on the basis of "usual, customary, and reasonable" fees—that made it easier for doctors to charge high fees without driving patients away. When the Medicare and Medicaid programs were adopted in the 1960s, government borrowed directly the payment methods developed by the Blues. This acceptance by government of the payment system so assiduously developed by provider interests was perhaps the high-water mark of the paradigm of a health care system in which fundamental choices were delegated to industry decision makers. Essentially, government agreed to underwrite whatever physicians and hospitals found it expedient to spend or charge.

Maintenance of the system of third-party financing preferred by providers required the suppression of alternative ways of paying for care. The medical profession was for a long time equal to this task. The problems that early HMOs encountered are well known. In addition, health insurers that were not subject to direct provider control found that, if they took cost-containment measures or tried to negotiate with providers individually, they ran into difficulties that inconvenienced their insureds and discouraged provider cooperation; indeed, the medical profession at an early date laid down specifications for lay-controlled insurance plans with which physicians could ethically cooperate and, when necessary, employed boycotts to enforce these requirements.[22] Ultimately, commercial insurers, perhaps accepting medical discipline in order to escape having to compete among themselves in the difficult task of cost containment, acquiesced in their prescribed role as passive bill payers and eschewed acting as aggressive bulk purchasers of providers' services.[23]

The mechanisms of self-regulation also included professional ethics prohibiting physicians from engaging in "contract practice," which meant letting an intermediary retail one's professional services. Also, the ideal of "free choice of physician" was used to contest early HMO development as well as efforts by insurers to steer patients away from high-cost providers. In short, by combining ethical controls over its own members with the threat of sanctions against corporate entities that threatened to force doctors into competition, health care providers, with occasional legislative assistance, found it possible to regulate in their own interest the development and behavior of independent financing and delivery mechanisms.[24] Thus, the options available to consumers in the marketplace were once again only a small fraction of the arrangements that might have been offered.

Public acquiescence in professional control. The medical profession was not without a legal warrant in seizing many of the decision-making powers described above.[25] Legislation frequently embodied the profession's view on specific issues or expressly deferred to the judgment of professional bodies. The profession also assumed additional authority that, while not expressly granted to it, was never challenged, an apparent reflection of the general deference to physicians that Starr describes as a cultural phenomenon. Even when the medical profession did not actively assume decision-making authority, the public frequently turned to it for guidance, either converting professional standards into legal standards or willingly accepting professional norms as appropriate standards for use in administering public and private health care programs.

An important manifestation of societal deference to the medical profession was the virtual exemption that medicine long enjoyed from the nation's antitrust laws.[26] This exemption, which was more de facto than de jure, rested in part on the vague notion that the so-called "learned professions" were different from other trades—indeed, that they were not engaged in "trade or commerce" at all. As a practical matter, however, the constitutional limit on the jurisdictional reach of federal law into local health care markets was probably a more important explanation of the paucity of cases. Indeed, the one notable exception to the general inaction of antitrust prosecutors in medical fields was a case arising in the District of Columbia,[27] where jurisdiction was not a problem. However one accounts for that famous 1943 case, which resulted in criminal convictions of prestigious medical societies for harassing an early HMO, the overall antitrust record into the 1970s was one of general acquiescence in professional control. Although professional groups could only occasionally be seen engaged in actions that would be clearly unlawful in ordinary business settings (boycotts, for example), there was a widespread view, supported by strong dictum in one Supreme Court decision,[28] that the profession would be left wide room to maneuver under the banner of ethics and the public interest. With the profession relatively free to act collectively in defense of its prerogatives, few in the private sector undertook to challenge those prerogatives.

The public's long and deep-seated deference to the medical profession as a decision maker reflected a deeply rooted misconception, one that was planted and carefully nurtured by the profession itself. In the public mind, medicine aspired to be, and therefore was treated as, an exact science. The medical profession was viewed as a single entity striving to solve purely scientific problems, and medical practitioners were seen as primarily engaged in applying received technical knowledge. Believing that there is a single right way, or sometimes a narrow range of acceptable ways, to diagnose and treat human disease, the public naturally accepted professional hegemony over all technical questions and even acquiesced in the view that cost considerations were undesirable impediments to the pursuit of professional objectives. Even as the cost problem became apparent, there was little challenge to the prevalent assumption that the system must operate under a single set of prescriptive standards. The possibilities for decentralizing decision making about what is acceptable care and what is wasteful spending went generally unrecognized. The prevalence of the egalitarian ideal—the belief that a single standard of health care should be available to all—played nicely into the hands of a profession anxious to keep control of the system.

One manifestation of societal acceptance of the view that a uniform standard of medical care should govern all physicians appears in the law of medical malpractice, which derives the legal duty of a physician primarily from the standards of the profession. Thus, it is an almost complete defense to a charge of professional negligence that the defendant did what other physicians in the community would have done under the circumstances; in contrast, courts judging negligence in nonprofessional fields give less than conclusive weight to custom and practice in the trade. Although there are some exceptions to the "customary practice" standard and some good practical reasons for adhering to it,[29] the effect of the rule has been to give the medical profession the power to prescribe, informally at least, its own standards. In practical terms, the customary practice standard meant that a plaintiff could hope to win a malpractice suit only if another physician were willing to testify that a professional norm had been breached. Because professional solidarity frequently made it hard to find such an expert witness, the profession became something of a law unto itself, at least until courts devised some alternative ways of proving the standard of care and until changes in the profession made the so-called "conspiracy of silence" harder to maintain. Consistent with the view that professional norms should bind the parties, courts were generally unreceptive to claims that a plaintiff had contracted for a higher standard of care than that generally prevailing among the defendant's peers.

Malpractice law's customary practice standard served as a sword as well as a shield. Under it, a physician who departed from the practices of his peers (general practitioners or specialists, as the case may be) risked becoming a guarantor of good results. Prevailing practice thus became mandatory, enforced rigorously by the threat of both financial penalties and a public labeling of the practitioner as a negligent professional. Physicians complain of being forced by this legal standard to practice "defensive medicine"; in addition, it is beginning to appear to many observers that the standards of customary practice may be seriously inefficient as the cumulative product of many medical decisions made without significant cost constraints, and often under pressure generated by the law itself to omit no arguably beneficial step. Nevertheless, the customary practice rule is a logical extension of the profession's own view that the public should look to the profession alone for rules of professional conduct. Another manifestation of this professional ideal is the prevailing judicial hostility to defendants' arguments that the plaintiff contracted for a lower standard of care than the law, borrowing from the profession, prescribes; the law has thus incorporated the dominant professional view that profession-sponsored norms, not consumer choice, should govern.[30]

Professional norms and standards have also been turned to for guidance on the appropriateness of spending public and private insurance funds on specific services or specific patients.[31] Private health insurance policies have commonly covered all "medically necessary" care or the equivalent; similarly, the original Medicare legislation committed the government to pay for care that is "reasonable and necessary." Inevitably, determinations of medical necessity and reasonableness were made by reference to prevailing medical practice. Indeed, in a particularly striking display of public deference to professional judgments, the Medicare program in 1972 turned over to profession-sponsored professional standards review organizations (PSROs) the definition of norms and standards to govern program payment for specific services. Disregarding the obvious conflict of interests, government in effect delegated to local professional bodies, with only limited oversight, the task of defining the limits of government's obligation to pay. Standards were to be drawn from customary practice. Once again, however, it may be observed that, because of the weakness of economic constraints on medical decision making, prevailing standards may not reflect appropriate attention to the marginal trade-offs between the benefits derivable and the costs incurred.[32]

In sum, the view that decision making on all vital points should be centralized and largely entrusted to the medical profession as an entity dominated most thinking about health policy well into the 1970s. Indeed, this idea remains widespread today even as traditional patterns are being broken and pluralistic influences are creeping in. Nevertheless, it should be clear from the history summarized here that the stage was set for major change.

Moves to substitute government as the dominant decision maker[33]

Under self-regulation, the health care industry fattened itself on reimbursement from passive third-party payers. The weakly constrained industry revealed an immense appetite for spending on technology and manpower and gobbled up whole percentage points of GNP—from 4.6 percent in 1950, to 7.7 percent in 1973, to nearly 11 percent today. These rising costs became the irritant that kept government constantly searching for a point at which to intervene, aroused previously complaisant purchasers of group health insurance, and ultimately brought about the collapse of self-regulation. Before telling this most recent chapter, however, it is appropriate to reflect upon government's efforts in the 1970s to replace, or supplement, the industry's own controls, both formal and informal, with government regulation.

Health planning and regulation by certificate of need. The earliest attempts by government to control health care costs sought to prevent "unnecessary" capital investments and associated higher costs by imposing certificate of need (CON) requirements tied to the decisions of local and state health planning agencies. These initiatives were unlikely to succeed, however, because they were based upon both a basic misconception of the cost problem and an overestimate of government's political ability to contest health care spending decisions taken in the private sector. Indeed, CON regulation was promoted by some industry interests precisely because it was limited to addressing certain symptoms of the cost problem and was more likely, because of the political context, to legitimize than to prevent high levels of health care spending.[34] Although the planning agencies that were expected to rationalize the system included consumers, few of the participants in the planning effort had any incentive to work for cost containment. Because consumer representatives were usually more interested in ensuring availability of services than in cost control, they could usually be co-opted or circumvented. Thus, there was no more than a minor shift in the locus of decision-making authority and no challenge at all to the dominant conception of a unitary, largely self-regulated system financed by payers committed to reimbursing all but demonstrably unreasonable costs. Because they did not seek to alter the monolithic character of the industry or to change payment ground rules, CON controls can be viewed in retrospect as highly conservative measures.[35]

Several specific misconceptions of the cost problem were reflected in CON laws. Among other things, they neglected the likelihood that, as long as open-ended revenue sources were available to be exploited, costs incurred by providers and patients would, like a partially constrained balloon, simply expand in unregulated directions. Experience under these regulatory programs suggested that any savings achieved in capital and related costs were indeed offset by increases in labor costs and in capital spending that regulation did not reach.[36] Moreover, CON laws, like programs to discourage unnecessary care through profession-sponsored peer review, were based upon the assumption that the cost problem is one of spending on facilities and services that are essentially worthless, both to society and to the patients being treated. Unfortunately, although some useless, "flat of the curve" spending does occur, the ultimate problem almost certainly lies in spending on services that, though arguably beneficial, are not enough so—given the small probability or light value of the health benefits sought or the existence of offsetting risks—to justify the outlay.[37]

Both CON laws and PSRO-type programs also proceeded on the unexamined assumption that publicly designated experts could reliably determine on a case-by-case basis how society should spend its resources on health care services and on the additional assumption that they could make their official judgments stick. Unfortunately, policy makers underestimated the ability of providers to rationalize high levels of spending, either by ignoring the trade-off between benefits and costs or by exaggerating the likelihood or value of the health benefits to be obtained. Faced with professional justifications for particular spending, politically accountable health planners and regulators found it difficult to deprive patients of allegedly obtainable benefits or to veto any desirable capital project that was not clearly duplicative of existing facilities. In a political world where professing commitment to unstinting provision of health services is a useful way of demonstrating compassion, it is difficult for publicly accountable decision makers to challenge authoritative professional judgments and to insist upon close comparisons of benefits and costs.

Thus, even when government tried to impose specific checks on the industry's spending impulses, it found that it was politically impossible to make much difference. Professional advocacy for patient interests was too effective to resist in most close cases. Also, there was no room at all to challenge a professional consensus where it existed. Not only were the potential cost savings that might have helped offset the weight of industry opinion effectively hidden by the financing system, but there were severe questions about the basic legitimacy of economizing at the expense of a few sick persons for the benefit of the public treasury or an insurer's deep pocket. In short, government found it virtually impossible to assume decision-making responsibilities that had previously been entrusted to professional decision makers. Its early efforts to ration medical care hardly made a dent in professional hegemony.[38]

Hospital rate-setting regulation. As the ineffectiveness of early forms of government cost containment became increasingly obvious throughout the 1970s, policy makers began to consider more far-reaching regulatory proposals. Several states adopted hospital rate-setting regulations, and in 1977 the Carter administration proposed a far-reaching hospital cost-containment bill that would have imposed a fixed percentage limit on the annual growth of hospital costs; roughly, the revenues of each hospital would have been allowed to increase each year at no more than the rate of overall hospital-cost inflation plus one percent. Although the original bill left a gaping loophole for the automatic pass-through of higher labor costs, its other features suggested a new potential for effective cost control.

In particular, the Carter proposal's formula-based approach stood in striking contrast to previous cost-containment efforts, which had relied upon explicit public determinations of the appropriateness of particular capital and treatment costs incurred. Because the proposed revenue constraint was purposely arbitrary and concerned only with a hospital's bottom line, it promised not to entangle government in balancing specific health benefits against dollar costs. By thus shifting the adversarial confrontations between government and health care providers to a point far removed from patient care, the proposal sought to increase the regulators' political ability to be rigorous. Although the efficacy of such regulation in controlling costs would still depend upon complex political factors, the Carter proposal had the potential virtue of allowing government to escape the political burden of confronting providers over specific outlays.

Unfortunately, the same arbitrariness that makes hospital rate setting somewhat promising as a cost-containment tool raises the possibility that any cost containment it achieves will be a very gross affair—as is any operation with a meat axe. The factor that the advocates of such regulation apparently count on to save it from its own imprecision and to ensure its sensitivity to patients' needs is providers' responsibility for deciding how the newly limited resources would be spent. Within each hospital, if the resources made available by the regulators were inadequate to do all that physicians would like to do, internal rationing decisions would have to be made, and it is apparently assumed that only fat will be trimmed. Although shifting the rationing burden to providers in this way would allow government to get rid of a political hot potato, it would raise the question whether providers can realistically be expected to serve primarily public needs rather than their own interests and values in performing the resource allocation function. In fact, proponents of regulation have given little thought to the intraprofessional or intrahospital political mechanisms that would be relied upon for rationing decisions if open-ended financing were replaced by the zero-sum game of a fixed hospital budget.[39] It is notable that proposals for hospital rate-setting regulation demonstrate virtually the same faith in professionalism that was implicit in the policies of the self-regulation era.

Being limited to hospital costs, rate-setting regulation would leave a great deal of nonhospital care unregulated, thus creating a gap that would eventually provide an argument for extending regulation to the entire system. Such all-encompassing regulation, which many regulation advocates acknowledge to be the logical outcome of their hospital cost-containment proposals, would make the level of spending on health care a subject for political struggle at the macro level, like the defense budget. It would seem that nothing less than total despair about arriving at satisfactory resource allocation by decentralized market mechanisms could make this approach to the problem seem attractive. Accordingly, it is little wonder that Congress balked at being led down this regulatory path until the alternative policy of market reform had been tried.

Shifting decision-making responsibility to consumers and their agents

Ironically, the same arbitrariness that promised to make the Carter proposal somewhat effective in containing costs proved to be its undoing. Beginning in 1977, interest groups scrambled for two years to get Congress to correct various actual or alleged unfairnesses in the bill, thereby eliminating much of its potential bite. Finally, Congress defeated what was left of the Carter proposal in 1979. This action put an end, at least for the time being, to federal efforts to solve cost problems by regulation, and the advent of the conservative Reagan administration ensured that no further regulatory proposals would be forthcoming from the executive branch for some time to come. Coincidental with government's retreat from its candidacy for the dominant decision-making role, the ability of previously dominant industry groups to exercise their customary self-regulatory powers was being seriously eroded by an intensive campaign to enforce the antitrust laws in the health care sector.[40] Coupled with a rapidly expanding supply of physicians (due to the efforts of the manpower planners) and an oversupply of hospital beds (despite the efforts of hospital planners and CON regulators), the antitrust initiative opened the way for competitive developments that expanded opportunities for meaningful consumer choice.

Recent developments.

Once government dropped its aspiration to regulate hospital costs, the debate over health care cost containment shifted to new ground. The federal government began to concentrate its efforts solely on controlling the costs of its own programs: Medicare and Medicaid. In so doing, it moved to phase out the strategy of directly challenging provider-incurred costs and to substitute a payment system based not on retrospectively determined costs but on price. Pursuant to the Social Security Amendments of 1983,[41] the Medicare program has introduced a prospective schedule of payments for hospital services based on diagnosis. In contrast to the old cost-reimbursement approach, prospectively fixed payments will impose on the hospitals the burden of controlling their own costs so that they can live within, or maximize their profit from, the fixed DRG (diagnosis related group) allowance. Government's decision to act solely as a prudent, though powerful, purchaser rather than as a regulator bent on controlling industrywide costs was a major step in the direction of decentralizing decision making. Although payment by DRG is widely regarded as regulation—and certainly feels like regulation to the providers affected—it is fundamentally distinguishable in principle from the Carter administration's proposals to regulate all hospital costs.

Other payers, both public and private, have begun to follow the federal government's lead toward more aggressive buying and are negotiating with individual hospitals and physicians over the price of specific services. In a pathbreaking move, Medi-Cal, the California Medicaid program, required hospitals to bid competitively for the right to serve program beneficiaries. Many private purchasers, especially large employers, that had previously assumed either that health care costs were beyond their control or that government would sooner or later take the needed regulatory actions are now uncertain of help from governmental quarters and are beginning to challenge providers on their own. As both government and private payers begin to act for the first time as prudent buyers rather than as passive intermediaries, providers are responding in competitive ways, particularly by organizing or joining so-called "preferred provider organizations" (PPOs), whose members agree to provide services for less or to submit to special cost controls.

HMOs have shown particularly rapid growth since 1980 as purchasers have actively sought more efficient arrangements. Although federal subsidies to HMOs in the 1970s represented a government-sponsored expansion of consumer choice, they reflected only a limited tolerance for departures from traditional arrangements. HMOs were heavily regulated as a condition of government support and thus found themselves handicapped in many respects in competing with traditional insurers and providers.[42] HMOs did, however, keep the flag of competition flying throughout the 1970s and revealed forcefully that arrangements departing from provider-dictated norms could be acceptable. Nevertheless, the federal HMO program was designed more to inject a little controlled pluralism into the system than to promote vigorous price competition or to entrust significant decision making to consumers and their agents in the private sector. Indeed, it seems probable that the federal government's support of HMOs, by signaling which models were acceptable to the system's central manager, channeled the industry's innovative energies into a narrow range, causing other possible innovations, such as PPOs, to be neglected; in the last analysis, the focus of industry entrepreneurs throughout the 1970s was more on pleasing government than on pleasing consumers. More recent market developments, though usually described as the result of increased cost-consciousness on the demand side of the market and increased competition on the supply side, can be understood even more fundamentally as manifestations of real decentralization, of a relaxation of government control over alternative delivery systems, and of a true widening of the range of private choice.[43]

The role of hospitals in controlling the quality and cost of physician services has grown dramatically over a long period. Increasing exposure of hospitals to tort liability necessitated closer scrutiny of physicians in the 1960s and 1970s, but the necessity for hospitals to influence physician behavior has increased once again with the introduction of prospective payment and the intensification of price competition. Although organized medicine continues to use its influence over the JCAH to enforce its belief that physicians should enjoy special job security in hospitals and independence from institutional control and should be organized collectively in self-governing medical staffs, various pressures are beginning to weaken physicians' insulation from accountability to hospital boards. Following a recent change in JCAH policy, accredited hospitals are now allowed for the first time to grant clinical privileges and staff membership to the nonphysician practitioners.[44] This decentralization of decision making on staffing issues to the individual hospital level, which occurred because of the JCAH's antitrust fears, reveals once again the operation of antitrust law in undermining professional authority. A recent legal analysis of hospital/physician relations suggests that hospital medical staffs should have their role in decisions affecting hospital access by their competitors reduced to a truly advisory one by applying antitrust law in such a way that no special deference is shown to decisions that are preempted by physician interests.[45] Gradually, in one of the most significant developments of the current era, hospital boards are beginning to assert their own authority, as agents of consumers, over organized physicians.

Outlines of a choice-driven system. Although the process of change in the health care marketplace has begun in a promising fashion, it has further to go before consumers can be said to be controlling the system effectively. Nevertheless, the outlines of a system based on consumer choice are fairly clear. Cost-consciousness on the demand side, especially on the part of government financing programs and large employers, is the new force that is changing the system's traditional shape. As cost-conscious purchasers—acting as agents of taxpayers and beneficiaries or of employees, as the case may be—increasingly question the way their money is being spent, the system is being forced to respond with arrangements that offer consumers better value for their money. Such arrangements include financing plans that strive to control the "moral hazard" problem by limiting their coverage of services in strategic ways, either by excluding some services from coverage altogether or by imposing cost-sharing requirements. Alternatively or at the same time, a plan may follow a strategy of selecting providers of covered services on the basis of price and cost considerations and either exclude other providers altogether (as HMOs do) or cover their services on a less favorable basis (as in PPO arrangements).

In general, cost-conscious selectivity by middlemen acting as consumer agents is an important key to making the market translate consumer preferences into provider behavior.[46] Consumers, through their agents, must seek efficient financial protection and must be prepared to make more cost-conscious decisions, frequently with professional advice, about which providers to patronize and which services to purchase out of pocket. Insurers and other fiscal intermediaries must be prepared to select and reward efficient providers, both categorically and individually. Provider intermediaries, such as medical group practices and hospitals, must select competent, cooperative physicians and be prepared to let cheaper nonphysician personnel expand their roles. The notion of "free choice of physician" must be recognized as a deception that, while holding out the illusion of consumer choice, weakens competition as a force for efficiency by eliminating the all-important cost factor and preventing ignorant individuals from employing sophisticated corporate agents to assist them in choosing.[47]

Current market developments, particularly HMOs and PPOs, reflect serious experimentation with new approaches to controlling provider behavior in the interest of consumers. A great deal remains to be learned, however, about how these basic tools can be used most effectively to provide good quality care at a reasonable cost. Many of the mechanisms in use are still primitive. Nevertheless, the process of innovation and reorganization and the weeding out of defective plans have begun. Although there remains a great deal of hesitancy to adopt new approaches and to push new cost-containment mechanisms to their full efficiency-enhancing potential, this hesitancy is in part a reflection of the difficulty of reeducating consumers, their agents, and providers to new realities and possibilities. One might wish, of course, that learning curves in health care cost containment rose more sharply than they appear to do, but at least the process of reeducation of the various parties, best illuminated by the formation of purchaser coalitions in local markets, is well underway. The market, with its rewards for fast learners, would seem the best way to bring home to everyone concerned the urgency of addressing the trade-offs that must be addressed.

Finishing the job. Although providers of medical care are today more responsive to consumers and their cost concerns than ever before, there are reasons for thinking that consumers are not yet in a position to exercise the full range of choice that they are capable of exercising. Some barriers to meaningful choice are the result of public policies and industry practices held over from the earlier era of regulation. Although each is amenable to elimination or minimization by some form of public action, it is not essential that all of these problems be solved before the procompetition strategy in health policy can be declared a success. Even if the public lacks the will to move forward on all the various fronts suggested here, competition and consumer choice may still serve as useful instruments of social control over the evolving health care industry.

Incentives for consumers to reexamine their options. Consumer incentives to economize in purchase of health insurance are currently diluted by unlimited tax subsidies. Because employer-paid insurance premiums are not subject to income or payroll taxes, there is a powerful inducement for taxpayers to pay as many health bills as possible through employer-purchased insurance. As long as such subsidies are retained (although questioned by many, they survived the 1986 tax reforms), health insurance will feature suboptimal use of cost sharing, will cover many routine services that consumers would otherwise pay for out of pocket (with normal economizing incentives), and will reduce the sense of urgency about cost containment on the part of all concerned. Although debate continues concerning how consumers would behave under different tax treatment of insurance premiums, there should be little doubt that the entitlement mentality that prevails concerning health benefits in employment settings owes much to tax policy. By the same token, putting a "cap" on the subsidy—or, better yet, switching to subsidies in the form of limited tax credits[48]—would induce people to reexamine their current behavior and speed the development of new options that offer consumers better value for the funds invested. Perhaps the significant lowering of marginal tax rates in the 1986 legislation, by reducing the effective discount obtainable through employer financing, will induce some needed redesign of insurance coverage.

The continued presence of hospital rate regulation in some states and the threat of it in others are additional factors diluting the private sector's incentive to restructure itself to deal effectively with the cost problem. As long as government holds itself out as being responsible for private health care costs—even if it does not act—private interests are less likely to take cost-containment initiatives themselves, either because they assume that government has the answer or simply because they are waiting to see what government will do. For this reason, although regulatory schemes can leave room for HMOs to coexist with traditional payers and even to bargain for discounts from regulated rates, states that can definitively reject regulation and convince private actors that they must defend themselves against higher costs should show faster progress toward establishing an effectively competitive market.

An important step in removing the political threat of regulation and opening the way for competitive developments would be the provision of new resources to cover the cost of caring for uninsured patients. Historically, such costs have been financed in large measure out of excess revenues that hospitals, protected against price competition, were able to earn from paying patients and passive third-party payers. Because much of the new pressure for regulation is prompted by concerns that competition will have harmful side effects on health care for the poor,[49] direct attention to this problem seems vital to providing a political climate conducive to the emergence of competition. (There are, of course, as later discussion will show, other good reasons for attending to this problem.)

Improving the flow of information. The supply of information to consumers is another matter requiring attention if health care markets are to work well. Data sharing now under way is helping bulk purchasers make sensible choices, and progress is being made in developing measures of health care quality that can facilitate comparative evaluations of providers by consumers and overcome the claims of government and professional interests that they alone possess the secret key to quality assessment. Government might be able to assist consumers and their purchasing agents by collecting quality and cost information or mandating disclosure.[50] Although the sensitivity of quality-related data frequently makes its disclosure highly controversial, the better policy is probably to make information available and to encourage those who are disadvantaged to respond in kind.

The control exercised by the medical profession's accrediting and credentialing programs over the supply of information and opinion concerning the quality of hospitals and training programs and the qualifications of health care personnel is another problem.[51] In the past, public policy has generally accepted JCAH accreditation and profession-sponsored educational accreditation as adequate substitutes for direct government regulation, without recognizing the opportunities that exist for philosophical biases and conflicts of interests to affect accreditors' judgments. Although government should rethink its acceptance of professional judgments on these complex issues, it should also resist the temptation to undertake the quality assurance task itself. Tools are at hand to let consumers have a greater voice.

A recent proposal to use antitrust law not to police the quality of information and opinion being produced by profession-sponsored accrediting and credentialing bodies but to increase the flow of information from competing sources offers another approach to consumer information problems.[52] The analysis supporting that proposal suggests, among other things, that the JCAH, as a joint venture of several dominant organizations each capable of publishing its own somewhat different views on the quality of hospitals, is a Sherman Act violation on its face—in effect, a conspiracy of its sponsors to speak with one voice and to deny consumers the benefit of competing opinions. A successful attack on the JCAH under this theory would significantly increase the freedom of hospitals to serve consumers well and to deal aggressively with physicians. It is striking that the JCAH is only just beginning to rate hospitals on the basis of actual outcomes of patient care as well as on their compliance with organizational requirements favored by organized medicine.

Antitrust theories are also available to attach the medical profession's domination of accrediting and credentialing in the allied health occupations, the practice of grandfathering (obscuring relevant differences among practitioners) by medical specialty boards, and the division of the market for credentialing services that has occurred under the auspices of the American Board of Medical Specialties. All that is required to end the medical profession's domination of the supply of vital consumer information in health care is recognition for antitrust purposes that the production and dissemination of such information is itself a business that should be operated on a competitive rather than a monopolistic basis. First Amendment considerations support this market definition[53] and suggest, in addition, the desirability of recognizing that health care is in many respects a marketplace of ideas in which consumers listening to providers' competing claims offer our best hope of inspiring good industry performance.

Antitrust initiatives to enhance the role of corporate middlemen. Antitrust law has other things to contribute to the strengthening of consumer choice and the decentralization of decision making in health care. One important antitrust goal should be to clarify that independent corporate middlemen and procompetitive joint ventures enjoy fairly wide discretion in excluding providers from desirable market opportunities as long as they stand in a vertical rather than a horizontal market relationship to the provider in question or have a satisfactory business justification for their actions. Thus, a hospital should be free to deny admitting privileges to a physician or other practitioner on any rational basis—and with only minimal accountability to an antitrust court—as long as it acts independently (though perhaps with the advice of its medical staff) and does not simply delegate decision-making responsibility to its physicians.[54] Likewise, HMOs, PPOs, health insurers, and other corporate intermediaries should also face no significant antitrust risks when, acting as agents of consumers, they exclude a provider from some desirable privilege. Although there is some confusion on these matters at the moment, the conclusions needed to strengthen competition by strengthening the hand of these various middlemen can be reached without much modification of existing precedent.

Antitrust law also needs to address some of the remaining protections that providers enjoy against aggressive purchasers of their services. Although things are changing in many health care markets, most Blue Cross and Blue Shield plans have conscientiously refrained, throughout their history, from exerting their potential buying power in dealing with providers. This policy was rewarded by explicit provider support for the Blues—most conspicuously in the form of hospital discounts for Blue Cross plans and physicians' participation agreements with Blue Shield plans in which they accepted peer review and plan allowances as payment in full. Although these concessions by providers may appear to have been extracted by the Blues through exercise of buying power against competing sellers, they were in fact conferred on the Blues by providers acting in concert[55] and betokened a cozy relationship that benefitted both the Blues and the respective provider cartels. Because it is not clear that provider cartels have finally broken down in all markets under the pressure of HMO and PPO development, it is necessary to elaborate a bit further how active competitive bargaining at the interface between financing plans and providers was for so long effectively suppressed by the collaborative efforts of the Blues and colluding providers.

Hospital and physician interests gained two things by collectively granting Blue Cross and Blue Shield plans substantial competitive advantages over other insurers. First, they ensured the survival of their respective cartels. These cartels would have quickly collapsed if the Blues had ceased to offer consumers "free choice" and begun to channel patients to lower-priced providers; with the largest purchaser of their services neutralized, however, providers were able for a long time collectively to resist demands from other, smaller payers seeking discounts and participation agreements.[56] The other benefit that providers enjoyed by virtue of their special treatment of the Blues was the Blues' continued friendship, which manifested itself in the acceptance of discounts smaller than could have been obtained by aggressive purchasing and in the provision to consumers (at rates effectively subsidized by providers) of comprehensive, first-dollar insurance coverage—which, by leaving moral hazard unchecked, kept demand for provider services high. For their part in this mutually advantageous relationship, the Blues benefitted from the provider cartels' ability to exclude or discipline other plans. They also enjoyed a large cost advantage over any actual and potential competitor—larger than they could expect if other purchasers could also obtain discounts or other concessions in a competitive market.

The long-standing alliance between providers and the Blues, which began in the 1930s, allowed the hospitals and medical cartels to operate successfully for nearly fifty years. It is an empirical question whether in each local market today this unholy alliance has finally broken down or whether the Blues are still collaborating with provider cartels to raise the costs and reduce the entry prospects or competitive effectiveness of alternative plans seeking to purchase provider services on competitive terms. In markets where a problem of this kind continues to exist, antitrust law should have something to say about it. In addition, recognition of how a collusive relationship between a dominant provider group and a financing plan retailing its members' services can facilitate the operation of a provider cartel should alert antitrust enforcers to the hazards associated with new provider-controlled financing plans that have been increasingly appearing in local markets. In particular, some individual practice associations (IPAs) and PPOs are under control of physician groups comprising a majority of area physicians. These plans are often welcomed—as were the original Blue Cross and Blue Shield plans—as desirable developments. But to the extent that they are creatures of provider cartels, they pose hazards to competition comparable to those that the Blue plans—first controlled by and later collaborating with provider interests—have posed since their beginning.

Unfortunately, although the FTC once expressed appropriate concerns about prepayment plans dominated by provider interests,[57] it has not followed up that initiative with any formal complaints. Its staff apparently views the plans it has looked at only as procompetitive joint ventures, not as joint selling agencies possessing enough market power to engage in unlawful maximum or minimum price fixing.[58] Until the antitrust agencies recognize that such plans can serve (as the

Blue plans have also served) as convenient vehicles for cartel-sponsored limit-entry or disciplinary pricing, physician cartels may continue to resist effectively the market developments they most fear. As long as provider cartels retain any of their previous ability to resist aggressive purchasers of provider services, the decentralization process cannot be said to be complete. Despite the progress that has been made, truly effective competition cannot yet be certified to exist in many local markets.

Reducing governmental and judicial limitations on consumer choice. The federal government has so far not gone much further in the direction of decentralization of decision making than to remove itself as a threat to assume authority over the entire system. It remains dominant in two of the largest health care plans, Medicare and Medicaid, and in that role essentially monopolizes decision making for large segments of the population. The possibility of operating those programs on a more decentralized basis exists, however, and is beginning to be regarded favorably. In several state Medicaid programs, as well as under Medicare itself, program beneficiaries have been given the option of joining an HMO at public expense; moreover, in a few places Medicaid beneficiaries must select a prepaid plan and can no longer rely on the government program for fee-for-service benefits.[59] As the potential for private cost containment is realized and as it is recognized that private plans freely chosen by consumers may have a comparative advantage in economizing over politically sensitive public programs, interest in such "voucherization" should increase, especially if adverse selection problems prove manageable.[60]

Essentially, the objective of using vouchers to provide public subsidies for personal health care would be to shift from an entitlement approach to a decentralized, contractual approach. Although the government would certainly screen the options available to individual beneficiaries (unfortunately, Medicare and Medicaid recipients have few opportunities for group purchasing and thus need special protection against unscrupulous providers), it should eschew a highly prescriptive role with respect to benefit packages, leaving consumers to decide what to purchase with the government contribution. As Medicare's problems with an aging population and an increasingly out-of-date prospective payment system mount in the next few years, it seems likely that the idea of cashing out benefits and offering vouchers in the place of a statutory entitlement will gain favor; the Health Care Financing Administration is already thinking in these terms, largely out of an appreciation of the virtues of decentralization.

Other government-imposed obstacles to the emergence of a health care system driven by consumer choice also can be overcome. State regulation—particularly occupational licensure, CON regulation, and certain restrictions on the freedom of health insurers to design coverage and select providers—remains a problem, but states are reexamining many of their most restrictive policies.[61] Repeal of CON laws should become increasingly attractive as the financing system changes and as competitive pricing emerges as a deterrent to the creation of excess capacity. CON repeal as of a fixed future date would give public and private insurers and insurance purchasers the time they need to introduce defenses against increased costs attributable to inappropriate capital spending. In general, legislatures should be thinking in terms of forcing payers to become responsible purchasers of health services and of expanding the range of consumer choice.

Important limitations on consumer choice also result from judicial attitudes toward private contracts. Although the courts have a legitimate role in scrutinizing transactions to detect overreaching of consumers, many courts are unduly willing to second-guess private agreements and to refuse enforcement of them where some hardship to an individual plaintiff would result. But, judged *ex ante* rather than *ex post*, contractual provisions that limit a patient's tort rights against a provider or that restrict his insurance coverage in some way may well be rational economizing measures that courts should be willing to enforce. The tendency of many courts to misconstrue such risk-allocation contracts or to declare them unconscionable or violative of public policy or of the "reasonable expectations" of the insured reflects the increasingly outmoded belief that the legal system must structure relationships in the medical field.[62] Only if privately negotiated arrangements are not viewed by the legal system as an invitation to litigate their validity can the benefits of decentralized decision making be fully realized.

In general, changing industry circumstances are opening new opportunities for informed consumer choice and for economizing innovations that depart from conventional views of what is desirable or right. Within broad limits, the legal system should respond to these new developments by increasing the leeway allowed to private decision makers. Because market developments are putting new pressures on old assumptions and old barriers to the effective exercise of consumer choice and to the growth of provider competition, those who previously viewed as hopeless the task of creating market conditions conducive to consumer choice should look at the situation again.

Some reflections on the trend to decentralized decision making

As a lawyer, I am most comfortable in arguing the general case for a market-oriented health care system on the basis of general democratic principles embodied in the antitrust laws (with their presumption favoring consumer sovereignty) and in the Constitution (with its guarantees of personal liberties and a free marketplace of ideas). Nevertheless, the argument for competition and consumer choice also seems to me to be supported by ethical or moral considerations. In this final section, I offer some tentative reflections on this theme, more to help structure the debate than to settle the issue.

The ethical virtues of expanded choice. Health care is a highly personal matter, often involving value-laden choices among technological options and consisting of moral support and counseling in the face of life's crises. I would therefore suppose that most people would find it hard to deny the basic desirability of letting people make their own choices in such matters. Although some choices would inevitably be mistaken and occasionally even life-threatening, the same can be said of many other important choices that the state still treats as private matters—such as the choice of a job, a mode of transport, or a recreation. Greater state intervention in health care choices than in these other matters can only be justified, it would seem, by reference to the consumer's comparative inability to make reasonably informed choices in practice. Whether such arguments for state control hold up or not is primarily an empirical, not an ideological, issue. Nearly everyone would agree that choice, in principle, is nice.

It is instructive, and useful in narrowing the issues, to observe that the health care system has always assigned some value to consumer choice. Thus, the tenet of "free choice of physician" was widely honored in part because it appealed to a basic value, however much it undercut that value by reducing consumers' freedom to hire allies other than a physician to help them confront professionals and their intimidating expertise. In addition, the principle of "informed consent" has long been given a high place in law and medical ethics—though a skeptic might see that principle as mostly an attempt to legitimize the monopolistic model of medical care by seeming to redress in individual doctor/patient encounters the power imbalance that results from denying consumers information, allies, and market opportunities for choice.

Because choice has always been given lip service in the system, the real policy issue is not whether there shall be any choice at all but how much of the discretion that goes into designing and operating the system shall in fact be exercised by consumers and how extensively certain choices shall be subsidized. This article has argued that the U.S. system has in the past assiduously limited the range of consumer choice, controlled the flow of information, denied the consumer corporate allies, and resisted letting price or cost considerations influence choices. Not only did the medical profession and the health care industry as a whole find it advantageous to have consumers denied options and insulated against costs, but opinion leaders on the political left have likewise believed that choice should be limited, that corporate middlemen are objectionable characters, and that price should not be a barrier to consumption. This coincidence of views between industry interests and their liberal critics led to a powerful consensus on the need for central control and caused the policy debate to focus almost exclusively on who would exercise that control. As we have seen, the changes currently occurring in the system are giving consumers a wider range of choice, more information, and more assistance, while simultaneously imposing more cost constraints on private choices than have been customary.

Just as the policy issue before the public at the moment is not whether consumers shall have any choice at all, neither is it whether consumers shall be granted unlimited choice. The market that is emerging in health care is not the laissez-faire world that is sometimes portrayed, and there is little support for throwing the ignorant consumer unaccompanied and helpless amidst the wolves that might roam an uncontrolled marketplace. It seems certain, for example, that a panoply of licensure laws and quality assurance regulations will remain in place, though some liberalization is certainly possible and desirable. Moreover, the rule of caveat emptor is not likely to be reinstated in health care, depriving consumers of their right to sue providers for breaches of implied obligations to provide a reasonable standard of care. In addition to the quality assurance incentives created by the tort system, society also supplies protections against overeconomizing by shortsighted individuals and against abuses by middlemen. Enrollment in private financing plans is likely always to be subsidized to some extent by the tax system, and in-kind benefits, perhaps in the form of vouchers, are more likely than the provision of cash allowances for public program beneficiaries. Moreover, private health plans are likely to remain subject to substantial regulation, particularly where individual (as opposed to group) coverage is concerned.

In addition to the many protections against overeconomizing and mistaken individual choices that the law supplies, the marketplace offers consumers numerous opportunities to make their health care choices collectively rather than individually, thereby overcoming the difficulty of becoming personally informed concerning the available options. Most consumers will continue to purchase provider services through employment groups or government programs, thus pooling their resources in order to search the market better and to bargain effectively. In addition, numerous corporate middlemen—HMOs, group practices, PPOs, insurers, hospitals, and so forth—will offer themselves to act as the consumer's agents and, being accountable for their performance of that function in the marketplace as well as to regulators and in the courts, will perform valuable screening functions, protecting consumers against incompetent or unscrupulous providers. The sufficiency of the numerous market and nonmarket protections against mistaken choices—protections that benefit even the most ignorant or complaisant consumer—can be debated, of course, but their existence should not be ignored or underestimated by providers or others who advocate arrangements that narrowly limit choice.

Despite the numerous forces available to keep a choice-driven health care system on a path marked by societal values, it may be possible to believe that such a system will still permit too many deviations, either intentional or inadvertent, from the straight and narrow. This concern implies a greater degree of agreement on values than seems to exist in reality and may betray the critic's desire to impute his own values to society as a whole. This final possibility draws attention to the question how the values that the system implements should be discovered and given effect—whether primarily through explicit or implicit delegation of vital choices to professional control, primarily through political mechanisms in which public officials (turning often to academic experts) prescribe the permissible range of choice, or primarily through a multiplicity of voluntary private arrangements.

If the issue is framed too starkly in these terms, of course, the debate over decentralization begins to look like a gloves-off ideological struggle between a libertarian ethic on the one hand and the authoritarianism/paternalism of both the Right and the Left on the other. Nevertheless, the potential for ideological conflict would seem greatly mitigated by the system's many collective features (group insurance and government programs, for example) and by the regulatory and legal controls that American society will inevitably maintain to prevent seriously mistaken choices. Given the many departures from the pure free-market model, the residual danger that excesses or catastrophes will occur should be tolerable. On the other hand, letting consumers both enjoy rewards from their successes (in economizing, among other things) and suffer some of the consequences of their mistakes should inspire them to look out for themselves, mostly by seeking reliable allies to assist them. Consumer responses to these incentives should in turn stimulate beneficial behavior on the supply side of the market.

To my mind, consumer choice, under cost constraints, is an ethically attractive way to deal with the difficult value questions that pervade the provision of health services. Health care is characterized by ubiquitous and often extraordinarily difficult trade-offs between cost and perceived benefits. Because of the emotional context, the symbolism, and the competing values at stake in many of the choices that must be made—the so-called "tragic choices"[63]—the ethical, legal, and political legitimacy of any economizing effort will always be open to challenge. Economizing on health care is especially vulnerable, however, when it benefits someone other than the individual whose health might be adversely affected. For this reason, effective cost containment, sacrificing benefits that are desirable though not cost-justified, is more likely to be ethically and politically tolerable where both the benefits and the burdens of economizing accrue privately to a single individual or family unit; even then, cost containment will probably be acceptable to society only within limits.

Privatization of these hard choices—that is, rationing care through market choices rather than through governmental mechanisms—has always seemed to me to be preferable, on balance, to bringing them out into the open for emotion-laden public debate and decision.[64] Congress revealed its own inability to say "no" to questionable spending to save identified lives when it responded to a well-orchestrated political campaign by creating the end-stage renal disease treatment program under Medicare; other publicly accountable decision makers have found it equally difficult to economize at the expense of identifiable patients.[65] For these reasons, it should seem wiser—and more satisfying on ethical grounds—to preserve substantial opportunities for private economizing in these especially sensitive matters. "Tragic choices" such as those regarding the treatment (or nontreatment) of newborns and the terminally ill must of course be made one way or the other, but society need not make them through the already overburdened political process. I once had occasion to write in connection with the artificial heart that, in order to spare government the demoralizing dilemma of whether to sacrifice its humanitarian image or to incur unwarranted costs, death and suffering from catastrophic disease should continue, to the greatest extent possible, to be perceived as "more an act of God than of the Legislature."[66] One of the greatest virtues of the market mechanism is its ability to relieve government of a myriad of complex and difficult decisions. Few decisions could be more debilitating to the body politic than value-laden life-and-death choices of the kind that health care frequently forces us to make.

This article has sought to show both the poor record of professionally contrived solutions to the problems of health policy and the poor prospects of governmental solutions and then to suggest that a market-oriented policy would yield results that are preferable, on balance, to these alternatives. Nevertheless, one might also argue that consumer choice is an absolute ethical imperative. On this basis, it would be possible to deny the relevance of certain "empirical" questions. Some observers have demanded, for example, that market advocates supply a complete description of the system as it would evolve and function under competition in order that the questioners can judge its acceptability. But, in demanding proof that a competitive system would be superior to some alternative, these observers miss the strong ethical point that the competitive process, precisely because it is based on choice, may validate the outcome whatever it may turn out to be. Thus, even if a competitive, choice-driven health care market should produce levels of health care spending which were unjustifiable under objective criteria and which exceeded what spending would be under regulation, it might still be regarded as preferable to a regulated system. Under this view, the only relevant empirical issues would be those relating to whether the process had truly given people what they want—whether they were freely choosing without perverse incentives, with adequate information, and with access to the help they need in order to choose well.

A plausible response to the argument that a health care market driven by con- sumer choice ipso facto defines the public interest might be mounted on the ground that consumers are irredeemably ignorant and irrational about health care. Such a response would draw strength from findings in psychological research that individuals are easily influenced by the way choices are framed and indeed are systematically inconsistent and incoherent both in their weighing and treatment of risks and in their valuations of alternative outcomes.[67] Although these findings may be seen as undermining the paradigm on which market theory depends, the foregoing defense of consumer choice in health care is still not untenable. That argument bears many resemblances to the case for democratic political institutions, whose legitimacy depends much less upon the actual rationality of voters than upon the accountability of elected officials. It is a fairly telling debating point against those who advocate government regulation on the grounds of con- sumer irrationality that citizens who are deemed incapable of making rational market choices are not likely to behave any more rationally as voters whose whims ultimately influence the performance of the regulators; indeed, public choice theory demonstrates that voters have less incentive to inform themselves on political issues than consumers have to prepare themselves to make choices in the marketplace.[68] Finally, a preeminent advantage of competitive markets is that they serve minority tastes and interests and, unlike political institutions, give no special weight to the preferences of the majority.

The argument for public control and against markets naturally assumes that regulators, unlike consumers, act rationally and have good information. Political circumstances, however, frequently require symbolic rather than rational, informed action—especially in the highly charged area of health care. Moreover, regulators can never know the medical circumstances of particular cases, the subjective preferences of individuals, or the societal preference for particular services or for health care in general versus other goods and services. Indeed, it is far from clear that politically accountable regulators score any better on rationality and omniscience than real-world consumers and their privately procured agents.

If rationality is what is sought, a plausible case can perhaps be made for an authoritarian system run by technically competent decision makers who are *not* significantly accountable for their day-to-day actions to citizens either in the marketplace or in the political process. Indeed, the medical profession's hegemony was long defended and accepted on just this ground. Claiming scientific expertise and altruistic purposes (like the central planners of Marxist nations), the medical profession was freed from normal market accountability to consumers, especially for the costs incurred in pursuing its mission. Although the profession-dominated system failed badly on the cost front, recent regulatory proposals have sought to correct for the open-endedness of health care financing by substituting a fixed budget constraint for the previously blank check. This approach can be seen as a reasonable attempt to perpetuate reliance upon the presumed rationality of professional one-party rule while publicly controlling the flow of funds. Framing the argument for health sector regulation in just these terms would appear to sharpen the policy issue and the empirical questions requiring study. Indeed, in light of the earlier discussion of the political setting of hospital cost containment, it may be that these regulatory proposals strike the best possible balance between reliance on professionalism, with its presumed scientific rationality, and acceptance of political oversight. Although I have never seen economic regulation clearly advocated as a way of preventing scientific rationality from being overwhelmed by either consumer *or* political irrationality, this formulation of the argument seems implicit in many statements by liberals who reject the market mechanism but are content to impose only relatively gross controls on the physician-dominated system.

Whether medical science and professionalism would be a sure guide to efficient industry performance if constrained by a fixed hospital or global budget is an issue worthy of more extended discussion than can be provided here. The assumption that a scientific monopoly is an entirely rational enterprise can be disputed, however, on the basis of Thomas Kuhn's observations of the way in which invalid intellectual "paradigms," coupled with the arrogance and self-interest of supposedly objective scientists, have often curbed scientific progress.[69] In addition, medical science has been shown by such researchers as David M. Eddy frequently to base its conclusions concerning the efficacy and cost effectiveness of treatments on seriously inadequate research and analysis.[70] Moreover, medical practice has been shown by John Wennberg and others not to reflect in any very systematic way the findings of medical science.[71] Finally, antitrust and other experience reveals numerous instances in which professional actions have been inspired by economic self-interest, not altruism or scientific principles. Although improvements in centralized decision making and in mechanisms for translating learning into action are certainly possible, it is not self-evident that preserving the monopolistic model of health care under new cost constraints would serve consumers well. Such an approach also implies a degree of egalitarianism in the distribution of health care that has not yet been accepted in American political life.

Although the argument for a constrained,[72] profession-dominated, egalitarian system is respectable, there is as yet no basis for rejecting the alternative hypothesis that competing health care plans, each responsible for developing alternative offerings at an attractive price, can draw upon and implement scientific learning, can introduce desirable incentives, and can improve overall industry performance. Consumers may be just rational enough to recognize their own irrationality and to entrust the making of difficult decisions concerning risks and complex trade-offs to experts or entities of their own choosing. To my mind, a health care system driven by consumer choice still seems preferable to any other for ethical and practical reasons that have already been stated: first, through mechanisms that are still being developed, it can make providers accountable to consumers; second, it permits diversity in response to varying preferences; third, it should be able to develop reasonably effective mechanisms for facing, however unsatisfyingly, the difficult trade-offs encountered in the no-man's land of tragic choices; and fourth, it encourages experimentation and innovation in the efficient delivery of health care. Both ethically and practically, this approach still seems to me the best way to negotiate treacherous territory and to put our scientific and economic resources in service to consumers.

The issue of equity. There is, of course, another ethical or moral issue that is frequently paramount in discussions of these matters—the question of equity in the distribution of health care. The market-reform strategy for improving the health care system's performance does not in itself, however, deny the claims of social justice. Indeed, although some proponents of the strategy appear to place a low priority on meeting obligations of this kind, the most responsible expositions of the strategy expressly contemplate that government will discharge its responsibilities in this regard. These expositions ask only that government pursue its redistributive projects in ways that preserve both the principle of choice and the essential incentives to economize. Advocacy of voucher systems, for example—such as the Enthoven Consumer-Choice Health Plan[73] and the capitation alternative under Medicare[74]—reflects a serious and constructive effort to combine redistribution with competition and consumer choice.

It has long been recognized by responsible critics of regulation that competition, though improving the system's efficiency, would also seriously impair the system's ability to generate from healthy premium payers and paying patients the excess revenues that the system has long used, at least in part, to cover the cost of treating those who cannot pay and lack adequate public support. And, indeed, the current transition to a more market-oriented health care system is apparently having some disturbing effects on the health care system's ability to care for underinsured populations. It is a truly regrettable consequence of the emergence of competition in health care that society must remake its historic, though often implicit, commitment to provide care for those who cannot pay their own way. Although hardships are being felt in many places, some state and local governments are coming up with new direct subsidies to replace the hidden ones previously depended upon. One can wish, of course, that the federal government were more inclined or in a better fiscal position to replace some of the revenues that its procompetitive policies and prudent purchasing strategies are denying the system.

One casualty of procompetitive developments has been the goal, once widely endorsed, of maintaining a single standard of medical care for all. That goal was always more symbolic than realistic, however. Moreover, as a rallying cry to resistance against anything that might permit "second-class medical care," it blocked decentralization of decision making. It also served to unite, in a curious alliance against competition and consumer choice, both liberal advocates of government intervention on behalf of the poor and professional interests seeking to preserve their own dominance. In general, the egalitarian ideal has proved more a barrier to desirable change and consumer choice than a practical social objective. Even if it served to expand somewhat the accessibility of health services to the poor, those gains appear to have come at a high cost in the form of sheltered inefficiency.

The President's Commission for the Study of Ethical Problems in Medicine and Biomedical and Behavioral Research performed a useful public service when it pronounced in 1983 that it would be sufficient, as a matter of ethics, if the disadvantaged were assured a decent minimum standard of health care.[75] This acceptance of a degree of inequality significantly reduced the force of egalitarian arguments for using regulation or other central control to find the one right way. At the same time, it did not let government off the hook for providing an adequate level of support for disadvantaged populations. Most important, the commission's finding opened the door for the emergence of a multitiered—not merely a two-tiered—health care system based on decentralized decision making and consumer choice. Nevertheless, as this writer has stated recently,

... even though access to a single uniform standard of health care seems no longer to be generally regarded even in theory as an entitlement of all Americans, health care in this society surely remains a merit good—that is, a commodity that people value for others besides themselves and do not wish to see allocated solely on the basis of ability and willingness to pay. Even as Americans increasingly purchase health plans and health services for their own consumption in the same way that they would purchase a new car or other consumer good, they still regard health care as something special when it comes to providing it to those who cannot pay. Like education, basic health care is deemed vital to ensuring equality of opportunity, and its provision to disadvantaged citizens helps Americans believe in the basic justice of their society.

Although some will regret the demise of the egalitarian ethic and many will fear that the majority will provide inadequately for the disadvantaged minority, it is doubtful that Americans, with their new sophistication concerning the value of marginal health care, will return to the naive view that everyone is entitled to some centrally defined quantum and quality of health services.[76]

Conclusion

The editor of this journal once wrote that the policy choice in health care "does not lie between a libertarian, freespirited, incentive approach honoring consumer choice and an oppressive, coercive, regulatory approach forcing narrow options down the throats of a resistant populace."[77] In his view, proposals to rely on markets to allocate resources to health care have too often unfairly invoked the attractive ethical norms and simplistic rhetoric of libertarianism:

> If the new approach were described accurately—as, for example, "centrally planned social engineering by the federal government involving the manipulation of material rewards and penalties to trigger major behavioral changes"—instead of in code words with ancient and honored libertarian connotations, the nature of the enterprise and of the policy options would be much clearer.[78]

Because this article may be subject to a similar criticism in some circles, it seems appropriate that I defend my somewhat tentative and, I hope, not rhetorically offensive invocation of libertarian values in defense of recent developments in health policy and in the health care marketplace.

Professor Brown's article incorporating his protest against libertarian rhetoric was principally concerned with analyzing specific proposals to have the federal government introduce cost sharing and HMOs into health care financing schemes and alter the tax treatment of employer-paid health insurance premiums. In fact, the emergence of competition in health care in the 1980s has owed surprisingly little to "centrally planned social engineering by the federal government." Aside from enforcing the antitrust laws, the federal government has had very little directly to do with what has in fact happened; indeed, PPOs are entirely a privately inspired development, and HMOs have prospered more as federal support for them has diminished. Proposals to limit federal tax subsidies for the purchase of private health insurance, though taken seriously, have encountered opposition from powerful interests and have not been enacted; moreover, because such proposals were aimed only at capping an existing subsidy and letting people make unbiased (at the margin) choices concerning the nature and extent (including the extent of cost sharing) of the insurance or other protection they obtained, they cannot fairly be described as endorsing "the manipulation of material rewards and penalties to trigger major behavioral changes." Finally, although the move to prospective payment under Medicare may accurately be characterized in such terms, payment by DRG is only a halfway house on the way to a capitation or voucher system in which public beneficiaries will have real freedom of choice and government's role as central planner will be dramatically reduced. In fact, the decentralization of decision making visualized in this article is real and requires of government little more than a decision to let it happen. Although that policy choice is a political decision, it is not the kind that is likely to come up for an affirmative vote in Congress. If, however, a federal policy entailing redesign of public subsidies, antitrust enforcement, and benign neglect of the private sector is "social engineering," so be it.

   Another criticism of a market-oriented health policy is that of Professor Rand Rosenblatt, whose primary concerns are distributive inequity and professional dominance. Observing that some market advocates do espouse "expanded benefits to low-income persons" and appear to favor "preventive and primary care," he notes that they "propose to achieve these values with a minimum of social decisionmaking—'politics' in the broad sense of the word."[79] His doubts about such a policy spring from a distrust of "the policies that a government dedicated to the market is most likely to pursue."[80] Rosenblatt seems guilty here, however, of jumping to the conclusion that any government that would allow the market to function in health care would also necessarily fail to meet appropriate redistributive goals. Although the Reagan administration might seem to some to confirm the thesis that a preference for markets bespeaks a hard heart, a government that is not ideologically "dedicated to the market" might still choose to employ its mechanisms in the health care sector. Indeed, adoption of market-oriented health policies might result not from right-wing impulses but from liberal pragmatism, some of which was evident in the Carter administration.[81] Even Joseph Califano, the chief proponent of the original Carter hospital cost-containment bill, has recently emerged as a powerful advocate of letting the private sector tackle the problem of health care costs.[82] Although Professor Rosenblatt is right to observe the role of ideology in these matters, it is also possible that he and others overstate the ideological dimensions of the issue.

The thesis of this article has been that viewing the past decade's developments in health care in the United States as decentralizing decision making and expanding the domain of consumer choice—and not simply as increasing "competition," "deregulating" the industry, or restoring "free enterprise," or in some other doctrinaire terms—is the best way to appreciate the true historical and ethical significance of the major changes that are under way. In the last analysis, the changes that are occurring represent an important political shift from a system in which basic decisions and information were tightly controlled by a dominant elite to a system more compatible with American pluralism and democratic ideals. Perhaps, after all is said, it is best simply to view this democratic revolution as Winston Churchill viewed democracy—as a terrible idea except in comparison with the alternatives.

Notes

1. The market has become operative in the health care sector not because Congress expressly voted to rely on competition and consumer choice but because changes in the political climate and antitrust doctrine unleashed innovation in the private sector. *See* text accompanying notes 2, 40–43 *infra*. In the absence of a definitive political decision, it is natural for critics of a market-oriented approach to hold out for a reconsideration of today's de facto policy. In similar fashion, this author refused to accept government regulation as a foregone conclusion in the late 1970s—and was criticized for so doing. Weiner, *Governmental Regulation of Health Care: A Response to Some Criticisms Voiced by Proponents of a "Free Market,"* 4 Am. J.L. & Med. 15, 20 (1978) (criticizing my alleged failure to propose "constructive changes" in regulation, "given the current realities of active health care regulation and of the likelihood that such active regulation will continue into the future"); *see also* Havighurst, *More on Regulation: A Reply to Stephen Weiner,* 4 Am. J.L. & Med. 243, 249–51 (1978). Later discussion in this article suggests that, unfortunately, continued uncertainty about fundmental policy may inhibit market performance. *See* text accompanying notes 48–49.
2. Goldfarb v. Virginia State Bar, 421 U.S. 773, 785–788 (1975) (rejecting the idea that the so-called "learned professions" enjoy an implied exemption from antitrust prohibitions).
3. P. Starr, The Social Transformation of American Medicine 3-232 (1982).
4. *Id.* at 5.
5. *Cf.* Brandwein v. California Bd. of Osteopathic Examiners, 708 F.2d 1466, 1468–69 (9th Cir. 1983) (reporting attempts to merge osteopathy and allopathic medicine in California). *See also* Blackstone, *The A.M.A. and the Osteopaths: A Study of the Power of Organized Medicine,* 22 Antitrust Bull. 405, 425 (1977):

   > [T]he policies organized medicine has employed toward osteopaths are consistent with the monopoly preservation hypothesis. Initially, such policies as advertising that osteopaths were "cultists" and opposition to their licensure minimized the impact of the lack of control over the supply of osteopaths. Later, organized medicine shifted to a strategy of trading its recognition of osteopaths for control over their supply. . . .

6. *Cf.* Wilk v. AMA, 719 F.2d 207, 213 (1983), *cert. denied,* 467 U.S. 1210 (1984) (reporting AMA efforts through a "Committee on Quackery" to stamp out chiropractic).
7. *See generally* Kessel, *Higher Education and the Nation's Health: A Review of the Carnegie Commission Report on Medical Education,* 15 J. L. & Econ. 115, 121 (1972) (discussing the homogeneity of medical education); Kessel, *The A.M.A. and the Supply of Physicians,* 35 Law &

Contemp. Probs. 267, 269 (1970) (observing that there is less diversity in medical training than in any other field).

8. The peak year for FMG licensure was 1973, when 7,419 FMGs were granted initial state licenses; this number represented 44.9 percent of the total of initial physician licenses received that year. Office of the Inspector General, Department of Health and Human Services, Medical Licensure and Discipline: An Overview 3 (Control No. P-01-86-00064, June 1986).

9. *Id.* at 2-8.

10. A. Flexner, Medical Education in the United States and Canada (Carnegie Foundation for the Advancement of Teaching, Bull. No. 4, 1910). The widespread impact of this study is discussed in Starr, *supra* note 3, at 118–26, 131, 224; Kessel, *Higher Education and the Nation's Health,* *supra* note 7, at 116; Kessel, *The A.M.A. and the Supply of Physicians, supra* note 7, at 267–72.

11. *See* Summary Report of the Graduate Medical Education National Advisory Committee to the Secretary, Department of Health and Human Services (1980) (concluding that there will be a substantial oversupply of physicians in 1990).

12. R. Stevens, American Medicine and the Public Interest, 318-47 (1973).

13. *See* Havighurst & King, *Private Credentialing of Health Care Personnel: An Antitrust Perspective* (pts. 1 & 2), 9 Am. J.L. & Med. 131, 263, 264–95, 308–14 (1983).

14. *Id.* at 300–307.

15. *In re* AMA, 94 F.T.C. 701 (1979), *modified and enforced,* 638 F.2d 443 (2d Cir. 1980), *aff'd by an equally divided Court,* 455 U.S. 676 (1982) (per curiam). State laws restricting professional advertising have also been called into legal question, thus opening the door further to alternative information sources. *Cf.* Bates v. State Bar of Arizona, 433 U.S. 350 (1977).

16. Havighurst & King, *supra* note 13, at 264–95.

17. *See Selected State Statutory Provisions Relating to the Insured's Choice of Providers and to Reimbursement Practices,* 11 State Health Legis. Rep. (AMA 1983). For a discussion questioning the validity of these state laws, see Note, *ERISA Preemption of State Mandated Provider Laws,* 1985 Duke L.J. 1194, 1216 ("[M]andated-provider laws should be [deemed] preempted as applied to insurance policies purchased by employee benefit plans regulated by ERISA.").

18. Havighurst & King, *supra* note 31, at 147–50.

19. *See, e.g., The Report of the Joint Task Force on Hospital-Medical Staff Relationships* 21, 26–28 (American Medical Assoc. and American Hospital Assoc., Feb. 1985).

20. *Cf.* Virginia Academy of Clinical Psychologists v. Blue Shield, 624 F.2d 276 (4th Cir. 1980) (physician-controlled prepayment plan held to violate Sherman Act by refusing to pay for services of clinical psychologists unless billed through a physician).

21. *See generally* Havighurst, *Doctors and Hospitals, An Antitrust Perspective on Traditional Relationships,* 1984 Duke L.J. 1071, 1077–92. The model of hospital governance preferred by physicians might well have recommended itself to many hospitals, especially those seeking to attract the most competent and professionally trustworthy practitioners. *Cf.* Majone, *Professionalism and Nonprofit Organizations,* 8 J. Health Pols., Pol'y & L. 639 (1984). Hospitals dealing with less reliable professionals, however, might have served consumer interests better by imposing more direct control.

22. *See generally* Havighurst, *Professional Restraints on Innovation in Health Care Financing,* 1978 Duke L.J. 303, 306–19; Goldberg & Greenberg, *The Effect of Physician-Controlled Health Insurance: U.S. v. Oregon State Medical Society,* 2 J. Health Pols., Pol'y & L. 48, 55–60 (1977); Comment, *The American Medical Association: Power, Purpose, and Politics in Organized Medicine,* 63 Yale L.J. 937, 976–96 (1954).

23. *See generally* Havighurst, *Explaining the Questionable Cost-Containment Record of Commercial Health Insurers,* in The Political Economy of Health Care (H. E. Frech ed., forthcoming).

24. *See generally* Havighurst, *Professional Restraints, supra* note 22.

25. *See generally* Clark, *Why Does Health Care Regulation Fail?* 41 Md. L. Rev. 1 (1981). Clark states,

"[T]he medical profession enjoys enormous autonomy. Its determination of its own worth is *not* significantly controlled by patients, . . . nor by judges, . . . nor by the states, . . . nor by hospital managers. . . . [T]he medical profession gives the law to itself, and all others defer." *Id.* at 22–23.

26. *See generally* Havighurst, *A Comment: The Antitrust Challenge to Professionalism*, 41 Md. L. Rev. 30 (1981).
27. AMA v. United States, 317 U.S. 519 (1983).
28. United States v. Oregon State Medical Soc'y, 343 U.S. 326, 336 (1952) ("[T]here are ethical considerations where the historic direct relationship between patient and physician is involved which are quite different than the usual considerations prevailing in ordinary commercial matters. . . . [F]orms of competition usual in the business world may be demoralizing to the ethical standards of a profession.").
29. *See* Havighurst, *Altering the Applicable Standard of Care*, Law & Contemp. Probs., Spring 1986, at 265, 265–70.
30. *See generally* Havighurst, *Private Reform of Tort-Law Dogma: Market Opportunities and Legal Obstacles,* Law & Contemp. Probs., Spring 1986, at 143.
31. *See generally* Havighurst, *Decentralizing Decision Making: Private Contract Versus Professional Norms*, in Market Reforms in Health Care 22, 23–31, 38–41 (J. Meyer ed. 1983).
32. Havighurst & Blumstein, *Coping with Quality/Cost Trade-offs in Medical Care: The Role of PSROs*, 70 Nw. U.L. Rev. 6, 9–30 (1975).
33. Several paragraphs of this section and the next have been adapted, with the permission of the American Enterprise Institute for Public Policy Research, from Havighurst, *The Debate Over Health Care Cost-Containment Regulation: The Issues and the Interests,* in Incentives vs. Controls in Health Policy 9, 9–15 (J. Meyer ed. 1985).
34. *See generally* Payton & Powsner, *Regulation through the Looking Glass: Hospitals, Blue Cross, and Certificate-of-Need*, 79 Mich. L. Rev. 203 (1980).
35. They were so characterized in Havighurst, *Regulation of Health Facilities and Services By "Certificate of Need,"* 59 Va. L. Rev. 1143, 1156 (1973).
36. *See, e.g.,* D. Salkever & T. Bice, Hospital Certificate-of-Need Controls (1979); Sloan & Steinwald, *Effects of Regulation on Hospital Costs and Input Use*, 23 J.L. & Econ. 81 (1980). *See also* C. Havighurst, Deregulating the Health Care Industry 53–76 (1982).
37. Schwartz & Joskow, *Medical Efficacy versus Economic Efficiency: A Conflict in Values*, 299 New Eng. J. Med. 1462 (1978); Havighurst & Blumstein, *supra* note 32, at 9–20.
38. *See generally* C. Havighurst, *supra* note 36, at 25–52; Havighurst & Blumstein, *supra* note 32.
39. *See* Harris, *Regulation and Internal Control in Hospitals*, 55 Bull. N.Y. Acad. Med. 88, 96–101 (1979) (discussing internal rationing procedures in hospitals).
40. *See generally* Havighurst, *The Contributions of Antitrust Law to a Procompetitive Health Policy*, in Market Reforms in Health Care 295 (J. Meyer ed. 1983).
41. Pub. L. No. 98-21 § 601, 97 Stat. 65, 149–63 (amending § 1886 of the Social Security Act which was added by the Tax Equity and Fiscal Responsibility Act of 1982, Pub. L. No. 97-248, § 101(a)(1), 96 Stat. 331, 331–36).
42. Starr, *The Undelivered Health System*, 42 Pub. Interest 66, 68 (Winter 1976) ("The original purpose of the HMO strategy, which was to create self-regulating institutions and thereby minimize federal involvement, has been utterly frustrated by the most elaborate regulation imposed by Congress on any part of the health system.").
43. Since the original federal HMO legislation of 1973, a series of amendments and new legislation specifying the place of HMOs in the system have allowed increasing flexibilty and a wider range of consumer choice. New federal laws have reduced benefit, staffing, and other requirements for federally approved HMOs, increased favoritism for HMOs subjected to CON legislation (culminating in an exemption of sorts), and provided for new alternative delivery forms (including so-called "competitive medical plans").
44. Joint Commission on Accreditation of Hospitals, Accreditation Manual for Hospitals/1984 97–98 (rev. ed. 1983). *See* Havighurst, *Doctors and Hospitals, supra* note 21, at 1090 n.57.
45. *Id.* at 1108–42, 1157–62.
46. *See generally* Havighurst & Hackbarth, *Private Cost Containment,* 300 New Eng. J. Med. 1298 (1979).
47. *See* Olson, *Foreword*, in A New Approach to the Economics of Health Care xv, xv–xvi (M. Olson ed. 1981).
48. *See, e.g.,* Enthoven, *Health Tax Policy Mismatch*, 4 Health Affairs 5, 12–13 (Winter 1985) ("Congress ought to . . . create a refundable tax credit or direct subsidy to qualified health plans. . . . Such a credit would be equally valuable to a person with a low income as to a person with

a high income. It would give everyone an incentive to buy a health plan up to the subsidized limit, but would make them fully cost conscious above that limit.'') In 1985, Senator Durenberger introduced S.1211, The Health Equity and Fairness Act of 1985, which would limit tax-free employer contributions but extend the same deduction to individuals.

49. *See* Havighurst, *The Debate, supra* note 32, at 15–24.

50. *See* National Conference of State Legislatures, What Legislators Need to Know About Health Data/Cost Information Programs 1 (1986) (''[b]ooklet . . . intended as a resource both for legislators and others considering whether to establish a health data/cost information program'').

51. For a complete listing of organized medicine's current activities on behalf of the ''quality of care'' (almost all of which involve the production of authoritative information and opinion), see Statement of the AMA to the Subcommittee on Health and the Environment of the House Committee on Energy and Commerce, 99th Cong., 2d Sess., July 15, 1986 (statement presented by Raymond Scalettar, M.D.). Although such professional activities may seem to perpetuate its dominance, they do not offend antitrust or other public polices or unduly limit the range of consumer choice unless they are unthinkingly embodied in government policy or accompanied by anticompetitive actions. For a series of articles defending professional generation of information and opinion but opposing efforts to suppress diversity and competition in the expression of alternative views, see Havighurst & King, *supra* note 13; Havighurst, *Doctors and Hospitals, supra* note 21; and Havighurst, *Professional Peer Review and the Antitrust Laws*, Case W. Res. L. Rev. (forthcoming).

52. *See generally* Havighurst & King, *supra* note 13, at 295–325 (1983).

53. *Id.* at 194–97.

54. *See generally* Havighurst, *Doctors and Hospitals, supra* note 21, at 1108–39.

55. *See, e.g.,* Travelers Ins. Co. v. Blue Cross, 481 F.2d 80 (ed Cir. 1973) (Blue Cross discount upheld without recognizing significance of collective bargaining by hospitals).

56. *See* Goldberg & Greenberg, *supra* note 22; Havighurst, *Professional Restraints, supra* note 22.

57. FTC, *Physician Agreements to Control Medical Prepayment Plans*, 46 Fed. Reg. 48,982 (1981); FTC, Staff Report and Proposed Trade Regulation Rule, Medical Participation in Control of Blue Shield and Certain Other Open-Panel Medical Prepayment Plans (1979).

58. For a more hostile view of physician collaboration, see Arizona v. Maricopa County Medical Soc'y, 457 U.S. 332, 356–57 (1982) (medical organizations found not to be integrated joint ventures producing a new product or service and therefore to be subject to per se rule applicable to price fixing by competing entrepreneurs). *See also* Havighurst & Hackbarth, *Enforcing the Rules of Free Enterprise in an Imperfect Market: The Case of Individual Practice Associations*, in A New Approach to the Economics of Health Care 377 (M. Olson ed. 1981).

59. National Governors' Assoc. Center for Policy Research, Affording Access to Quality Care 201– 41 (1986); on Medicare, see Ginsburg & Hackbarth, *Alternative Delivery Systems and Medicare*, Health Affairs, Spring 1986, at 7–8.

60. *See, e.g.,* Luft, *New Rules for the Adverse Selection Game*, Milbank Mem. Fund Q. (forthcoming).

61. *See* Alpha Center for Health Policy and Planning, The Deregulation of Services from CON Review (Oct. 1985); State Legal Initiatives: Legal Developments Report No. 4 (American Hospital Assoc. March 1984).

62. *See* Symposium *Medical Malpractice: Can the Private Sector Find Relief?* Law & Contemp. Probs., Spring 1986, at 143–303 (exploring ''private reforms'' in the area of medical malpractice); Havighurst, *supra* note 30, at 170 (observing how ''some features of malpractice law—such as its faith in professional custom as a benchmark for judging professional performance, its exclusion of efficiency considerations, and its assumption that the legal system must define all rights and duties— distinctly manifest the old paradigm of a centrally regulated health care system supplying a uniform product''); Havighurst, *supra* note 29, at 270–75 (arguing for judicial acceptance of contractually specified standards of care in malpractice suits, including a limitation of liability to cases of ''gross negligence''); Havighurst, *supra* note 31 (criticizing judicial hostility to private contracts limiting tort remedies and the scope of insurance coverage).

63. *Cf.* G. Calabresi & P. Bobbitt, Tragic Choices (1978).

64. *See generally* Havighurst, Blumstein & Bovbjerg, *Strategies in Underwriting the Costs of Catastrophic Disease*, Law & Contemp. Probs., Autumn 1976, at 122.

65. *See* Havighurst & King, *Liver Transplantation in Massachusetts: Public Policymaking as Morality Play*, Ind. L. Rev. (forthcoming).

66. Artificial Heart Assessment Panel, National Heart and Lung Institute, The Totally Implantable Artificial Heart 247 (DHEW Pub. No. (NIH) 74-191, 1973) (separate views of C. Havighurst).

67. *See* Kahneman & Tversky, *The Psychology of Preferences*, 246 Sci. Am. 12 (1982); Tversky & Kahneman, *The Framing of Decisions and the Psychology of Choice*, 211 Sci. 453 (1981).

68. *E.g.*, D. Friedman, Price Theory 442 (1986) ("it is rational to be ignorant if the cost of information is greater than its value").

69. *See* T. Kuhn, The Structure of Scientific Revolutions viii, 10, 175 (2d ed. 1970); *see also* Kissam, *Government Policy Toward Medical Accreditation and Certification: The Antitrust Laws and Other Procompetitive Strategies*, 1983 Wis. L. Rev. 1, 5–6, 21–27.

70. *E.g.*, Eddy, *Clinical Policies and the Quality of Clinical Practice*, 37 New Eng. J. Med. 343 (1982).

71. *E.g.*, Wennberg, *Dealing with Medical Practice Variations: A Proposal for Action*, 3 Health Affairs 6 (Summer 1984); Chassin *et al.*, *Variations in the Use of Medical and Surgical Services in the Medicare Population*, 314 N. Eng. J. Med. 285 (1986).

72. Perhaps the best exposition of the case for regulation and against the market, which uses a line of analysis similar to that suggested here, is Rosenblatt, *Health Care, Markets and Democratic Values*, 34 Vand. L. Rev. 1067 (1981). That article is expressly premised on a preference for equality, however. *See* text accompanying notes 79–82 *infra*.

73. A. Enthoven, Health Plan: The Only Practical Solution to the Soaring Cost of Medical Care (1980).

74. *See, e.g.*, Ginsburg & Hackbarth, *supra* note 59.

75. President's Commission for the Study of Ethical Problems in Medicine and Biomedical and Behavioral Research, Securing Access to Health Care 1–6 (1983).

76. Havighurst, *Private Reform, supra* note 30, at 155–56.

77. Brown, *Competition and Health Cost Containment: Cautions and Conjectures*, 59 Milbank Mem. Fund Q. 145, 178 (1981).

78. *Id.* at 179.

79. Rosenblatt, *supra* note 72, at 1115.

80. *Id.*

81. By the time the Carter administration left office, several prominent officials—most notably, Alfred Kahn, the administration's chief inflation fighter—were becoming comfortable with the idea of relying more on market forces in health care. *See, e.g.*, Kahn, *Health Care and Inflation: Social Compassion and Efficient Choice*, 12 Nat'l J., 1294, 1297 (1980). The kind of thinking that might lead liberals to such a conclusion is typified by Charles L. Schultze, chairman of President Carter's Council of Economic Advisors, who has warned against an "output-oriented, command-and-control approach to social intervention which is not only inefficient, but productive of far more intrusive government than is necessary." Schultze, *The Public Use of Private Interest*, Harper's, May 1977, at 43, 61 (summarizing Schultze's 1977 book of the same title).

82. *See* J. Califano, America's Health Care Revolution: Who Lives? Who Dies? Who Pays? 9–10 (1986):

> For more than a decade, I was convinced that the job of reining in health care costs was too big for the private sector, that only government could do it, and that government had to do the whole thing. That's why, as Secretary of HEW, I proposed an across-the-board cap on hospital charges that would have controlled payments by all private insurers as well as by the government. My years at HEW, and six more outside government, lead me to believe that the great hope of containing health care costs lies in an aroused private sector. Government has to do its share, get its house in order. But a Congress whose members depend on private contributions for election campaigns, who must satisfy constituencies in their home districts and states, and who will always worry about offending hospital trustees and influential state and local medical societies cannot do the job alone. Our best hope to change the health care system rests in an awakened, competitive world of business purchasers demanding and bargaining for high-quality care from a variety of providers at much lower cost.

Although Califano's natural instinct was to seek a governmental solution, he turned to the private sector because he came finally to appreciate that the political system was incapable of doing the job. Although most Americans would probably start with the opposite presumption (that government command-and-control mechanisms should be employed only when technical factors make the market incapable of working tolerably), it is still notable that someone of Califano's liberal persuasion now sees, on the basis of practical experience, the wisdom of letting market forces and consumer choice operate in the health care field.

Index

Contributors

Lawrence D. Brown received a Ph.D. in government from Harvard University in 1973. He then spent three years as an assistant professor of government at Harvard, followed by seven years in the Governmental Studies Program at the Brookings Institution. Since 1983, he has been associate professor of medical care organization and adjunct associate professor of political science at the University of Michigan. He is director of Michigan's doctoral program in health policy, which is funded by the Pew Memorial Trust. He is also editor of the *Journal of Health Politics, Policy and Law*. His main area of interest is the politics of public policy, with particular emphasis on health care issues. Among his publications are *Politics and Health Care Organization: HMOs as Federal Policy* (Brookings, 1983); a staff paper, *New Policies, New Politics: Government's Response to Government's Growth* (Brookings, 1983); and various articles on competition, regulation, and administrative issues. He is currently completing a manuscript on the implementation of health regulatory programs, and (with Catherine McLaughlin) is evaluating the community programs for affordable health care launched by the Robert Wood Johnson Foundation.

Robert G. Evans received his B.A. in political economy in 1964 from the University of Toronto, his A.M. in 1966 from Harvard University, and his Ph.D. in 1970 from Harvard. He was consultant to the Ontario Hospital Services Commission 1968–70. He has been consecutively assistant, associate, and full professor at the University of British Columbia since 1969, and has held the National Health Scientist Award there since 1984. He was Visiting National Health Scientist in the Department of Health Administration, University of Toronto, 1977–78. He is a member of the main advisory committee of the National Health Research and Development Program in Ottawa. He is also a member of the board of editors of *Journal of Health Politics, Policy and Law; Health Services Research; Journal of Health Economics;* and *International Journal of Technology Assessment*. Dr. Evans's publications include a textbook, *Strained Mercy: The Economics of Canadian Health Care* (Butterworths, 1984); "Illusions of Necessity," *Journal of Health Politics, Policy and Law* (Fall 1985); "The Welfare Economics of Public Health Insurance: Theory and Canadian Practice" in *Social Insurance,* ed. Lars Soderstrom (North Holland, 1983); and with M. L. Barer and G. L. Stoddart, *Controlling Health Care Costs by Direct Charges to Patients: Snare or Delusion?* (Ontario Economic Council, 1979).

Theodore R. Marmor received his A.B. and Ph.D. degrees from Harvard and taught at the Universities of Wisconsin, Minnesota and Chicago before coming to Yale in 1979 as the chairman of the Center for Health Studies. He is professor of public management and political science in the Yale University School of Organization and Management and Department of Political Science. Professor Marmor is the author of *The Politics of Medicare* and numerous articles on the politics and policies of the welfare state, particularly emphasizing Social Security, national health insurance, and health planning. A number of these articles have recently appeared in a volume of essays published by Cambridge University Press, *Political Analysis and American Medical Care*. He is an editor and contributor to *National Health Insurance: Conflicting Goals and Policy Choices*. He was editor of the *Journal of Health Politics, Policy and Law* 1980–84. Professor Marmor served as special assistant to the HEW undersecretary in 1966, was on the staff of the President's Commission on Income Maintenance Program 1968–70, served on the recent Presidential Commission on a National Agenda for the Eighties, and most recently was an advisor on health and other domestic policy issues for Democratic presidential candidate Walter Mondale. A fellow of the National Academy of Social Insurance, he is co-director of an interdisciplinary research project on Social Security in American politics.

Harvey M. Sapolsky is professor of public policy and organization at the Massachusetts Institute of Technology. He received a B.A. from Boston University and a Ph.D. in political economy and government from Harvard University. He specializes in health policy and defense policy. His books on health are *Health Planning and Regulation, Federal Health Programs, The American Blood Supply*, and, most recently, *Consuming Fears: The Politics of Product Risks*. Currently he is completing an evaluation of the New Jersey DRG experiment.

Frank J. Thompson received his B.A. from the University of Chicago and his Ph.D. from the University of California (Berkeley). He is currently professor of political science and department head at the University of Georgia. His past experience includes work for the U.S. Public Health Service on problems relating to health care for the disadvantaged. He has also published books and articles on health policy implementation, including *Health Policy and the Bureaucracy* (MIT Press). His recent research has focused on the role of the states in implementing the Occupational Safety and Health Act.

Deborah A. Stone holds a Ph.D. in political science from MIT. She is currently the David R. Pokross Professor of Law and Social Policy at the Heller School of Social Welfare, Brandeis University. She formerly taught in the Institute of Policy Sciences of Duke University and the Political Science Department of MIT. She is the author of *The Limits of Professional Power* (University of Chicago Press, 1980), *The Disabled State* (Temple University Press, 1984), and a forthcoming book on political analysis in public policy (Little Brown, 1987). She is on the executive board of the *Journal of Health Politics, Policy and Law* and serves as book review editor.

Clark C. Havighurst is William Neal Reynolds Professor of Law at Duke University, where he teaches courses in antitrust law and health care law and policy and directs the Program on Legal Issues in Health Care. His scholarly writings include articles on most phases of regulation in the health services industry, the role of competition in health care financing and delivery, antitrust issues arising in the health care field, and medical malpractice. His book, *Deregulating the Health Care Industry*, was published in 1982, and he is currently preparing a book of teaching materials to be entitled *Health Care Law and Policy*. Mr. Havighurst is chairman of the management and executive committees of the *Journal of Health Politics, Policy and Law*.